"SOME PEOPLE EVEN TAKE THEM HOME"

D1056565

"SOME PEOPLE EVEN TAKE THEM HOME"

A disabled dad, a Down syndrome son, and our journey to acceptance

Tim J. McGuire

Tim J McGuire

Scottsdale

To Jean, my inspiring partner and collaborator in life, parenthood and on this book

CONTENTS

INTRODUCTION

I stared unbelieving at the list of 25 different topics the Aquinas College sophomore English instructor had offered from which we could choose to write five papers during the semester. It was 1968 and I was laser-focused on one of the topics, which read, "You've just been told you have a disabled child, describe the sadness and disappointment."

At the time I was unbelievably defiant, if not in denial, about my own physical disability. I was born in 1949 with badly crippled limbs. The diagnosis was Arthrogryposis Multiplex Congenita. Despite my protruding butt, my profound limp and twisted hand I spent most of my adolescence trying to prove to everyone that I was just like everybody else. In my college years my quest for normal was so energetic I darned near killed myself with ill-advised reckless behavior.

So, the heat rose off that theme paper when I argued that having a disabled child wasn't a problem at all—as long as the child had his mind. If he had all his mental abilities he would be a blessing, not a disappointment. I remember I got an "A" on that paper, but the instructor's comments made it clear he was seriously taken aback by my vehemence.

Ten years later, I got the official news that our first son, our second child, was not like all the other kids. That sophomore English paper was one of the first things I thought about when the aging doctor, with a bedside manner out of *The Exorcist*, told me and my wife Jean that Jason was "Mongoloid or what they now call Down syndrome."

He then uttered the words that have hovered over all of our decisions, disappointments and triumphs: "Some people even take them home."

It is impossible to imagine not taking Jason home and not experiencing the happiness, wisdom, frustration and tenacity he has brought us. It is incomprehensible to me that Jean and I and our other two children, Tracy and Jeff, would have missed the mystery of Jason—that he is 35 and 5 at the same time. At his essence, Jason is simultaneously a little boy, with all the fears and emotional immaturity of a child, and the smart-alec, somewhat experienced adult who has watched countless movies and TV shows and poignantly wishes he had somebody with whom to share his life.

Jason has no real cognitive skills but his incredible savvy drives us to laughter and a deeper family sharing. Clearly, he is the emotional glue for our family, but the journey to acceptance and appreciation of our experience was unpredictable and sometimes ragged.

Shortly after the devastating words from the doctor we promised that we would take Jason home unless and until he jeopardized our marriage or our family. He never did because his good nature and our family's sense of adventure and irreverence helped us survive the madness of such things as three years of toilet training and two years of incessant running and countless other challenges and frustrations.

We all had our roles. Jean was always the clever problem solver. Tracy, the third parent, was destined to be a Special Ed teacher because caring for a Down syndrome brother seemed so natural to her. Jason's younger brother, Jeff, from the time they stole cookies from the cupboard together, was his close buddy. As the disciplinarian I could usually control Jason with a stern look and then moments later we would fall over in laughter from "jerking each other's chains."

One of the few real tensions between Jean and me, and the great ground for on-going compromise, was that my own battle with disabilities had made me tough and independent with a fairly large chip on my shoulder. I believe the way you deal with a disability is to dig deep into your reservoir of strength and rise above it. No coddling allowed.

My parents were coached never to pick me up when I fell for fear of spoiling me. I spent two weeks practically every summer in the hospital and only saw my Mother every other day. Jean has always been low-key about it, but she made it clear monkeys would write Shakespeare before Jason spent a night alone in a hospital. Fortunately, he wasn't in the hospital often.

By watching and helping Jason through the years I continually gained more perspective on my own physical condition until one day, when I was 43, I ditched years of defiance and denial and I finally checked the disabled box on a census form. It was time to admit to myself and to others that my disability had shaped me, and it had shaped my relationship with my physically disabled son.

This book is about a family, especially a father and a son, coping with two disabilities. It is a story full of laughter and love, of insights and lessons about life and disabilities; a story that demonstrates the importance of tackling one challenge at a time. It is also a story of a child shaping his father as much as the father shapes his son.

It is also a story that took a dramatic, devastating turn in mid-2014, a turn that redefined challenge for our family and offers a new set of lessons as we create the next chapters of our lives.

One person who has not read this story, and never will, is Jason. I deeply regret that. When he and I discussed it I am not sure how much he grasped and his only real reaction was that the book idea "gives me goose bumps."

CHAPTER 1

TIM'S BEGINNING

M y tiny wrists were twisted like useless little clubs. My feet were laid up against the inside of my newborn legs. The right side was clearly more damaged than the left. My skinny right leg stuck out like a stiff stick. It looked as if it would never bend. The rigid right elbow would never throw a curveball.

Jim McGuire, the short, tough-guy World War II veteran, had been in the waiting room for eight hours anticipating the moment when the doctor would come out to tell him all that "healthy-baby, mother-doing- fine" stuff every dad is anxious to hear. The kind, small-town doctor, Frederick Balz, did rush out immediately after the birth. But he couldn't hide his sorrow. He had delivered a lot of babies in this peaceful central Michigan town of Mt. Pleasant, but he hadn't seen anything like this for a long time.

The doctor warned my dad that I wasn't the perfect child most of the

other dads had welcomed into the world. But as my dad stared into the
nursery he hadn't expected anything like this. The former all-conference
football guard at 118 pounds, the guy whose reputation for an Irish temper
got him into more than his share of scraps, stood in front of that nursery
glass and bawled. He was beside himself. He cried for me. He cried for himself. He cried out of fear. How was he going to tell his bride of 10 months
that her first-born, the little boy they had decided months before to name
Timothy James, was badly deformed?

Jim McGuire had known bleak days. From the time he was eight until
he was 11 he languished in an orphanage after his mother died in childbirth
with her eighth child. In those depression years Jim grew up hard and he
grew up fighting tough with a dad overwhelmed by eight kids. Money was
always tight and hunger was too much a part of his childhood. Tears and
emotion were not allowed. But here he was crying and fretting on the day
that was supposed to be the best day of his life.

Dreams of success, money and status were unfulfilled dreams stuffed
deep in his pocket, and now he couldn't even father a decent child. Wallowing in guilt, he kept muttering over and over, "I even screwed this up!"
There had been a lot of bad days, but this one was the worst. His little boy
was *crippled!*

Yet, one thought overpowered every other: "How in God's name was he
going to tell Anita?" Anita was 24, but she wasn't as worldly as he was. He
was 28. He'd spent four years in the army and worked supply lines behind
the front at the Battle of the Bulge during the war. He drank hard and he
played hard. The year before this bleak March day in 1949, it had come time
to say the "I dos," settle down and start a family. Anita was a country girl,
and she wanted this baby so much he feared this would break her.

Jim had to pull himself together and figure out how he was going to
break this horrible news to his wife. He knew he couldn't do it alone. He
didn't have a mom, but he sure wished he did. Anita would need her mom
at a time like this. Could he afford to take the time to get Matilda Starr in
from her rural home 20 minutes away?

He had no choice so he had to stall for time. He would bluff his way
through, as he often did in card games. He was so good at poker he went
deer hunting without a gun to make a little extra money at the deer camp
poker games. He had crappy cards this time but he simply had to run this
bluff. He was not ready to show me to my mom.

He gathered himself and walked into her room at 7:15 a.m. March 24, 1949, with as much bravado as he could find in his devastated soul. He kissed Anita and told her with enthusiasm, "It's a boy and he looks just like me." He struggled to find his confidence and swagger, but Anita knew he had been crying. She just assumed it was the excitement of his first child, or perhaps he was as relieved as she was that it was all over.

SEEKING HELP

Jim survived his secret-keeping for only a few minutes before he begged out. He told Anita he'd be back soon. She seemed comfortable with that. He stumbled out of the hospital into a March day that was as dark and cloudy as his spirit. He was as unsure of himself as he had ever been in his troubled, mucked-up life.

He had the presence to order roses for Anita that he couldn't afford. Then he hurried to his aunt's house, where his Dad lived, to tell them both. He could have picked up a phone and called the Starrs, Anita's parents, but they were on a party line. He was sure to break down if he tried to deliver this news over the phone. Jim hated the goofy telephone anyway. He would always drive somewhere to deliver a message rather than making a call that invited the whole damned world to eavesdrop. Even years later, it fell to Anita to talk to the kids on the phone. Matilda needed to be told in person and he needed to bring her back to the hospital fast.

In his personal fog he tried to move quickly, but a million thoughts pelted him like a spring sleet storm. He did slow down enough to change clothes. He couldn't deal with these doctors and Anita's mother dressed in the casual clothes he wore to the hospital late in the night. He was a poorly paid hotel clerk at the only downtown hotel in Mt. Pleasant, but he wore a tie every single day and usually a sport coat or a suit. The crisis and the horrible thoughts about potential choices and decisions stopped long enough for him to clean up, don a white shirt and put one of those garish, wide, flowered ties around his neck. It might be the worst day of his crappy life, but, by God, that was no excuse to look like a bum.

He climbed into his late '30's pre-war Pontiac, and took off for the Starr homestead. The car was in bad shape, and he had recently spent $500 to have the engine replaced. He would later become a committed Chevy man, but in those post-war days of quotas and restrictions on the sales of cars you took what you could get.

At least half the trip was on unpaved, rutted roads. He drove fast, but he had wasted some time and he knew Anita was going to wonder where he was. He flew across the too-familiar, too-bumpy roads still trying to figure out what he was going to say and how. Anita's mother Matilda simply had to have better ideas than he did.

But it was going to take a while to get that answer. Matilda was as upset as he was by the news and it took some time to calm her down. She was a worrier and giving her an actual reason to worry was worse than teasing a shark with raw meat. Telling my grandma and her gruff, hard-talking husband Bill, that Anita's first child was badly deformed was almost as hard as he thought telling Anita was going to be.

Then the dithering started. Matilda could not go to the hospital without cleaning up and dressing up. Her small-town inferiority complex required her to "gussy up" before she journeyed into town to comfort her daughter.

Nobody is alive today to tell us what Jim did as he waited or what he thought, but the image is not an attractive one. He was distraught, his wife was waiting and his mother-in-law was dressing up to go to town. His temper and patience must have been stretched as thin as his waistline and close to a pack of cigarettes were probably puffed as he waited. It would be more than 20 years before he impulsively flushed the cigarettes down the toilet one night during a coughing and choking episode.

MOM FRETS

Jim's con had worked with my mother as she drifted in and out of sleep. As she woke up she recalled speeding to the hospital at 11 p.m. the night before when the contractions started. Prenatal classes were in the distant future and first-time mothers might as well have been sliding into the middle of a volcano for all they knew about the birthing process. Anita shivered when she remembered the hideousness of the ether. She hated that stuff since she had her tonsils out in fifth grade. The spinal block was pretty horrible too. She never even gave a thought to the fact that she had to go through child-birth alone and asleep. That was the way it was done. Period. No discussion.

Anita was pleased she had a little boy, but she was still weary from the delivery and her heavy sedation. While it was difficult to keep her eyes open there was a slow dawning of surprise, and then concern that she hadn't held her little boy. The more aware Anita became, the more her comfort with Jim's departing words faded. She slowly realized that not only had she not seen her baby, nobody would tell her why. Everyone seemed to evade the questions she had. The woman in the next bed cuddled and cooed with her baby twice that morning.

The minutes dragged by and they turned into hours and Anita still had not seen or held me. The worst thoughts edged into her mind every time the nurses ignored her questions.

Anita was hyper-aware, more than a little naïve, but pretty damned sharp. She was born and raised just outside a little German farming community called Beal City. Her dad ran the community sawmill and hired out to neighboring farmers for thrashing. Beal City was 10 miles and 10 years from Mt. Pleasant. There were a lot of intermarriages between Mt. Pleasant and Beal City, but the allegedly more genteel city folks never really approved. Fifty years later some people still kept track of the "tainted" intermarriages and people like my Mom knew who the "scorekeepers" were.

Anita was one of the best students at tiny Beal City High School. But she was innocent and a rule follower. Medicine, science, authority were all scary, elusive concepts. Women didn't have a lot of rights in 1949 and they had less power. She had no idea how much she could question these doctors and nurses. Certainly they knew best. But why were they keeping secrets? Why were they stonewalling her? Why would anyone be so cruel?

The fears rose in her throat. Her baby must be dead. If he wasn't dead she would have seen him by now. But if the baby was dead, where was Jim? He wouldn't leave her if the baby died, would he? Her hopes rose again when she received a beautiful bouquet of roses from Jim with a card that read "To mommy from daddy." Jim wouldn't have sent a note like that if the baby had died.

The way the staff avoided and evaded her forced her through a gamut of emotions from indignation to concern to anger. Mostly, she was just afraid.

That fear exploded about noon. More than four hours after he left the hospital, and almost six hours after her baby was born, Jim appeared at the doorway to her semi-private room with her mom and Dr. Balz. Anita's mind did a million calculations in a heartbeat when she saw the three of them. She knew something dreadful had happened. Tears flowed. She cried out with desperation, "What's the matter?"

MOM MEETS ME

Dr. Balz masterfully commanded the conversation to rescue Jim and Matilda. Matilda had already seen me and had dealt with her personal devastation. Dealing with Anita would not be as easy. If the German-American stereotype of cold, mechanical reserve is justified, Matilda is hugely responsible. Communication and comfort were not her strengths. Jim had still not figured out what to say to his new bride about this calamity.

The doctor emphasized the positive. "The baby is darling," he said, "but he has problems." Anita had never heard a bigger "but" in all her 24 years. To her, it was an overwhelming earthquake of a "but." The doctor clinically described her little boy's twisted limbs. He never offered cause or prediction. He concentrated on describing the extent of the defects. As he nervously watched Anita's anxiety build, he ordered a nurse to bring me to the room.

It was the first time my mom ever saw me and she wasn't allowed to hug me. He gently placed me on the bed and peeled back the blankets to give everyone in the room an anatomy lesson they never wanted to learn. He showed parents and grandparent each deformity and explained it in horrible medical detail. Only a little bit of that detail was retained because the doctor never said why this had happened or what it was. He never uttered a diagnosis and that was scary. The doctor did not know if the baby was retarded, the operative word of the day. The doctor was sure I was healthy, so healthy that he dismissed the Catholic parents' desire for immediate baptism. With a stubborn allegiance to church doctrine they ignored him and I was baptized for the first of two times in an emergency ceremony that night. My mom's baby wasn't going to Limbo, by God!

Dr. Balz's strongest message was an optimistic one. He insisted a lot could be done for me. He emphasized it was crucial to start as soon as possible. He knew an outstanding orthopedic specialist named Dr. Donald Durman in Saginaw, 50 miles away, and he promised to make an immediate appointment.

Anita heard little the doctor said and understood even less. If tears were money she would have been a Rockefeller that day. Dr. Balz talked, mom cried. Dad asked questions, mom cried. Mom thought of all the dreams she had for her baby boy, assumed they were lost dreams, and cried some more.

Dad hated tears. He ran from sadness, and he despised discomfort. Suddenly he was drowning in all of it. By the time he and mom were alone again all that was left was to hold each other and pray. In that hospital room they began a nightly ritual that continued for more than 15 years. Together they said prayers to St. Jude, the patron saint of desperate cases, and to St. Anne de Beaupre, a saint known for miracles for the disabled. When I was two or three mom and dad took me to her shrine in Quebec City, Canada. They tried not to pray for a miracle, but they always made it clear that they would accept one.

They mostly prayed for a positive outlook on life. I can't be sure if they ever got that positive outlook, but I certainly did.

Even that first night they instinctively knew something all parents of a disabled child know: Despair is the mortal enemy.

The conversation that night and for the next few days had little form. A thesaurus of emotions for sadness and suffering would have been exhausted but their fear trumped sadness. The thought of coping with everyday life was overwhelming. Even shame made a guest appearance as it often does for parents of a disabled child.

My sweet smile reminded them both that this was their baby and I deserved all their love. I would get that, but how would the rest of the world react to this twisted, crippled child? Would they think less of Jim and Anita? Would they mock their little boy? They seriously discussed keeping me a secret. They wouldn't show my twisted limbs to anyone. They would just take care of me and love me far away from prying eyes. They couldn't shake the belief that it would be so much harder for anyone else to love their little baby because I was so different.

Mom constantly thought about Agnes, Monica, Theo, Pauline, Loretta and scores of other friends and relatives who had given birth to healthy children. What had they done right and what had she done wrong? She considered every little sin and every mistake and wondered if that was the cause of this horrible accident. She knew in her heart those mothers had not lived a better life. They didn't deserve their good fortune and she didn't deserve to be punished. It wasn't fair. Then my mom prayed some more.

The frightened couple pondered and feared the worse for my future.

What if I didn't have my mind? What if I didn't grow? Would I ever walk? How would they cope? How do you raise a crippled child?

Just as that endless and fruitless angst threatened to explode, money would hijack their thoughts. Jim had a mediocre job at the Bennett hotel that paid little and their car was a wreck. Dr. Balz was sending them to a smarty-pants specialist in Saginaw and that wasn't going to be cheap. There were a lot of question marks concerning their hopes and dreams for me. But there was no question about finances. They were in trouble, deep trouble.

TAKING ME HOME

After the required stay in the hospital, it was decided that Anita should go home a few days before me to get used to the idea of being a mother of a, ah, uh, what? What do we call him? Crippled, deformed, disabled, a freak, an accident, a mistake? What should anyone call this baby who had brought so much sadness and terror into the lives of a young unsophisticated couple? Those thoughts may seem cruel or overwrought if you've never experienced something similar, but this petrified couple was on the edge of an unexplainable abyss that parents of disabled children know and people with other frightening diagnoses can understand. As frightening as that abyss is in 2014, it was absolutely terrifying in an age of little information and absolute doctor authority.

My mother went to grandma's house to rest, recover and get used to the idea of being the mother of a very different child. The respite damaged more than it helped. Matilda's worry genes had dropped straight down the genetic pipe to Anita. The glass wasn't half-empty. The damn thing was as dry as a bone. She tried to imagine a bright future, but those images strangled before they saw light. The challenges and the uncertainties grabbed my mom somewhere around her rib cage and bubbled in her throat, hour after hour.

Three days later Dad brought me to grandmother's house. His schoolmarm aunt, Mayme, carried me in the front seat. Seatbelts, car seats, and mandatory laws about where a baby could sit were decades away. The Aunt Maymes of the world carried babies in their arms in the front seat, and people would have found any other solution most odd.

Aunt Mayme was a pioneer female school teacher in Mt. Pleasant. Years later an elementary school would be named for her. But on this day in 1949 the fact that Mayme had never married and bore children loomed as a far more momentous issue. She may not have been the perfect choice for baby carrier. My dad told me many times over the ensuing years that Mayme handled her cargo as if it was an already broken piece of china that she didn't want to be blamed for damaging any further. Mayme never forgot that trip. For years whenever she was affronted by some slight or another, she would brag about that day she carried me home to my mommy.

That night some friends of my mom came to visit. I never made a sound from supper until late in the evening after the guests had left. I never cried. This was it. I was dying. Something was horribly wrong. Babies are never quiet this long. The doctor was mistaken. I was not in good health. Here I was dying the first night I was home.

Anita desperately looked to her mother for help and consolation. Matilda did her best, but she was as upset and discombobulated as Anita. She had raised four healthy children. Healthy children. That was the huge difference. Were the rules for her crippled grandchild child different than rules for normal children?

Nobody knew the answer and nobody in that country house that night knew that they were asking the defining question that would haunt Jim, Anita, and haunts every parent of a disabled child. Is my child behaving this particular way because they are a baby, or because they are a *disabled* baby? The question consumes parents from infancy through adolescence and every parent answers it differently every time it is posed.

One man in that room that night reacted to all the drama, and to this special little guy causing all the tension and fear, in ways that surprised everyone. William "Bill" Starr, Anita's dad, was not a talkative man. He was flinty hard. People knew him as honest but not someone you'd ever casually hassle. Beal City folks would have told you that drilling down to Bill Starr's sentimental core would yield a dry hole. They were wrong. I received the oil of love immediately. By this time William had several grandchildren, but while I was causing all the heartbreak, I melted him in ways none of the others did. My mother speaks with deep pride when she recalls how much my grandpa loved my visits. He roughhoused with me just as he would play with any infant. He frolicked with me on his sickbed the night before he died, a year later.

THE FIRST OF MANY TRIPS TO SAGINAW

Ten days after I left the hospital that old beat up Pontiac sputtered and coughed its way to Saginaw on a trip that transformed four lives. Dad and mom presented me, their fragile, deformed infant with the unnamed, undiagnosed crippling to Dr. Donald C. Durman. They knew he had a stellar reputation, but the balding, 50ish doctor captured the room and mesmerized the young Mt. Pleasant couple in a way that surprised them. He was grandpa, confidant and college professor in one dynamic package. It was clear he knew his stuff.

He offered the label they had been searching for since my birth. I had Arthrogryposis Multiplex Congenita or Arthrogryposis. Translated from the Greek, that literally means "curved or hooked joints." For the first time, mom and dad knew what they were dealing with and they had some sense of a prognosis.

Dr. Durman carefully explained Arthrogryposis is a muscle disorder that causes limited motion in multiple joints. He carefully demonstrated the problems in each of my joints. He showed them my club feet, the flexion problem in my ankles, right knee and my right wrist. He pointed out the severely affected hip. He told the nervous parents that his course of treatment would include casts, braces and surgeries to correct the current deformity and to shape the feet and knees in a way that would allow me to walk. The doctor predicted a long and probably expensive treatment, but he was convinced that one day I would walk and move fairly easily.

My petrified parents hemmed and hawed. They finally asked the question that had dominated their thinking and their conversations for the first 10 days of my life. Would my mind be okay? Was I retarded? That was the word of the time and nobody tried to sugarcoat it.

Durman didn't want to answer that one. He wandered with his answer. This was a very rare disease (about 1 in every 3,000 births) and not a lot was known about it. Finally, the doctor did admit that he had one other Arthrogryposis case and that child was profoundly mentally impaired. He was quick to add that he had heard of plenty of other cases in which mental function was just fine and he'd heard of several cases where the IQ of the patient was very high. But the bottom line was there was no bottom line.

That left the critical conversation that began moments after birth and continues to this day. Why? What caused Arthrogryposis? Why did this happen? Was there a genetic problem with one of them? Could it have been the bumpy ride over bad roads to Pontiac in my mom's second month of pregnancy? My frightened mom peppered Dr. Durman with scores of ideas about the cause. She made it her mission for many years to figure out the reason, analyze every action of every day of her pregnancy, to find an explanation.

At that first meeting and for the next several years Dr. Durman asked, suggested, demanded and commanded that Anita stop torturing herself. He told her to think about it as an act of God and move on with her life. That message damaged and distressed more than it helped because she could not believe God intentionally did this to her. My mother was and is a worrier so there was no way she'd ever stop searching for a cause.

She is convinced now she has solved the mystery. In the early stage of her pregnancy she had an abscessed tooth. The dentist tried to pull it. (In today's world that would never be done until the infection was killed by antibiotics.) He shot Novocain into my mother's gum but it didn't take effect. That didn't stop the dentist. He still wanted to pull the tooth without deadening it. But the pain was unbearable and Anita thought she was going to die in the dentist's chair. Finally, everyone marched to a medical doctor's office where she was administered gas and the tooth was extracted. Anita never mentioned she was pregnant, and the doctor never asked. Anita is convinced that caused my Arthrogryposis.

There is some scientific evidence that chemicals and gases can affect the pregnant mother and cause the birth defect, but it seems the root cause is that something limits joint movement in the womb during the pregnancy. It can result from a lack of amniotic fluid, maternal fever or an abnormally shaped uterus according to Arthrogryposis.net. Genetics is the cause of 30 percent of Arthrogryposis cases.

Some doctors also believe an undiagnosed viral infection during the pregnancy can result in the fetus experiencing limited overall movement which causes the deformity.

However, that analysis requires everyone to believe the condition is no one's fault, just the roll of the dice, and that's often the hardest explanation to accept. Things are always so much easier psychologically in disabled cases if someone can be blamed. It has to be somebody's fault. I am convinced that's why lawsuits are so prevalent in obstetrics cases. Parents desperately need their tragedy to be someone else's fault.

On that day in April of 1949, Dr. Durman spent all the time the couple desired and after carefully detailing the treatment plan he made an appointment and sent the young couple back to Mt. Pleasant. As they left he was convinced he had a new patient and his treatment plan would continue uninterrupted.

"JUST SEND THE KID OUT TO THE HOME"

Then the winds of well-intentioned friends and relatives started blowing. Mom and dad believed the birth of their badly deformed little boy was an extremely personal thing. They really thought they could fulfill their hospital room fantasy and hide their scandal from everyone. They didn't discuss it with other people any more than they had to, but Mt. Pleasant was a small town and soon it seemed as if everybody knew about the "tragedy."

Mom had the constant feeling every person she saw was looking at her oddly. Everybody was nice to the point of being syrupy. Half the time you might have thought her baby died, people were so sympathetic. Few of those reassuring words helped. Anita was more than a little cynical about the sympathy they received. Some of it, especially from her family, seemed genuine. To her, a few of Jim's relatives seemed sincere, but not all. She just couldn't get past the feeling that most people were "just thankful that they were not us."

While sincere sympathy might have been in short supply, opinions were not. Everyone had one. One of Anita's aunts tried to make everybody feel better with an "oh maybe he'll grow out of it," comment. A few guys Jim knew from around town sidled up to him and gently suggested he bite the bullet and "just send the kid out to the home."

Mt. Pleasant State Home and Training School was based in Mt. Pleasant and those "well-wishers" just assumed if I was crippled I was mentally damaged. Institutionalize him now and save the heartbreak was their message. Fifty-five years later Anita said about all the misguided wisdom: "It is hard to explain how stupid people were about medicine in those days. Those days were so different."

Despite my mom's memories of support from her family a recent conversation indicates even her family feared the worst. My oldest cousin, Don McDonald, the son of my mom's sister, Valeria, was nine when I was born. With tears welling in his eyes, he recently told me he remembers my birth vividly. "Everybody was crying and I remember my mother saying 'they're probably going to have to have to take him out to the state home.'" Don passed the state home often and while he didn't exactly know what happened there, he knew it made him sad to think that the infant child of his favorite aunt, the woman he called "Nanny," might end up there.

Years later when I was a successful newspaper editor, I enjoyed recounting my near-miss with institutionalization, always using the seriously voiced punch line, "and now many people believe a mistake was made." That's a real knee-slapper until I start seriously wondering how many perfectly normal kids were unjustifiably sent to mental institutions because their bodies were deformed. That thought is not so funny. My cousin Don made the same observation when we talked recently. "I have often wondered how many intelligent people ended up there. What a waste."

Well-wishers suddenly knew somebody who knew somebody, who heard this doctor or this treatment was sensational. Mom and Dad were looking for the perfect solution so they talked to several of the therapists and specialists recommended. Practically every expert they saw tried to be optimistic, but they were all honest. This was a tough case. They predicted I would eventually walk, but everything in the McGuire family was going to be a battle from now on. Nobody should think it would be easy.

Two weeks after that first appointment the family returned to Saginaw where Dr. Durman positioned a bar from one foot to the other. This was designed to bring my feet away from the legs and hold them in place. Several weeks later, Dr. Durman put casts on my tiny feet, but I was incredibly active and I often wiggled out of them almost immediately. Back to Saginaw everyone would go for new casts. Throughout this process my feet did not flex. When I stood I was practically standing on my toes. Over the next few years Dr. Durman cut the cords in my feet so I could actually stand on them.

Even though the treatment was in high gear so was the search for the pot of gold, the perfect solution to our problems. About six months after the birth, Jim and Anita made an appointment with a famous orthopedist in Grand Rapids. By reputation he was the best. He was certain to be the answer to their prayers. In many ways he was.

He was blunt and tough. His message was unmistakable in its clarity: Dr. Durman is right. The baby does have Arthrogryposis. Durman's treatment proposal is absolutely correct. Durman is an excellent doctor, and it is time to stop running around the country looking for a miracle. There will be no miracles. Only quality care and hard work will improve this situation. It is time to start both.

Mom admits now that during that time "Dad and I did sort of shut down. We made so many dumb decisions. We took a long time to sort everything out." It is hard to think the assertive, sharp parents of my adolescence and adulthood made a lot of dumb decisions, but the cataclysm of bringing a disabled child into the world does that to parent's psyches. Confidence is shaken. There are no answers and too many answers. Heartbreak and rational thinking are horrible bedmates.

The Grand Rapids doctor's stern talk was a call to arms. It bounced both of them out of their lethargy and convinced them they had to move ahead.

SAINTS AND DEVILS

Throughout those early days there were saints and devils in their lives.

Dad had a Blue Cross insurance policy and my mother had a policy with another company. An insurance man named Richmond went out of his way to remind Jim that Blue Cross needed to be notified of my birth and my problem within 10 days of the birth if I was to be covered. Without that friendly word of advice my very expensive treatment might not have been insured. Richmond's own son had been born months earlier with a cleft palate. Jim and Anita always wondered if the insurance man's personal trauma prompted him to step in to save them from certain financial disaster. It didn't really matter. If his act of kindness and attention didn't make him a saint, he was at least their small town hero.

Another saint was Mrs. Steimel, the owner of the hotel where Jim worked as a desk clerk. The job didn't pay much, but Mrs. Steimel liked Jim a lot. She showed her empathy for his newborn in lots of ways. She gave Jim a baby buggy, a play pen, and she used to slip him extra money every now and then.

But there were devils as well. Not too long after I was born, Mrs. Steimel changed her will. She willed me $500.00. That's $4,861.49 in 2012 dollars. That would have been a huge boost at the time and would have at least started the college fund in the right direction. However, when a man close to her found out about the will he convinced her to change it. The motives for that kind of meanness will remain a mystery, but a witness to the will told my dad that story many years later.

During the early stages of my treatment some well-meaning people suggested that Jim and Anita seek some help from county and state agencies. Again, that insidious grapevine went to work. They were told by someone who knew someone that a child mom and dad knew had her whole treatment paid for by the county. She was the daughter of some people "they" thought could well afford to pay.

So Jim went to see the Probate Judge who was in charge of the Crippled Children's Fund. Jim presented the problem matter-of-factly, but the devil obviously grabbed the judge by the throat that day, and imperious beyond belief, he glared down at the tough guy Irishman and said, "What's the matter, you can't care of your family yourself?"

My feisty dad never hesitated. He leaped from his chair. He set his feet and returned the judge's glare. He said to His Honor, in all his Irish eloquence, "You can go straight to hell!" Dad never waited for a response and he never crossed the judge's doorway again.

Mom was not pleased with the actions of her "hot-headed" husband, but when they discussed the issue with Dr. Durman the following week he was grateful they had not worked out a deal with the Crippled Children's Fund. He explained if they went that route, I would have to be a part of a cattle call of disabled kids on Saturday mornings. Dr. Durman fretted that under those circumstances he wouldn't be able to give me the special care my case required.

For reasons dad and mom never really understood Dr. Durman said he could work with them. In that doctor as king-lord-hero era, before the HMO's captured the kingdom, he told them he would charge $75.00 a year. That's $729 in 2012 dollars, a huge sum for my parents, but certainly piddling compensation for an outstanding orthopedic specialist. By today's standards Dr. Durman's kind offer was laughable and laudable.

In those days doctors could order hospital stays for hangnails. Dr. Durman told them that when he thought it was needed, he would put me in the hospital and do a procedure. That way he could collect from the insurance to help compensate him for his work on my difficult case. Most of the early procedures were clipping cords in my feet to form them correctly.

Dr. Durman's kindness was puzzling, but there were a number of possible explanations. He may have taken a particular liking to the young couple. He may have seen some signs that I was not mentally challenged. The prospect of working with an Arthrogryposis patient of normal or even exceptional intelligence could have excited him. And, it was possible that this case of Arthrogryposis was a special challenge. The affliction was rare and the challenge clear.

It was just as possible that he was simply a good man who saw an opportunity to do a good thing. Dad decided years later that was the best explanation. But he didn't ever argue with my mom's view because he knew she could be right. Mom believed, to the bottom of her soul, Donald C. Durman was one of the many ways her fervent prayers had been answered.

He was more than a doctor and surgeon. He became a family counselor. He advised the couple on how to navigate the bureaucracy and, most importantly, he held mom's hand during her incredible ordeal of future pregnancies.

HIS LIMBS WERE PERFECTLY FORMED

When I was only six months old mom raced to the toilet early one morning and, as her sobs resonated through their rented house, she suffered a miscarriage with her second child.

Two years later, in early 1952, mom was eight months pregnant. Her sister, her cousin and several friends were also pregnant. Everything had been going well. Confidence was rising and hopes were high. Things were going to be okay.

One cold February night mom and several friends, including many of the pregnant ones, journeyed out to a brush party at Liz Theisen's house. Shortly after the brush demonstration, mom went to the bathroom and all her fears and insecurities about childbirth hemorrhaged into the toilet and all over Liz Theisen's bathroom rugs.

It was bloody, but there was no evidence the baby was lost so mom's best friend, Betty Smith, rushed her home and my dad, full of panic himself, drove her to the hospital. Doctors examined her and sent her home for bed rest.

Mom, petrified and bordering on hysterical, tried to follow the instructions precisely. She stayed in bed for three days when labor started. Dad frantically called the hospital three times. The doctors kept saying that the sensations Anita was feeling were "just things going back in place."

By 10 p.m. the third night, both of them knew things were terribly wrong no matter what the doctors said. They defied the medical advice and resolutely drove to the hospital. When the "experts" actually saw Anita they rushed her to the delivery room, and she delivered Patrick Joseph McGuire.

Patrick weighed 1 3/4 lbs. His internal organs were poorly developed. As Jim would say for almost 50 years, always with tears welling in his eyes, "The poor little guy never had a chance." It was always obvious that he was editing out the expletives he felt.

The doctors did not equivocate. The baby was going to die very soon. Did the couple want to see him? My mother said that if he was going to die, she did not want to see him. Looking at the baby who would never grow up would destroy her. My father did want to see Patrick. He had a clear agenda. Was his little boy deformed? Did he have the same problems I did? He had to know. He had to see if he and Anita were doomed to deliver crippled children.

Patrick's limbs were perfectly formed.

But he was dead.

He never had a chance.

Mom was convinced her heart would break. Her world was a mess. She had a severely crippled boy, one miscarriage and one dead baby. And all of her friends had babies without problems. It seemed as if every other mother in the world had the perfect baby. It was so unfair. There must be a clear cause for all this heartbreak.

It was then that Dr. Durman ordered her to quit torturing herself, and his nurse Dorothy Burns suggested a gynecologist. Fancy pills and painful treatments for both mom and dad followed and in September of 1953, when I was four and a half years old, Marty McGuire was born healthy and well-formed. He became the mischievous, mobile, whirling dervish Jim and Anita had prayed for.

DAD'S JOY

The challenge of raising me never relented during all the pregnancy heart-break but there was also some joy. As each day passed it became more and more obvious that I was not mentally disabled in any way. I did all the intellectual developmental things kids are supposed to do and I did them on time. Relatives and friends were constantly amazed at my charm. More than once my recovering parents were told, "My, what a sweet little boy." As I began to talk, people become more amazed at my bright personality and my ever-expanding vocabulary. My parents were starting to realize that despite my profound disability, I was pretty smart and in remarkably good spirits, especially considering what I was going through. That upbeat personality in the face of adversity was my calling card even as a toddler.

The family was racking up the miles traveling back and forth to Saginaw for new casts every six or eight weeks. The heavy, clumsy plaster of Paris casts were omnipresent. They made moving around a chore and I was still standing on my toes. Every movement seemed to be a genuine strain.

One Sunday afternoon when I was 18 months old, with casts on my feet, I was playing in the side yard at my Aunt Mayme's house. My grandpa lived there and Sunday afternoons at the big house near downtown were common. The clan talked in the front yard. A family friend named Judy Chisek was playing and talking with me. Without warning she suddenly screamed to everyone who could hear, "Timmy is walking! Timmy is walking!"

Everybody in the yard scurried to see the miracle of a toddler taking his first steps in clumsy casts. Tears and congratulations filled that September day. Unbridled happiness gripped family and friends. There was back slapping, kisses and hugs. I got attention like few toddlers ever have. I am convinced I had to know how much I pleased everybody present that day. Pleasing people became crucially important to me.

One of the most relieved people on the planet was my dad. He couldn't help but think about the day I was born when he first saw my twisted, deformed little body. In his mind those first steps were nothing short of a blessing from God.

Chapter 2

JASON'S BEGINNING

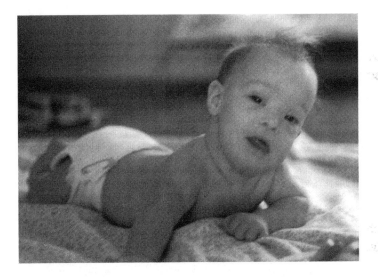

J ason came fast, faster than expected. The doctor ran from across the street to the hospital and literally caught the emerging baby. Everybody around the birthing table laughed at the entrance and pronounced how healthy the baby looked. For me, this was the future center fielder of the Detroit Tigers. Jean and I had a few doubts when our daughter Tracy was born 20 months earlier, considering my own disability, but she was perfectly healthy and our second child would be too.

After that almost-acrobatic birth Jean was in an especially festive mood. Everybody found it hilarious that Jason had come so quickly I had forgotten to take pictures. The doctors and nurses did their routine checks and proudly announced he was perfectly healthy. There was some dissent that we didn't hear about until later. As the nurses wheeled Jason's bassinet away, the pediatrician's nurse, who knew us from Tracy's birth, remarked that he looked "just like his daddy." The hospital nurse had a very different take. She whispered out of our earshot, "This baby looks funny."

I'm a hyper-sensitive guy. I score off the charts on the Intuitive scale on psychological tests. Sometimes I just know things ahead of other people. Perhaps it was paranoia, or it could have been insight, but I immediately focused on the ridge on Jason's stomach. It unnerved me but when I raised the issue I was assured it was nothing. That ridge was ever present in my mind but I didn't discuss it with Jean beyond that birthing room inquiry. I was happy and pleased but I had a gnawing sense in the back of my mind that something was very wrong. That ridge protruded on the baby's stomach like a mountain disturbing a desert.

The ridge couldn't have been more than a one-inch bulge, but through the years it has grown in feet in my mind since April 6, 1979, when Jason made his abrupt entrance into the world. The doctor had decided to induce labor for Jean that sunny Friday before Palm Sunday because, according to his calculations, our baby was 10 days late. That date had changed three times during the pregnancy after two sonograms signaled very different information about the due date. Red flags could have been hoisted right then, but nobody was suspicious.

The doctor didn't want the baby to surprise him over the weekend. Jean had been induced when Tracy was delivered by the same doctor in the same hospital 20 months earlier. Both children were born in Winter Haven, Florida, 12 miles from our Lakeland home, because the foot-draggers running the Lakeland hospital didn't allow fathers in the delivery room. That was a non-starter for us.

The decision to induce labor was the most controlled, planned thing about that hectic day.

The nurses started the process with an intravenous line at 8 a.m. The labor was surprisingly intense and fast. Jean was a veteran of Lamaze so she knew she shouldn't push until she was told to and that allowed the nurse time to call a shocked doctor. Jean never pushed once, but Jason and the doctor arrived about the same time a few minutes before 11 a.m. He announced we had a boy. Jean cried out "it's a Jason!" We had chosen the name Timothy Jason before the birth of our daughter, and throughout this pregnancy we knew a little boy would be Jason. And I had desperately wanted a little boy for all the reasons most sports-crazed fathers do.

While I had instantaneously focused on that ridge I was assured it was probably a "slight hernia." It seemed obvious I was overreacting when the nurse announced our little guy had a perfect Apgar score of 10.

The Apgar test is given to newborns at one minute and five minutes after birth. It measures pulse, breathing rate and effort, activity and muscle tone, reflex irritability and appearance. Babies are given a score of 0-2 on each of those five characteristics and a perfect 10 made it dancing time in the delivery room.

Tracy had also scored a 10. She was a perfect little child so all was right in my tiny, self-absorbed world. In retrospect, Winter Haven Hospital suffered from acute Apgar inflation. Today a rating of 10 is rare according to the Kid Health for Parents website. A close friend, Cindy Dawson, is an accomplished neonatal nurse and she says she's never given a 10 in her career.

But that morning I clung to that Apgar 10 as you would a raft on Class 5 rapids. That 10 told me my unease was unjustified, silencing all the natural anxieties I brought into the whole birthing process because of my own disability. I had been repeatedly assured that my birth defect was not genetic, but without a written guarantee from God I was going to worry. My mother had apparently passed her worry gene to me. Twenty months earlier when I had called my mom to tell her Tracy had been born without problems she tearfully said, "Then you really were just an accident." Those were not the most reassuring words my mother has ever spoken. I have never been comfortable considering myself an "accident!"

The afternoon was a typical one for parents of a second child. We were veterans and knew the program. We played with our new son when he came in for nursing and like every parent in the universe we thought he was beautiful. He had a little eye problem that required drops, and he wore a little eye cone, but it was not a significant concern.

Tracy was safe at home with a retired registered nurse babysitting (that's the kind of thing you do with the first child.) I was the top editor of the Lakeland Ledger newspaper, but my number two, and good friend, Will Corbin, assured me he had things under control. So when I left the hospital I decided to enjoy a relaxing dinner at a neighborhood Italian restaurant in Lakeland. I had a couple of drinks and savored clam linguine.

I distinctly remember the dish because midway through the meal that damn ridge leapt into my mind. I stared long and hard at that linguine. To this moment I cannot explain the source of my uneasy feeling, but that odd emptiness in my stomach is an overwhelming memory because it was a prelude to one of the most important spiritual moments I have ever experienced and I was totally unprepared.

Moments like these do not advertise themselves. They do not send you an advance message to be on guard. They possess you, you do not possess them.

I have been blessed with three inexplicable interventions from "out there" in my life. My Catholic faith tradition tells me it's the Holy Spirit. Some people of every faith, and even some non-believers, know that feeling of an "Other" inserting itself into their raggedy, unworthy life.

This was my first such "intervention." The other two would come many years later. One was job related and the other involved a serious surgery. In each of the three cases I can affix the exact location of the source of the intervener. This one was over my left shoulder and it felt very close to my ear. The second intervention was in the same location and the other was out in front of me, to the right.

The haunting thing about this moment the night of Jason's birth was that it brought simultaneous thoughts and emotions. I knew with a strange, unequivocal certainty that the ridge on my son's stomach was bad news, that my fears were completely justified. Yet, at the same time, there was a palpable, comforting presence assuring me everything would work out. Fear and comfort locked in mortal battle, but comfort, with the "Other" on its side, clearly won.

I am uncertain why, but I didn't tell Jean about that simultaneous fear and assurance for many years. I walked out of that restaurant soothed and calm. I was also convinced our little boy had a serious problem.

The oddness of this story does not escape me. I have always struggled to explain that when I left the restaurant I was reassured and completely under control. A cloud of doom did not hover above me and I was not ensnared by tension. I can be a control freak. I seek order and certainty. That night, sated by the clams and linguine and guided by that "Other," was one of the few times in my anxiety-ridden life that I truly believed "what will be, will be."

It would be a long time before I was that sanguine again.

"JASON HAS A PROBLEM"

Jason spent Friday night under the bilirubin or phototherapy lights to address a minor case of jaundice, but Jean knew that was no big deal. The nurses brought Jason to her a few times overnight. In the morning they rolled his bassinet into the room and Jean played with her little boy just as all the mothers did. It was a far cry from the isolation my mother felt shortly after my birth.

Jason was Jean's beautiful, perfect child through all that playing and nursing. The central Florida sun shone brightly through the blinds into Jean's hospital room as she celebrated her good fortune. We now had the girl and the boy so many families desire. Her family was complete. We had never planned on a big family.

Around 9 a.m. the hospital's staff pediatrician, a serious, somewhat inarticulate man came into Jean's room. He announced that "Jason has a problem." Jean didn't react because she was sure the doctor was talking about Jason's minor eye problem and she said so.

"It's more serious than that," the doctor said. "I'm pretty sure Jason is mongoloid. It's also known as Down syndrome." Mongoloid was an old-fashioned term that you would never hear today. It has racist overtones because it refers to the wide set eyes, expansive forehead and flat nose of ethnic Asians. It was already objectionable at the time this 60ish doctor used it with Jean. It was not the last objectionable thing this oafish man would say.

Jean didn't have a clue what a mongoloid was, or what Down syndrome was, but she knew it was bad. She had some distant memory that it happened to older mothers. But she was young. She cannot remember if the doctor uttered the words "mentally retarded" or if she knew that instinctively. Her tears fell and her imagination hit overdrive as she conjured images of 'mongoloid idiots' portrayed in books and film. She immediately flashed back to a child she had seen at Disney World a few months before Jason's birth. The parents were pushing the child around that magic place on something that looked like a hospital gurney.

The doctor expected the tears, but they flustered him. He struggled to remain clinical so he walked to the basinet and picked up Jason. Just as Dr. Balz had done with me 30 years earlier, the doctor laid him on the bed and started explaining the symptoms of Down syndrome. He showed her

Jason's rounded ears, the Simian crease right across the middle of the hand, the broad flat nose and the slanted eyes. He even explained the ridge. Jason's stomach muscles didn't interlock correctly, a common problem for Down syndrome babies. Jean listened as intently as she could and observed all the things that were wrong with her son.

Yet, Jean couldn't help focusing on how cute and lovable he was. So many things seemed right, but the doctor was standing here telling her everything was wrong.

Jean was absorbed by what was normal and abnormal about her son when the doctor exploded her world again. "Should I call your husband or do you want to call him?" Talking to me was way down the list of things Jean was prepared to do at that moment. She asked herself, "How can I tell Tim his son is—what in the world is he?" Jean remembers knowing there was no way she could explain to me what she didn't yet understand. She knew her tears could not be controlled and her sobbing would panic me. The tears flowed again as she told the doctor to call me.

As she began her long wait, Jean wrote these first words of a diary/letter to Jason:

> *"And then I lay here in bed waiting for him to walk in. You and your father have a lot in common. He was born with a birth defect, a physical handicap. He's always been a sports nut and I know how much he wanted a boy who could be a star quarterback or a centerfielder for the Detroit Tigers. That's what keeps going through my mind."*

With so much time to think, wild thoughts about the pregnancy and delivery bounced around her brain. "If they hadn't induced me, Jason wouldn't be born yet and I wouldn't feel this heartbreak. Then all of this would be better." Then she remembered the doctor had changed her due date three times. Could that be because Jason's head was too big? She wondered if all Down syndrome kids have big heads. She knew some did.

Then the guilt started. It always does. Did I eat something I shouldn't have? Did I do something bad? Did Tim's disability cause this? Self-recrimination was certainly the first option, but she could not imagine what she had done. At some point or another everyone in the genetic pool would question their own role in Jason's fate even though Down syndrome is unequivocally not hereditary.

Jean's wrestling match with guilt and 'what-ifs' was interrupted twice.

First, my younger brother Marty called with congratulations. Jean chose the lying option–a big lie, not a little lie. She told Marty her little boy was perfect and beautiful and she didn't cry when she said it. Jean had no idea what she was going to tell people about her Down syndrome son, but she wasn't going to tell anybody anything before I even knew. She needed to cry some more before she got to that point. So she lied and made a feeble excuse to get rid of Marty quickly.

The doctor who cared for Jean was on duty that morning but all three doctors from the Ob-gyn practice trudged into her room. Her doctor knew he should come to her room when he heard the news about Jason, but it was apparently clear to him he could not face that duty alone. None of the normally confident, fun-loving young doctors had ever delivered a Down syndrome baby before.

Their books told them this was possible, but those books had not prepared them to deal with a heart-broken mother. None of them examined Jean that morning. This was not a medical crisis. It was the kind of crisis medical schools don't teach. The three of them leaned against a chest of drawers as Jean sobbed. Jean remembers none of the few words they spoke. She only remembers them staring at their shoes as she cried some more. After several minutes of crying and staring, Jean began to feel as if she should do something to make the doctors feel better.

I KNEW WHAT DOWN SYNDROME WAS

I have blurry memories of my call from the veteran pediatrician. It was about 9:30 on Saturday morning. Loitering around the house before I went to the hospital was enjoyable. I was a daddy of a boy and a girl. Things were, as I liked to say, "hunky-dory."

The large, playful Mickey Mouse phone rang out innocently on the kitchen counter. My heart jammed in my throat when the caller identified himself as the staff pediatrician from Winter Haven Hospital. I knew from the halting seriousness of his tone he was not calling to discuss the Detroit Tigers' spring training performance in Lakeland.

The doctor told me I needed to get to the hospital quickly. The red flags practically flew out of the phone and I wasn't going to hang up until I knew why I was being called to the hospital. After a lot of desperate wrangling with a doctor who had been taught to deliver bad news only face-to-face, I was told my second child and firstborn son had been diagnosed with Down syndrome. I can't be sure of much from that conversation, but I don't believe he used the word mongoloid with me. And I don't think he used the words mentally retarded either.

He didn't have to. I knew what Down syndrome was. My Cousin Joey's parents never said those words out loud, but I always assumed he had Down syndrome. Joey was ill-behaved, huge, and impossible to control. He had a really big head. Joey was only a few years younger than I was, but I knew he never read and never went to a real school. Joey died before he was 12. My cousin Joey was retarded, and so was my son.

"My son is retarded" are four difficult words for anyone to get their head around. There were no softening words. The appropriate words today like cognitively delayed, mentally delayed, developmentally disabled didn't exist in 1979. The accepted word was retarded and I use it here to demonstrate how those four harsh words devastate everybody. However, my world crashed particularly hard because I worshipped at the altar of brains. At that time, I judged every person and every act in relation to intellect. Glib responses, quick analysis of tough situations and artful writing were my currency. Sadly, no matter how much shame it brings me now, a facile mind was my measure of human worthiness.

My memories are jumbled but I knew my most important task was to get Tracy cared for without communicating all the sadness, anger and panic Daddy was feeling. I do remember that all those emotions started out slowly and then slammed me like a deranged middle linebacker. When every neuron in my brain hit overload as I stood in the middle of my living room not knowing where to go next, I realized I couldn't trust myself to drive to Winter Haven. This was not the time for pretense. I needed help to manage the next few hours so I called Corbin.

Will was as much friend as he was top deputy. He was a hard-driving, hard partying, bearded man with an incredible intellect. He had high expectations for excellence, but believed life should be enjoyed always. He immediately said yes, he would drive me, but it became clear as we drove the longest 12 miles of my life that Will was way out of his element. In all his maleness in the late 70's, Will did not do feelings well. Here was his crying boss sitting in the passenger seat dealing with the reality of a mentally disabled son. The loquacious Corbin was a very quiet man that day.

I tried to stash my tears for my meeting with Jean, but when I walked into that hospital room we grasped each other as if we would never let go. We cried and held and cried some more. Ignorance at that point was our most distinguishing characteristic. We knew something was wrong with our son, but like my parents years earlier, we didn't have any conception of what 'bad' meant and how 'bad' would play out in our lives.

The pediatrician returned to Jean's room like a principal coming back to an errant classroom. I did not care for the man from the moment I met him. He had made my wife cry. He was delivering me the worst possible news, so a lifelong friendship was unlikely. His clumsy bedside manner exacerbated a horrible situation.

He actually began the conversation with good news, but his delivery rankled more than it comforted. He had ordered an x-ray which revealed Jason's esophagus was connected to his stomach. That's not always the case with Down syndrome children. And, as far as the pediatrician could tell there were no heart problems, which is the other huge risk factor for Down's babies. Jason was perfectly healthy except for that pesky mental problem. That blessing of good health didn't impress us much that morning, but we have thanked God for Jason's exceptionally good health practically every day since. We are acutely aware that so many Down syndrome families struggle mightily with stomach, esophagus, lung and heart problems. We are grateful we dodged those troubles.

The doctor dealt a sliver of hope when he said he would not be certain of the Down syndrome diagnosis until he did a blood test. Then he proceeded to smash the sliver by showing me all the things he had shown Jean. He was showing me the slanted eyes and the gap between Jason's big toe and the one next to it, but the conversation slammed to a halt when he showed us the Simian crease. I had the same line across the center of my palm!

That was my first introduction to the guilt game since I obviously wasn't mentally delayed. Did I have some traits of Down syndrome which caused Jason's problem? I would later find out that my sister Mary Beth has the same Simian crease and that my mother worried for years that Mary would have a Down syndrome baby. Her two children were born healthy.

We later learned it is not unusual for a normal individual to have one or two of the characteristics.

The primer on Down syndrome the doctor gave us that morning should have assured me there was nothing hereditary about this condition but that didn't stop me from taking my turn in the guilt barrel many times during the next several months. The guilt game goes to the very center of the experience of parents of disabled children. It's embarrassingly universal and yet it's an emotion we all try to convince ourselves is unique to us. Nobody is as guilty as I am!

The doctor fidgeted, stammered and stumbled as he explained Jason's situation. He communicated his discomfort with every action, but he finally explained he was skittish because two parents had "yelled" at him several months before for the way he explained the affliction. If his behavior this day was evidence, the scolding did only a little good.

Jean worries that I am portraying the doctor too negatively. She thinks his heart was in the right place but he was simply ill-prepared. I paint him darkly because I think his lack of preparation and sensitivity was sinful. And, as a journalist, I know the messenger always has to take the spear.

Well-intentioned or not, the doctor explained the technical details of Down syndrome as if he was reciting some long-forgotten page from a musty med school manual. He said Down syndrome is also known as Trisomy 21 and he used the ugly "mongoloid" word again. To us, in 1979, "mongoloid" was just as ugly as the word retarded is to parents now.

The doctor dully recited the facts. Every person inherits 23 chromosomes from each parent. An accident can cause one of the parents to give the child an extra chromosome and when the extra chromosome is the 21st chromosome Down syndrome is the dramatic result. After he explained the round head with the flat back, the small mouth with a protruding tongue and all the other telltale physical signs he knew he had to move away from the clinical.

Jason would certainly be mentally impaired, he said, but he had no idea just how impaired he would be. His bumbling got worse as he talked. He held out some hope that Jason might be "Mosaic," a condition which means some cells of the body have Trisomy 21, and some have the typical number of chromosomes. Mosaics are often more intelligent. Like many Down syndrome parents we grabbed on to that piece of news as if it were the last life preserver on the Titanic. We found out some weeks later that particular life preserver was not ours.

The age of enlightenment on mental issues dawned in the early 1970s. The Rehabilitation Act of 1973 introduced a flawed, but passionate advocacy for special education and mentally disabled children. Parents passionately believed love could overcome and that hiding mentally disabled children harmed those with potential and harmed the families. As was the case with many social issues, Florida escaped the enlightenment, and our pediatrician managed to burrow himself in a hole far from the light.

In his horribly misguided attempt to be humane the doctor informed us that we could put Jason in a foster home or an institution. The tone of his voice indicated, in fact, that was the preferred decision. Then he uttered those incredibly insensitive words which have shaped our conversations for the past 34 years: "But, some people *even* take them home." That word "even" sounded as if it was in capital letters and over the years the type has gotten much larger.

Later we found out there was a philosophical battle raging among pediatricians, especially in the central Florida area, over whether keeping a Down syndrome child at home was advisable. Doctors hesitated to subject their patients to what they felt might be "undue influence" to persuade them to take the children home. I thought our pediatrician bent over too far the other way and left us with the impression we would be more than a little nuts if we took Jason home.

I don't know if I am the revisionist on the doctor's behavior or if Jean is. I didn't like him when he walked in and as he walked out I wrote him off as a buffoon. But he scared the wits out of me. Were we really facing a situation that might require institutionalization?

TALKING THINGS THROUGH

The pediatrician had put center stage an issue we had taken for granted—that we would take Jason home. That forced us to talk things through.

It wasn't a long conversation and it didn't feel particularly insightful at the time. In hindsight it is clear that conversation was full of wisdom, compassion and it was pretty astute for a couple of young parents whose world had just been blown apart. We agreed on some key issues:

We loved Jason and we wanted him with us.

We loved each other. Our marriage was paramount. Before we had children we agreed we had married each other, not our kids. Our marriage would always be central.

Tracy and any other children we might have were also vital. We loved Jason but Tracy had to be okay just as we needed to be okay.

That led us to the conclusion we would take Jason home with us and he would stay with us, unless he threatened our marriage or our family in any way.

That discussion was not as clinical or cold as it might seem now. Tears flowed and we clung to each other throughout. We had just been told we probably ought to warehouse our little boy—the little boy that I dreamed would be a star athlete. Warehouse was still the correct word for those times. I was haunted throughout the discussion by the McGuire family lore that several people had told my dad he ought to send me to the State Home and Training School.

I didn't want that for my son, and Jean kept looking at Jason and seeing a normal baby boy. We wanted our son with us, but we also wanted to protect and hold dear the great life we had. We worried that wouldn't be possible, but in those very brief moments we vowed we would give it our best shot.

Jean and I were of one mind about those issues, but we didn't enjoy a similar mind-meld on how we should deal with the rest of the world. Much like the temptations we would later discover my Mom and Dad faced with me, Jean wanted to hide. She wanted to close the curtains of that hospital room and snuggle Jason as I sat at her side. This whole nightmare could be our little secret. My ever-present sense of obligation started kicking into gear and I insisted we had to tell our families. Jean's remarkable letter/diary details this struggle.

"I can't handle it myself much less talk about it to anybody. Your dad is my strength. I isolate and cushion myself in my hospital room and ask him to head off all visitors. I don't want anybody to see me like this. To your dad fall the chores I can't face—like calling your grandparents. He says they have to be told as soon as possible. We can't shut them out, they'll be hurt. The nurse

offers me a sedative if I need it, but I don't want it. I have a low tolerance for medication and I'm afraid it will cause me to miss a visit with you. I want to breastfeed you and I worry that worrying will keep my milk from coming in. I persuaded your father to take your sister over to friends tonight for dinner. She's rather bewildered and upset about her missing Mommy and she needs her daddy. I just need to hide here and recuperate. Your dad and I agree you are here for a purpose, we just don't know what it is."

So I went off to inform the families that all was not well with their newest grandson. My instructions were to say that Jean preferred no visitors or phone calls. The call to Jean's parents in Texas went okay, but it felt very odd. I had never communicated well with the Fannins. I always felt they viewed me as some sort of Yankee intellectual snob. We lacked warmth with each other. Their reaction was kind but distant. There were no tears, just concern.

Jean's mother amazes everyone with her "what will be, will be" approach to life. Sometimes you wonder if she has a clue, she is so easygoing. At the same time she's tough and attentive so I knew she grasped the import of what I was telling her. She drawled simply, and in retrospect, eloquently, "Well, we'll just have to love him more." Even 35 years later I am amazed at the courage of that response.

But the other member of the family was not nearly as calm. Jean's father E.L. immediately accepted blame for Jason's condition. He was convinced something had happened to him during his time as a prisoner of war in Japan during World War II that caused his daughter to give birth to a mentally disabled child. That barrel of guilt is deep.

I dreaded making the call to my mother. It was my dad's birthday. Happy bleeping birthday, Dad, your grandson has Down syndrome! I knew I wouldn't be talking to my dad. He hated phones and he hated sadness. He would run faster than his Notre Dame football heroes to get away from this call.

Even now, all these years later, I clearly remember the call I made to my mother when Tracy was born much more vividly than I remember the one about Jason's birth. Her reaction to the news that Tracy was healthy was blunt: "Then you were just an accident." As I called to tell her that Jason was a Down syndrome baby those words, spoken 20 months earlier, rever-

berated in my ears. After all this was a woman for whom childbirth and
heartbreak had too often been synonymous. Her toughness could not be
questioned but she was human, too. This news was going to hurt.

Her reaction was everything I feared it would be. Anita was the director
of admitting for the Mt. Pleasant Michigan hospital so she knew her medicine. But she had a difficult time grasping the fancy term "Down syndrome."
I think I had to say, "They used to call it Mongolism." The crying was loud,
but you could also hear the personal guilt from all those child-bearing difficulties creep across the telephone lines. Everybody drinks from that foun-
tain of guilt.

Fear was the other emotion I remember. I could tell my Mom was genuinely fearful about being a grandma to a Down syndrome child. I found
that completely unnerving because, in truth, I was more than a little afraid,
too. By the time the phone call ended we were both weeping.

Mom was beside herself with sorrow, anxiety and guilt. Why Tim? Why
did Tim have to go through this again? The emphasis was on *again.* Tim
had survived his own disability, but now he had to deal with another one. It
wasn't fair. She admits to a lot of "why us, God" kind of thinking.

My youngest brother David, Jason's godfather, distinctly remembers
playing basketball at a neighbor's house when his hysterical mother drove
up. He said she got out of the car crying and shrieking, 'Tim's baby is a
mongoloid." David was 15 and Mongolism was a mysterious word that
meant little. He recalls going home to an encyclopedia where he read that
most such youngsters die when they are 12 or 13. He recently told me that
every year on Jason's birthday he privately exults, "Jason proved 'em wrong
again!"

My brother Marty, unaware that my bride had lied through her teeth
when he called the hospital, was stunned to find out the truth when he
and his wife visited my parents later that Saturday afternoon. One minute
everybody was celebrating the birth of our second child and now everybody was grieving the death of the baby's mind.

The next morning when Marty went to Catholic Mass, the Knights of
Columbus were outside church selling tootsie rolls to raise money to benefit retarded children. Marty says, "I ate a lot of tootsie rolls that day."

As I struggled through the process of informing family I started to pull
myself together. I still cried on the trip back home with Corbin, but began
to adopt the tough guy façade as that short trip ended. I needed to be

strong for Tracy, for Jean, and for my family. For that brief moment with Corbin when I recalled my college essay, I questioned my God. I had passing qualms about my faith and the mercy of God. None of that lasted long but it did lead to my ultimate recognition that this was not God's work. God is not a micromanager but is there to help. God did not make Jason a Down syndrome child.

Even though my mother was asking "why Tim" I wasn't. To this moment I do not understand where I learned or decided that it was cheap, improper and even a little immoral to ask "why me?" Even when people around me have asked why Tim, I can count on one hand the times that thought has entered my mind in my entire life.

In my perception, though my mother stands as contrary evidence, the greatest lesson taught to me by my Mom and Dad from their words, actions and their passionate card playing was "you play them as they lay." You can't cry about your lousy cards. You can still take the Euchre trick with poor cards. You play the cards as they are dealt and you do your best. Sometimes you bluff and bluster your way through. By late Saturday afternoon I was already arriving at the realization that this was my hand and I was going to play it. I was not going to be a self-pitying wimp and ask, "why me?"

And, by God, I was going to play it well! At that moment and for many months I entertained a lot of goofy thoughts about being the best father of a Down syndrome kid ever. That was my competitive streak merging with my acceptance gene in a super-hero fantasy. I needed to be the strong one.

People were crying and breaking down all around me. It had been clear to me since I was really young that I could not flinch in the face of pain. I must be the strong one. Or at least appear to be. It would take months, years and even decades for me to figure out that quest for strength and image probably meant repressing a lot of anger. It would explode in strange places with unsuspecting innocent people over a long period of time.

But that Saturday and in the succeeding days I donned my mask of invincibility and soldiered on. I would be the model of strength.

Jean could sense the mask, and she wrote this in her diary to Jason Saturday night:

"Your dad keeps saying not to worry about him. He says he long ago made a vow not to feel sorry for himself—not to say "why me?" I try to make the same vow—but I can't help it. I keep saying, "Why Tim?" Your dad has never

been able to handle my tears and I know it will be better for him to spend
the evening with Tracy. I don't want to upset him. I've always been afraid
that I'm a self-centered person—but I find myself worrying about your dad.
Maybe there is hope for me after all."

A NORMAL, HAPPY BABY

Palm Sunday, April 8, 1979, was the first day of my life I woke up knowing I was the father of a mentally disabled son. The day unfolded as a revelation and not as a sad day at all. Jean and I spent the day cuddling, feeding and playing with Jason in the hospital room. I learned what Jean had known for more than 24 hours—if you knew nothing of medical diagnoses and dire outlooks—Jason seemed like a normal, happy baby.

That peaceful Sunday in the hospital, as we pulled away from the world and enjoyed the sanctuary of our private room, revealed a truth to us that would guide us for the next three or four years. Jason was a baby who wet, pooped, sucked, cuddled and played like every other baby. He might struggle with some endeavors more than normal babies would and his development would be slower than others. He definitely was not the monster an active imagination could conjure. When he was out of sight, the *concept* of a Down syndrome baby was frightening and debilitating. But when you held Jason close to you it was easy to appreciate that, at bottom, he was a baby to love.

At one point I was overwhelmed by that emotion. I said aloud I wished the grandparents and our friends could see our baby boy right now. I convinced myself if they could see him just "be" they would cry less, worry less and move beyond the profound sadness I knew gripped everybody who knew us. My life-long curse has been that when people around me are sad I feel responsible. People close to me were inordinately sad this weekend, but I just knew if they could watch Jason squirm and cuddle all would be better. One other momentous thing happened that Sunday. Jean noted it in the last sentence of her diary entry for that day: *"We're even able to make small jokes."* It's a short sentence, but it was a sentence of hope and healing.

The humor, the irreverent jokes that would certainly offend outsiders, the wry, comical observations about our fate, all began that Sunday afternoon two days after Jason's birth. There was no way of knowing that evening that we had tapped into our essential lifeline, a lifeline of humor that would sustain us, nurture us and serve as a key survival technique for the rest of our parenting lives. We just knew the laughter felt great after two days of tears.

The laughter continued the next day when just like all the other mothers and newborns we left the hospital right on time. There was no need to keep our "perfectly healthy" baby in the hospital. He was ready for the world even if he wasn't ready for his big sister.

Tracy was 20 months old and verbally and socially precocious. She said "Hi" to people in the supermarket at seven months. A few months later I was playing with her on the bed and said, "Take it easy, Jack." She shot back, "me no Jack." She loved interaction and affection, so her first moments with her brother were precious. She hugged and kissed him and cried, 'baby, baby, baby." She posed for pictures and made a constant fuss over this brand new package in our house.

It did not take long though for Down syndrome to take a backseat to a more common and often dreaded disease—sibling rivalry. Jean wrote this in her diary on Tuesday, April 10th:

> "Sibling rivalry has set in full force. Your big sister is so jealous of you. Every time I sit down to feed you she thinks of a hundred things she has to have right now! Juice, cheese, whatever! She also has become accident prone. She falls off the couch twice during one feeding. She doesn't want you around, but when I put you in your room she can't stand to not have you around!"

Sibling rivalry is one of those troublesome things in most families that became a blessing in ours. Sibling rivalry is normal. Down syndrome is not normal. We loved normal. We craved normal. Jean violated doctor's orders on rest and recuperation so she could take the kids to the market, to the vet, and around the neighborhood, because those things are normal. Normal means no tears. Normal means no fretting about the future. Normal means everything is okay.

The neighborhood of young middle class executives where we lived in Lakeland was the closest-knit neighborhood we ever experienced. We had frequent neighborhood parties and everybody helped each other out. When we brought Jason home, neighbors lent us car seats and other necessary equipment for our transition and several took Tracy for play dates with their kids while Jean tended to Jason.

My first attempt to tell somebody from the neighborhood about Jason had not gone well. We had grown particularly close to Nancy and Jeff who lived at the end of the cul de sac. We had traveled with them to the Super Bowl in Miami in late January. Saturday afternoon when I got back to the house I knew I had to tell them before I told anyone else in the neighborhood.

Tracy and I walked down to their house. When there was no answer at the front door I went around to the back yard and saw Nancy about thirty yards from me. When she saw me she belted out a hysterical shriek that convinced me she had somehow learned about Jason from someone else. She raced toward me shouting and crying, "He left me, he left me." I rushed into her arms shouting and crying, "He's retarded, he's retarded." By the time we embraced each other, it slowly dawned on each of us that we were crying about completely different things. We were simultaneously unloading our greatest tragedies on each other, and the other person wasn't listening.

Nancy's husband Jeff had informed her that morning he was leaving her. The departure caught Nancy completely off guard. She had spent her entire morning in the backyard bawling and trying to find the courage to tell her friends. And here I was in her backyard trying to upstage her news with bad news of my own.

Once we sorted out our tragedies and comforted each other we were able to find our way to laugh about that remarkably funny, yet painful scene, of two people dueling with their bad news as weapons. My bad news is worse than your bad news. So there!

As Jean and I started to assimilate back into our world we discovered a remarkable thing. Down syndrome kids were everywhere. It's just like a word you think you've never heard. Once you hear it, you suddenly seem to hear it all the time.

The day before Jason was born we didn't know much at all about Down syndrome but within weeks of his birth we found a neighbor who had a DS grandchild. Another neighbor introduced us to friends who had a nine-month-old DS son. Friends told us about nieces and cousins and nephews. I went to the grocery store and encountered a mother and her DS daughter. My boss told me about his 37 year-old sister-in-law. It seemed like an epidemic of incredible proportions. Even today when strangers see Jason, they will often stop to tell us about a Down syndrome sibling, child or nephew. We usually do the same. Just recently we cried in our coffee shop with a woman who lost her Down syndrome child in utero two years ago. The bond of shared experience is potent.

Friends, neighbors and co-workers were kind and solicitous when they heard the news, but Jean thought she saw the same "I'm glad it's not me" attitude my mother thought she saw in 1949. Jean wrote this account in her diary letter to Jason on Thursday, April 12th:

"After we picked up the pictures we took them down to the paper to show your dad- and everybody really made a fuss over you. I could tell some people were a little leery about coming over to look at you, but you worked your usual magic and everybody was coming over before we left. Only one woman had to turn away from you to hide—or try to hide—her tears from me, but I'm sensitive to that and I noticed. However, she's a new grandmother and I'm sure most of her tears are caused by the thought that "there but for the grace of God is my grandchild."

Meanwhile, Jean and I were frustrated by our attempts at scholarship. Jean was every bit the journalist I was. She had "retired" as assistant managing editor in Ypsilanti, Michigan, when we got married in 1975. As good journalists we needed to know everything we could about Down syndrome but that was not easy.

On the way home from the hospital we had stopped at the local book store and found a couple of outdated books but real solid information was hard to come by. Now, the Internet is like a treasure trove for Down syndrome parents. We had no such rich discovery even though we longed for it. Knowledge was something we could control. Faced with the crisis of a disabled child, control is the water mirage in the desert. As you wonder about the future you thirst for any possible way to control that future.

MAKING A DIFFERENCE

Amid all his bumbling and outrageous statements, the one good thing the clumsy hospital pediatrician did was give us the name of parents who had formed a Down syndrome support group in Lakeland. When Jean called the woman she demanded to know who had given us her name. Jean thought she was angry as she quickly explained the doctor had given us the name. The woman was giddy in her excitement and exultation. The support group had been begging for hospital cooperation and hadn't gotten any. The fact that we had her name meant progress.

We reached out to them and to other Down syndrome parental veterans in those early days.

We were genuinely discouraged to find no one had any definitive answers to all our questions. They could not provide a road map for our journey. They were as mystified as we were about where treatment for our special children was heading. We wanted the truth, the answers, and most of all we wanted certainty. We found none.

We did accomplish a little bit of good though. We began attending weekly Wednesday night meetings with other parents of cognitively disabled kids under two. We called the gatherings our "Downs" classes and while the group commonly used the word retarded as a medical diagnoses our great accomplishment was shifting the language from "Mongolism" to Down syndrome. Every generation has its own language battles.

The classes were directed and coordinated by a county caseworker who donated her time and energy to the then unfunded program. There was a genuine question about how long the program could survive without proper funding.

Four months later, just before I headed to Minneapolis for a new job, I wrote a column about our son and the program. Miraculously, after the column appeared in the newspaper, the county suddenly found money to fund the program. Jean has always said that was the first "purpose" Jason achieved.

On April 13th, one week after Jason was born, Jean wrote this final entry in her diary describing the most difficult week of her life. Now she cannot remember why she abandoned the diary. The best, most believable theory is that the mother of two children under two preferred the sleep option over the diary option. This final entry lends insight into the strange mixture of acceptance and disbelief that marked her mood at the end of the most dramatic week in her life.

"Dearest Jason—today has been the roughest since last Saturday when we first got the news.

First, I was sorting out pictures of you to send your grandparents in Michigan and the ones taken in the delivery room really got to me. Your Dad and I were just glowing—and all of a sudden I was crying uncontrollably—why us, why you—why the son we waited for so long—had such great plans for.

Now all our plans are limited to tomorrow or maybe the day after that. Right now we have no idea of your limitations, but we do know you'll never be president or find a cure for cancer. It's hard on parents who have always felt they could be anything they wanted to be.

Again you saved me from wallowing in the depths of self-pity. You woke up and had to be fed and bathed and diapered.

Then something happened. I'm not sure why, but the clock caught my eye at exactly 10:50 —the time you were born exactly a week ago—and then you got your first mail—an Easter card from your Grandma and Grandpa Fannin which calls you an "egg-straspecial" boy.

I worry about your daddy too. He has been so strong and so positive—which is his nature—but I worry that he never gets depressed—is it only me who gets these spells —or does he just not talk to me because he knows I'll end up in tears and he's trying to protect me—or maybe because everything is so busy at work he can find an outlet for his emotions at work. I just don't ever want him to end up resenting us—you or me! I just don't want him to feel I'm forcing him to bottle up his emotions.

Sometimes when I hold you, I find myself denying the whole thing. The doctors are wrong—all of them. There's nothing wrong with you. I know your father and I agreed—no false hopes—but you're my son—and a new mother is hard to disillusion!

CHAPTER 3

TIM'S EARLY YEARS

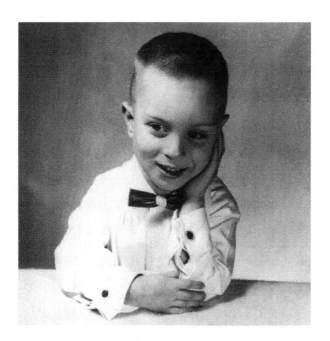

From that day when I first triumphantly walked at 18 months, wearing those hateful casts, I was a constant surprise to family and friends. I was more of a rambler than they feared despite those plaster casts I wore until I was about two. From that time until I was 12, I wore metal braces up to my knees whenever I wasn't forced back into casts to recover from surgeries on my feet. My feet had been turned dramatically inward and every medical procedure performed was designed to straighten them out.

It often wasn't elegant but I was quite mobile. I was stick-like skinny and those heavy braces prevented me from actually running. I walked and played with neighbor kids dragging my shorter right leg with a pronounced limp and hauling my always conspicuous protruding butt. My right wrist was bent downward until a later surgery released it.

It would probably not happen today, but I walked seven blocks to kindergarten every day through unpredictable and snowy Michigan weather with that eye-catching gait. Walking to school was never a question and neither was picking me up when I fell. Dr. Donald C. Durman bluntly told my parents that if they repeatedly picked me up and treated me as some sort of special child I would become coddled, spoiled and I would expect life to be handed to me. They made self-sufficiency such an article of faith, I never questioned that I would do what every other kid did. On those few occasions when I couldn't keep up physically I just pushed harder despite frustrations and setbacks.

Perhaps the biggest early setback was the battle between me and the two-wheeler. I distinctly remember my happiest Christmas ever came when I was six, three months before turning seven. Under the tree that Christmas Eve was the shiniest red bicycle ever made. It had training wheels but I just knew those were coming off quickly.

Those high hopes turned into a daily, humbling grind that went a long way to forming, or perhaps, defining my personality. I will never know if that determination was a native trait or an earned trait but from my earliest memories I felt ashamed if I didn't get up when I fell. The bike tested me.

I scrambled onto the bike. I fell. I got back up.

I mounted that shiny red bicycle 28 times in one city block in the center of Mt. Pleasant, Michigan (pop. 18,000). And, 28 times I fell off.

As I continued my valiant effort to ride that sunny day in 1956 I toppled more than 100 times. What ghoulish streak caused me to count, I will never understand. Over several weeks there were at least a thousand more crashes and a thousand more remounts. There were scores of scratches, scrapes and bruises. I was locked in a battle. A battle I had to win.

I was a preposterously skinny 7-year-old weighted down by four pounds of braces on each leg. My determined struggle fascinated friends and saddened my parents to the point of tears. Every neighbor on the block of older, middle class homes stared with gritted teeth as the tiny, disabled kid picked himself up and climbed back on that red bike. Drivers traveling Fancher street, the busy thoroughfare that bounded the east side of our block, slowed to a crawl as they watched me slam into a tree or waver off the sidewalk and tumble onto the grass.

Nobody ever laughed to my face. They tried to help, but not too much. Everybody, from my parents to the four-year-old down the street, intuitively understood that nobody could fight this battle for me. Nobody could ride that bike for me. They knew it was solitary combat.

The crusade went on hour after hour, day after day, and week after week. Some days I'd struggle to ride that bike on the sidewalks of our city block for five hours at a time—always falling, always getting up.

My mother is convinced I never gave people the satisfaction of seeing me cry. I consider that revisionist history. I distinctly recall my tears and my despair. I got angry too. I kicked that ornery bike with hopeless frustration. I called it silly, childish names. But I always climbed back on. Sometimes I'd stay on for 40 or 50 feet. Other times I fell after 10. Those were often hard falls. Nobody back then had ever heard of a bike helmet.

I talked openly about all the falls. The whispers from the neighbors would have reached Mom and Dad anyway. Many years later they told me they never considered telling me to back off my relentless efforts to ride that bike. My mother now admits that the struggle was hard on both she and Dad, but this "was the very kind of thing Dr. Durman lectured us about."

In the earliest day he told them when I learned to walk it was crucial that when I fell, they had to let me get up on my own. "Don't pick him up, no matter how much you want to, he has to learn to pick himself up." The doctor's words were wise. He told mom and dad the world is full of disabled people like me who think the world owes them, and if they constantly coddled me, "Tim will become one of those kids."

They never forgot those words and they did their best to live by them. It was hard advice. No parent ever likes to watch their child hurt and suffer. More than one person thought ill of them because they allowed me to fall and left me to pick myself up. I have never resented that choice for a moment. I consider it my parent's greatest gift to me.

I've never been certain why it was so difficult for me to learn to ride that bike. It's a mystery why so many scrapes and bruises had to be part of the bargain. I rode. I fell. I got back up. I don't know what knocked me off, but I know what kept me getting back on that bike. I refused to fail, just as I refused to fail through my entire life. I wanted to be viewed like other kids, a desire that drove me until middle age. They rode bikes and, by God, I would ride a bike.

Most importantly, I had to earn my freedom. For most kids learning to ride a bike was how they spent an afternoon. For me it was emblematic of my quest to be free. Walking long distances was hard, but on my bike the entire city of Mt. Pleasant would be mine to do what the other kids were doing. That independence smacked of normalcy. That was my childhood and adolescent Holy Grail—normalcy. Learning to ride was my Mt. Kilimanjaro and refusing to accept anything as insurmountable became a defining characteristic of my life.

Over the course of many weeks, I fell less and less. First I conquered the straight-away. After more crash-bang drama I learned to stay balanced around the corners. Then I earned the right to ride in the street. My freedom was won by raw determination.

I rode for miles with my thoughts and independence. When friends explored the city I was included. That inclusion had always been the primary goal. I was suddenly like the other kids. That desire is a signature memory of my childhood. No price, no number of bike crashes, was too high. The prize was worth the pain.

Some people who know me well as an adult are convinced that is the most defining story of my childhood. They look at my competitiveness, my accomplishments and doggedness and believe that anybody who survived all those falls from that bike was destined to become the editor of the 14th largest newspaper in the country and the president of the American Society of Newspaper Editors.

But many other people think the story about the grape thieves best defines the Tim they know.

Three second graders were stealing grapes from the Breezes, an elderly couple in the neighborhood around Sacred Heart Academy grade school in the mid 50's. Stealing grapes from them was just about as obligatory a tradition as First Communion.

But these three were a cut tougher, a bit meaner than most of the second graders. They ripped at the vines and ate the grapes with swagger rather than stealth.

Then they saw the funny looking kid on the other side of the fence. He was running around playing some silly imaginary game alone in his backyard, catty corner from Sacred Heart. The kid was almost as short as they were, but they knew he was a fourth grader, the funny looking fourth grader. He had steel things on both legs. When he walked his butt stuck out and he dragged his right leg.

He was different. Nobody walked as he did. He was crippled.

Suddenly one of them started to yell. "Hey crippled kid, you walk funny." Immediately all three were chanting, "Crippled kid, crippled kid, crippled kid."

The words snapped me out of my imaginary baseball game with a hateful wrench. I'd heard taunts before, but I'd never been alone with such bitter, incessant jeers. Always before, Mike Hackett, my big protector and my fourth cousin, or my close friend Bill McDonald, who would grow to be 6-7 and 290, or mom or dad or a teacher had been there.

I wasn't even quite sure what crippled meant. I only knew those three "little kids" were making fun of me because of the way I walked. I knew they were laughing at me just because I wasn't big and strong and able to play sports with friends. I was smart enough to know they were dismissing me and jeering at me because they figured I was scared of them.

And worst of all, they knew I was alone.

The loneliness and the taunts squeezed and squeezed until I exploded in anger. I cannot remember ever being that angry before that moment. I have seldom been as angry since. I was not going to be scared and I was not going to be mocked. Just like my dad, I was not going to run. I was ready to fight.

Tears streamed down my face as I charged the fence that separated me from the three teasing second graders. Without any real rational thought I tried to climb the fence. I had never been able to climb that fence before, and I still couldn't climb it, even fueled by raging anger.

By now, the tears were tears of hatred and my favorite juvenile expletive punctuated the tears. "You dirty idjits! I'll get you. I'll get you. You dirty idjits!" I raced to the corner of the fence and used my favorite cherry tree to get a higher start on the fence.

I got the boost I needed, but as I swung eight pounds of braces over the wire mesh, the right one got caught.

More than anything in the world at that moment I wanted to kill three second graders and my blasted brace was caught.

My anger and my childish epithets bored the three second graders. They strolled away leaving me and all that hate hanging on the fence.

Anger is a merciless teacher. By the time I was able to wiggle my foot out of that wire, the three second-graders were gone, and my wonderful opportunity had evaporated. I tearfully pulled myself off that fence. More than a half-century later I remember the cold dawn of logic in my 9-year-old mind. That fence saved me, because I wasn't going to effectively kick anybody's butt. I began to understand that if I was embarrassed over being different, I was going to have to get used to it. I was different. Play the hand.

I wasn't your basic tattle-tale. I took my normal ration of grief without complaining. I knew the rules of the game. To be accepted you had to be able to take the hassle.

But somehow, even in those days before bullying became a national issue, I knew deep in my bones the meanness I felt that fall afternoon was out of bounds. I knew those second graders had to know how much they had hurt me.

I tattled. There was an inquisition. The nice little disabled boy in fourth grade at Sacred Heart was picked on and he said Sacred Heart second graders did it.

The nuns went crazy. There would be hell to pay. "Okay, admit it. Which three of you did this terrible thing?"

It doesn't take a particularly bright second grader to know that volunteering to a nun that you are guilty of a crime that has her hopping mad is like entering the valley of death and running smack dab into the meanest S.O.B. in the valley. There were no admissions of guilt that day. Interestingly, I choked when it came time to finger my enemies. I said I couldn't be sure so I named no one. I gagged on my tattle.

That day taught me life is not fair. For decades I heard taunts, even when no one else did. I sensed every stare, curious or malevolent. Sometimes I'd foolishly castigate the person who held his or her look for a second or two too long. I always wondered if I was being judged as Tim or as the crippled kid of my memory.

That day and a few others like it are the source of a most undesirable character trait. Some people carry a chip on their shoulder. I am afraid for much of my life I carried a stone monument on my shoulder. It took the maturity and spirituality of a 50-plus man to bury most of it, but definitely not all of it. I still struggle with my conviction that things are different for me because of my disability.

GAINING INSIGHT

I faced relatively little other bullying in those early years. I was blessed with two great friends. I was with either McDonald or Hackett most of the time. They treated me as a buddy and it was just a coincidence they were very large second graders. Adults around us thought it was pretty funny that the tiny little guy hung around with two extraordinarily big youngsters.

Hackett and McDonald were impressive deterrents for bullies. My growing pluckiness helped. I was also maturing with the idea that I was different.

My brother Marty is four and a half years younger than me. He recalls a time when I was 13. A younger neighborhood kid taunted me with shouts of "cripple, cripple, cripple." An enraged nine-year-old Marty took off after the kid and caught him by the banana seat of his bike. Marty flung him to the ground and pounced on the kid.

I called him off.

Marty now says, "You told me to back off and I screamed at you, 'but he called you a cripple.' With the wisdom I was slowly gathering, Marty says I told him, "Yeah, but we can't beat everybody up who calls us names."

My sister, Mary Beth, recalled a similar tale for a magazine story about me in 2001. "One day (Tim) took us to the playground, kids came and they made fun of him. He told us there would always be people like that, people who don't know the person they are making fun of and that you should never judge a person like that. That made a big difference in my life."

People close to me often portray the childhood Tim as tougher, wiser, kinder and more forgiving than I remember myself. Yet, I know part of my thinking was the increasing realization that had been building since the grape incident that I was indeed different. I despised the word, but I was crippled. In retrospect, much of my early life was spent trying to sort out the best coping mechanisms for that stark reality.

Traumatic, instructive and life-shaping experiences abound in a childhood defined by a disability, casts and surgeries, but in many ways it was an idyllic 1950s childhood.

Our small town sat in the center of Michigan in a valley that belied the name Mt. Pleasant. There was little obvious poverty, but incomes were modest. The neighborhood we grew up in was fairly nice, even if it was a bit old. My parents rented a house on Michigan Street until I was almost seven, and then they bought our first house two blocks away on Lansing Street.

The Michigan Street house was home for my earliest memories. I remember a precocious Marty, riding his tricycle halfway around the block to the tire store at the age of two. He always scooted away with presents of gum and candy. Marty was a real pistol in his early years. I was silently jealous of his mobility and the perks it won him.

I was destined to attend the Catholic school across Michigan Street from our house, but at that time Sacred Heart Academy didn't have a kindergarten or a first grade. So every day I limped in my heavy braces seven blocks to Fancher public school. I usually walked with the Wendells and other neighborhood kids. I remember I often met my friend Marilyn Fabiano at her house a couple of blocks up Fancher Street.

Society and parents were not as protective then as they are now. Nobody ever questioned my walking to school. All the other kids did it, so would I.

It's pretty easy to imagine that making a child with braces walk seven blocks to school today would become a big deal with all sorts of protests and cruelty charges. Those objectors would be wrong. Normalcy was my supreme quest from the moment I started to hang out with other kids. Any special treatment would have made me feel more different than I already felt. It would have made me a "short bus" kid. That separation would have been an emotional hammer on my psyche. Pushing kids to exceed expectations takes a lot more courage than coddling them.

Protecting the braces from Michigan winters made for a major production. Every day I had to grapple with floppy oversized boots that zipped in front. Style never trumped practicality. The braces were expensive. It always seemed they were an unpleasant hit to the family budget and I got that message. They were a hassle to make because there was only one brace maker in the area. He was a hard case and not a nice man. His bluster was full of promises and short on delivery. The braces required change every time my feet grew and to complicate matters, my feet were different sizes. Braces were valued gems.

I was midway through first grade when my parents took a big gamble. They had been saving to buy a new house, but instead of buying a nice, small starter house, they bought a very large rooming house a block and a half away from our rented house. We moved from just across the corner *north* of Sacred Heart to 307 S. Lansing, just across the corner *south* of the Catholic school.

The house was 40 or 50 years old, and it had two kitchens upstairs. For the next 10 years my parents rented out two apartments in the upstairs of the house. The kids always shared the upstairs with renters. Some became close friends. Others, like the newlywed couple whose slightly opened door accidentally introduced me to gymnastic sex, considered us intrusions. I was continually fascinated and educated by the giggles and hilarity that emanated from their bathtub.

My parents, especially my mother, were smart about money and that rental scheme was probably the difference between the strapped child-hoods of most of my cousins and the more comfortable life I remember. Money was always at the root of family tensions, and we were never well off. Yet, we always took decent vacations and there was enough money saved for a memorable vacation to Disneyland and the Rose Bowl parade when I was 10.

My mother will tell you the braces, the trips to Saginaw and the hospital stays sapped our family income to the point of constant financial brinkmanship. Those tensions were never a secret and sometimes my parents "discussions" about the strains made for an ugly bedtime serenade. Before I really knew what college was, my parents talked scholarship. I was told to get a paper route when I was 12. As I got more involved in school activities Marty was an invaluable helper. We still have semi- playful arguments about who did the most work. Well, I think they are playful.

To my mother's credit, I never felt poor a day in my life. I always believed we were better off than most people I knew.

A few years after we bought that house a hot water heater exploded in the middle of the night in a downtown restaurant about four blocks away. The heater took off like a missile across town. It missed the bedroom in which Marty and I were sleeping by about five feet. We all awoke to find it burrowed into the ground in the next door neighbor's yard. I remember being miffed that the neighbor got her picture in the paper when Marty and I were the ones who almost got killed. Even today when the term 'hot water heater' is mentioned I flash on the realization that heater could have stopped this story of Tim and Jason with a fiery exclamation point.

The "Lansing Street house" and that neighborhood are at the core of my childhood memories. After second grade when I started attending Sacred

Heart Academy, simply called the "Academy," I could easily sneak home during recess to retrieve something I forgot. In high school I could usually pull off that feat during a class change so it was never important for me to remember permission slips or even homework. That proximity to school cultivated a habit of forgetting mildly important things that plagued me for a long time.

We remained close to downtown too, and a loaf of bread, a candy bar or a soda pop was always a short bike ride away.

Safety, comfort and camaraderie marked the neighborhood. Doors were never locked. At night, games of Hide and Seek, tag, or makeshift trivia games made it a pleasant, if noisy, refuge. And I needed a refuge. As idyllic as the little town and the charming neighborhood were, my early years from birth to 15 were largely prescribed by hospitals, surgeries and braces. Medical issues defined my childhood.

HOSPITALS MOLDED ME

Just about every summer, shortly after school was out, I would journey to Saginaw General Hospital for my annual surgery. It wasn't until I was well past 40 that I admitted those surgeries and the subsequent recovery periods were profoundly shaping episodes in my life.

Every toddler goes through separation anxiety. My degree of difficulty increased exponentially because I was left far away from home in the hands of people I knew were going to cause me pain. My mother remembers, with striking bitterness, hospital policy prevented her from picking me up from the hospital bed when I was a toddler. To this day she is mystified about why and how the hospital rule makers refined cruelty to such a high art form. It made her incredibly angry then, and it still does. She was convinced my toddler tantrums could have been controlled if she could have held me in her arms.

The first several surgeries of my early childhood sent Dr. Durman and the hospital staff into a frenzy because of my anxiety. I repeatedly spiked a temperature. Several operations had to be postponed because of those fevers. For several years Dr. Durman ordered me brought in on the day of the surgery so I could sleep at home and avoid the anxiety attacks.

Eventually bureaucracy won out and I was required to report a day ahead of time like other patients. My most overwhelming hospital memories are of fear and loneliness the night before a surgery. Saginaw was more than 60 miles away and in those days the drive always took at least 90 minutes and sometimes longer. Most of my 13 hospital stays were precisely and mysteriously two weeks long and day trips were hard for my folks. At best, I could count on seeing them every other day.

I remember being paralyzed with fear and isolation one night before a surgery when I was 10 or 11. I don't think I feared death or a disastrous outcome. I was more shaken by my aloneness and the incredible pressure of living up to everybody's expectations that I was the "strongest little boy" they knew.

By that time I had a reputation as the little tough guy who could handle anything. My reputation as the "perfect little patient' was vital to me even though I knew it was a sham. I was petrified to be alone in that dank, old hospital.

I don't know where the veneer of toughness came from, but crying was never an option. My dad never liked crying, for himself, or for his children. My mother is convinced I was just too ornery, even at a very early age, to ever show weakness. I stood silent while what I regarded as a myth grew around my toughness and courage. Despite what I was displaying to the world, I often felt weak, vulnerable and abandoned. Surviving those emotions was an essential building block in constructing a tough guy demeanor that for many years disguised a more sensitive guy.

I was usually the star of the show in the hospital and a staff favorite. After all, I was a regular. Even then, I knew making adults laugh was a ticket to better treatment. Nurses and aides were always attentive and nice to me, and sometimes even warm. Yet, it was an era of institutional control. Parents and authorities didn't worry about kid's "feelings" the way we do now.

As I struggled with my own fears and loneliness I knew those hospital stays were brutal on my mother. Dad was seldom involved. He was off selling candy through Northern Michigan for a wholesale company, or later, selling Chevrolets. Typical of the era, visits from Dad to the hospital were rare. That was Mom's job and it was a stressful one.

Leaving her little boy with strangers in a lonely hospital was bad enough. Then she had to balance the pressures of maintaining normalcy at home, economic concerns, part-time work at the telephone company and the exhausting 120-mile round-trips back and forth from Saginaw to Mt. Pleasant.

I vividly remember struggles over television. Renting a hospital television in the late '50's was a major financial investment. I considered it a necessity. Stretched budgets forced my parents to consider it a luxury.

I recall one time when my mother resisted my entreaties for a few days, but then she realized how abandoned and bored I was and relented. Of course, at that age, the costly family budget squeeze created by gas, food and babysitting, escaped me completely. My own isolation dominated my thoughts and reactions. The emotional survival of an 11-year-old does not depend on pragmatism or frugality. I do remember vague pangs of guilt but the comfort of a TV easily trumped guilt.

Often, the hospital experience taught me the most important lessons of my life about perspective and self-absorption. When I was 11 or so and still in a pediatric ward I contracted an infection. I was placed in protective isolation to protect against the dangerous spread of mysterious bacteria to other patients and staff. Everybody who came into my room, from nurses to doctors to Mom, donned surgical robes and masks. The desolation and loneliness of that imprisonment were suffocating until two surprising teachers arrived to show me how fortunate I was.

In the room next to me were two young people I never met. They had as profound an effect on me as anyone else in my 65 years. They were two year-old twin boys and they had been severely burned in a house fire. I knew the boys only by their constant and hideous screams. They were critically injured and their skin was obviously gravely tender. I listened to them yell in agony for hours on end. Horrible, piercing cries communicated unbearable torment. I shiver as I write this because 54 years later those screams are painfully vivid in my mind.

Even at my tender age I was sharp enough to realize that my own infection was small potatoes. Those boys taught me the true meaning of suffering. The doctors and nurses who treated them taught me about caregivers. Whenever I think about health care I think about those two terribly burned boys in an era when medicine was still searching for breakthrough treatments.

I have no idea if those little boys survived. What did survive was the belief burned into me by their screams that somebody down the street, or around the corner, or in the next hospital room always, *always*, has it worse than I do. That's why I try so hard to smile through tough times. I have worked hard to remember that lesson. Years later, when I was working at the Star Tribune in Minneapolis, I would sometimes start feeling sorry for myself for one reason or another. Every time I did, it seemed as if I bumped into the profoundly disabled man who worked at the newspaper. He had twisted arms and short malformed legs. He struggled to walk on two crutches. Whenever I saw him I was jolted into realizing how good I had it. I'd also think about those two burned little boys. Then, I'd utter a little prayer: "Okay, God, I get the point."

Dr. Durman performed most of the surgeries in mid-June right after school was out for the summer. That gave me the rest of the summer to recuperate, but it also ruined a good summer. The summertime play options were limited for somebody with at least one cast, and sometimes two casts up to the hip, but it was not hopeless for the imaginative.

With my friend Jim Russell, from around the corner, we took on all comers in my wheelchair. He pushed and I rode in frantic races against all forms of bikes, wagons and other make-shift contraptions. We tipped over my conveyance more than once. Those casts took an astonishing beating that constantly caused Dr. Durman to shake his head ruefully and ask, "Timmy, Timmy, Timmy, what am I going to do with you?" I never had an answer, but I always had the sense anything less than my outrageous antics would have disappointed him. Nothing discouraged me from squeezing more fun from my limitations than most would consider sensible.

Some years I escaped the wheelchair. Crutches were my preferred source of mobility. The metal arm crutches required far more forearm strength than I could muster. I used the old-fashioned wooden crutches, but I scoured the earth for comfortable armpit cushions. I needed to rest on the shoulder piece because my lack of arm strength prevented me from lifting my armpits off that incredible source of pain and irritation.

With those cushions protecting me, those crutches were my paintbrushes and I was a vain artist. I pranced, raced and maneuvered with an in-your-face boastfulness clear to anyone who watched. And I expected everyone to watch. One summer I danced four blocks every single day to get a cherry phosphate at Race's drugstore downtown. I didn't care who saw me. The truth is I wanted to be seen. The gritty kid on crutches motif was a good image. More than that, the camaraderie of the drugstore proprietor's two sons drove me. Lonely confinement at home was repugnant.

Activity was more goal than reality. Reading served as a blessed escape because I ended up sitting around alone far more than I liked. My mother often worked. Marty and the neighborhood kids had golf courses to conquer, baseballs to clobber and pools to swim. Summer was a feast to gorge on. I starved.

The more I sat, the more my dead skin inside the casts drove me to distraction and even tears. The skin flaked and itched on my atrophying legs to the point of obsession. I repeatedly proved my willingness to do anything to relieve that incessant, scabby itch.

Over the years I devised creative strategies that made Dr. Durman furious. I would use wet rags or even a glass of water to soften the cast right behind my knee. Once the cast softened it was easy to punch my way through to my maddeningly itchy skin. Then I inserted a pencil, a hanger, a ruler or some other foreign object and scratched my way to relief. The ruler was my favorite tool. More than once I overreached trying to get to a particular itchy spot and I lost the ruler or pencil. Usually I was only busted when Dr. Durman used his surgeon's saw to remove the cast. Other times the ruler or other dangerous object irritated and infected my leg. That made for one angry-as-hell doctor. His famed twinkle was nowhere to be found whenever I pulled that stunt.

HANDLING THE BATS LIKE DIAMONDS

My great refuge and a defining element of my childhood were sports. Participation and spectator sports were my hobby, my salvation and fuel for most of my fantasies and dreams.

Like our youngest son Jeff, born four years after Jason, I taught myself to read with the sports pages and I watched sports with my dad from the time I was a toddler. Just as they have been with Jeff, sports were the great bond between my dad and me. Despite strong pacifist leanings I am a boxing fan largely because the Friday night fights were such a crucial ritual for me and Dad. One Friday I went to bed early during an Emile Griffith-Benny "Kid" Paret fight. I woke up to learn that Paret had died as a result of punishing blows late in the fight. Today I find that appalling but our boxing ardor continued primarily because boxing and other sports brought us together like no other activity. My Dad was not loquacious. His traumatic upbringing as an orphan and his generation's unwillingness to show weakness prevented him from talking about feelings. My intellect and burning desire to succeed always confused him and maybe even frightened him.

My Dad taught me a lot by example, but the only piece of overt advice he ever gave me concerned potential predators. He took a lot of time one afternoon teaching me to "kick an attacker in the nuts, yell and run like hell." Today police advise kids to "run, yell and tell." They leave out that invaluable groin-kicking advice. That strange, but love-driven conversation and sports were some of the closest connections we had until he was on his deathbed.

At my mother's urging I filled a scrapbook with sports stories and pictures which captured my attention. As I look at that book some 50 years later I am befuddled why some stories fascinated me. The first entry shows a high school basketball game from Grand Rapids, Michigan. If I had a stake in that game, which I doubt, it is long forgotten. Items about college and pro football, again, some inexplicable, also dot the scrapbook.

Unsurprisingly there are several stories and photos of the Sacred Heart basketball team. Those players were my heroes. I remember attending basketball games with my dad and enthusiastically cheering for the Carey twins and other high school kids who would have been shocked they were held in such high esteem.

One football season when I was eight or so, I walked or rode my bike the 100 yards to the porch of the school where the Sacred Heart athletes donned their cleats before walking the seven or eight blocks to their practice site at Fancher School. I loved talking to the players and most of them were happy to have my company and enthusiasm. One day I happily carried home an autograph from one of the players. Embarrassment hit me hard when my laughing father explained to me that Babe Ruth did not play for the Sacred Heart football team. I later found out that young man's name and I never forgot him though I did forgive him helping to make a fool out of me.

I wasn't the fool often though. I developed an early reputation as an extremely knowledgeable little sports fan. I have a distinct early memory of a Christmas party at the Knights of Columbus hall when I was about five. While the other kids played children's games and waited for Santa Claus in the main hall, I insisted dad take me into the bar where the Detroit Lions football game was on television.

He positioned me on a bar stool with an easy view of my hero Bobby Layne as Dad's friends jabbed at him. They accused him of trying to show off and contended he was in the bar for his own interest and not mine. Dad simply shook his head and said "try him," inviting the men to test my Lions' knowledge. I passed with flying colors and the men decided I deserved to stay. In fact, they sent my dad back into the main hall where he had duties assisting Santa Claus and I stayed on the bar stool watching my Lions.

I had great affection for Layne, the famous Lions' quarterback, but my role model was Joe Schmidt, the middle linebacker. Schmidt *hit* people. He didn't get hit. Schmidt reveled in a dirty uniform and monstrous collisions with opposing ball carriers. He took the action to the opponent, and he was the general in charge of the defense. I admired and envied his aggressiveness. I never told people I wanted to be Bobby Layne. I dreamed of being Joe Schmidt. As unpractical as it was for a kid with braces, I aspired to be the hitter not the hittee. Many would argue I carried the intensity of a middle linebacker to high school debate and to my newsroom leadership.

The last two pages of that sports scrapbook feature two pictures taken when I was seven years old. Friends of my Dad knew of my intense interest in sports. One spring day Jerry Sheahan called Dad and asked him if I could be batboy for his highly successful Little League baseball team. Sheahan and his co-coach Bob Wohlscheid were both parishioners at Sacred Heart. They had known Mom and Dad for years. Without much notice, a uniform appeared at the house and that evening I was in the Roosevelt Oil team's dugout.

I arrived in the dugout that night more than a little confused. Jerry Sheahan briefed me on my duties, and I tentatively followed his instructions. I vaguely knew only a couple of the players. The game had barely begun when a photographer from the local newspaper, the Mt. Pleasant Times-News, showed up at the game to make me "famous." At the same time I learned some dubious journalism lessons I never forgot in my years as a newspaper editor.

At the time, I found the photographer's appearance at my first game a fortunate bit of luck. In retrospect, it is obvious somebody who knew more about what was happening in my life that night than I did, called the newspaper. The cynical might even think I was used to bring attention to Little League.

The photographer took one picture of my back looking onto the field.

My braces are prominent in the photo. Ironically, years later as editor of a major newspaper I constantly lectured photographers to avoid taking pictures of people's backs. I used to say nobody wants to look at butts. Show your subject's face. The Times-News photographer took considerable license with his cutline too. It read:

ANXIOUS TINY Tim McGuire, second assistant coach of Reesevelt (sic) guards the bat rack and worries about boys scoring in the third inning. He comes close to running out of his braces, he goes so fast after a bat to put in the rack. He can't play ball, but he is dynamite, a gallant sparkplug of Roosevelt. His instructions to his boys when he hands them a bat, "Hit a home run!" One of his boys did yesterday.

The second picture showed me handing a bat to a player well more than a head taller than me. It read:

SECOND-ASSISTANT COACH of the Roosevelt nine is Tim McGuire, 7. He is small even among the Little League boys and he has braces on both legs. But when it comes to zip and drive, he's a ball of fire. He handles the bats like diamonds and above he hands the bat to catcher Joe Feldman.

Those cutlines don't indicate it was my first night on duty, nor does it mention that I had never met Feldman before that posed picture. At the time I was no gallant sparkplug, and I don't think I had the good sense to tell anyone to hit a home run. I was a batboy, not a second assistant coach. There would come a day when I handled the bats like diamonds and all those characterizations would become more or less true. They were embellishments that night.

The photos are eye-catching and while the story was probably not worth a large two picture package and the space committed, the disabled batboy story was a good local human interest piece. Years later, as I interviewed a sports desk editor from the Lansing State Journal, the name of the photographer, Norris Ingalls, emerged in the conversation. I took the time to write Ingalls to remind him that our paths crossed 40 years earlier. He remembered nothing of his little feature photo package and seemed more interested in complaining about his perceived demise of the newspaper business.

For several years I raced out to get bats after hits and kept them meticulously stacked inside the dugout. The Roosevelt Oil team (later Leonard Refinery) and Little League became an integral part of my springs and early summers. Usually the season was close to complete by the time I headed to surgery. I still remember minute details of games and seasons.

Sheahan and Wohlscheid accomplished their apparent goal. The little kid who would never play baseball felt as if he belonged to a team. If the players regarded me as an oddity I never felt it. My sense of team, and self-esteem, was as strong as the fastball of the star pitcher, John Schade. Even today my friend Mick Natzel, an incredible Little League player, talks of when "we played Little League together."

I fondly remember team picnics at amusement parks and other team outings. I was always front and center in team photos and celebrations. One year the local newspaper had a contest for readers to select their favorite Little Leaguer. I received 46 votes from the community. It was good enough only for an honorable mention, but not bad for a kid who never took an official Little League swing. I won an autographed picture of Detroit Tiger pitcher Frank Lary, aka The Yankee Killer. Lary became a favorite of mine.

No Hall of Fame ever called, but I played sports whenever I got the chance.

During the few summers I didn't have surgeries, every day would find me playing whiffle ball a few blocks from our house at the junior high school. The school was guarded by six foot chain link fences and a very high fence stood forebodingly in what was our centerfield. We wrapped the whiffle ball in black duct tape and we doctored the whiffle bats too. The game that resulted bore little resemblance to the game the whiffle ball creators envisioned.

Every summer weekday my younger brother Marty and I joined five or six neighbor boys in a game akin to home run derby. I hit only a home run or two over the years, but I could pitch the ball across the plate accurately and harmlessly enough that the others could wallop their home runs. Sacrificial lamb was my role, and I played it enthusiastically. In many ways my enthusiasm and my presence were the two constants that held our informal league together.

Competition of all sorts was always important to me. My long-time friend Tim Fallon told this story at my newspaper retirement dinner in

2002. He later included it in his book: *What Jesus Said, (and why it matters now.)*

> *I changed schools at the start of third grade. On my first day in the new school, I encountered a crippled boy whose life has taught me much about Jesus' healing touch. It was impossible not to notice Tim—he came into class on crutches wearing braces* (they would have been casts) *on both legs. I later found out that he suffered from a congenital condition called Arthrogryposis that caused deformity in both his legs and his arms. On the first day I saw him, he was recovering from his usual summer routine—one or more serious surgeries to help him walk independently and increase the effectiveness of his hands and arms.*
>
> *While Tim's entrance into class captured my attention, it was nothing compared to what I experienced during recess. He became one team's quarterback in a pick-up game of football. The game began with a rules discussion because Tim wanted to play tackle! Fortunately for everyone, less courageous players won the argument, and they played touch. The next obstacle was that the teams had no football. Tim immediately took the arm pad off one of his crutches and it became the ball.*
>
> *Picture in your mind's eye a seriously crippled third grader. Tim's at least a head shorter than anyone else on the field and he's balanced on his crutches. He takes the snap from center and lofts a pass into the end zone for a touchdown. That scene repeated itself over and over during that recess and the ones that followed. Over the years, it connected with other images to help me recognize that this kid with a crippled body had an amazing spirit and two defining characteristics: courage and character.*

That story is fascinating to me because it illustrates how competing memories can be so strong and yet speak to the same truth. Clearly in Tim's mind my courage made an indelible impression upon him. As I've said, I am always surprised at how much people elevate my childhood courage. My self-image is more self-deprecating.

I would have told you the crutch pad incident occurred once or twice and that Tim is recalling the football games played with a pee wee football which pitted Mike Hackett and me against the world. Hackett became a 6-7

All State basketball center years later. It was easy for me to launch that little ball into his over-sized, outstretched hands.

When I first heard Tim tell that story I also questioned whether I really argued to play tackle. My memory is vague on that point, but Tim's is distinct. My wife Jean nods assent when she hears that story. It fits with her image of a reckless kid intent on playground acceptance. I will admit I held personal health and my encumbrances in astonishingly low regard if it allowed me to fulfill the driving desire to be "like everyone else."

That desire caused alarm and short breathing for a young student football coach from Central Michigan University. In late elementary school, Sacred Heart fielded a flag football team which played in a league with the public elementary schools. I had a fervent desire to play despite the fact that I was recovering from another surgery.

So on the first day of practice I showed up on crutches and sought out the young coach. I explained I wanted to play on the team. His eyes were panicked as he tried to explain my crutches were going to be a big problem. I found that hilarious but gently explained I was going to be out of the casts and off the crutches in a matter of weeks. True to my word, once the casts were off and I regained some strength in my atrophied legs, I showed up for practice. A pencil would have been just as formidable on the field but the coach made me a center. My job was to snap the ball and pray nobody blew me over with heavy breathing. My single claim to glory was a brief appearance on the third team in a game against Ganiard Elementary.

We played a form of the single wing and I long-hiked the ball to my friend Fallon. He was a bit more of a legitimate third-teamer than I was, but neither of us was destined to find great glory on the athletic fields. Fallon took my hike and ripped off an impressive touchdown run. Rather than celebrate his success I hungered for my reflected glory. I repeatedly asked him if the hike was a good one. It was all about me. Rather than hitting me upside the head as he should have, Fallon displayed the graciousness he has retained as an adult, lavishing great praise on my hike.

SECRETS CAN MAKE YOU SICK

Excessive pride and a hunger for attention were not my only childhood sins. Perhaps the greatest sin was my abject fear of being viewed as a "goody two shoes." The "normal" kids, especially my buddy Hackett, never struggled with such a reputation. My parents were proud of my reputation for upright behavior, but I bristled. There would come a day when I would damn near kill myself trying to escape it.

In those early years my forays to the wild side were brief and checkered, but my struggle between being the good little Catholic boy and being "like the other kids" was a defining element of my childhood.

At the age of 7, about to enter second grade at the neighboring Catholic school, I was sheltered and quite naive. But then there was Eddie McQuaid. Eddie lived on the next block and Eddie knew stuff. He was a real 7-year-old man of the world. I held him in awe.

So I paid particular attention when Eddie warned me, with much foreboding, that our second grade teacher was going to be the fearsome Sister Frances Mary.

Eddie described, with too much enthusiasm, the ruler Sister used on the heads of unruly students. He said she was really mean. My cousin, Mike McGuire, had survived Sister Frances Mary the year before and he boldly predicted I would not have the same survival success. Again, I was a rather protected, timid fellow, so this scared the heck out me.

That was the same summer I learned to ride my bike. By the beginning of the school year I had far more self-confidence than was justified by my riding performance. The day before I was to start second grade at my new school, Sacred Heart, I ran into the much feared Sister Francis Mary.

Kablam! I ran into her. I literally collided with the startled, defenseless nun on my bike just after barely missing an oncoming car. Sister was stern and few things frightened seven-year-old Catholic boys more than a stern nun. I came frighteningly close to knocking both of us over. Sister Francis Mary had never met me and she gave me the dickens for being reckless. She yelled and scolded, and I trembled.

I had crossed the nun I was about to face every day of the school year. I was a total mess. How was I going to face this scary nun ever again?

I fretted about my situation so much I had a mysterious flu for the first two days of my Sacred Heart career. I was too frightened to face Sister and I didn't have the courage to tell my parents why I was a nervous wreck. Fear of the unknown made me sick as I harbored my terrible secret. Finally, at the end of the second day, with my parents growing impatient, I came clean about my horrible misdeed.

My parents took the news remarkably well and, to my shock, Sister Francis Mary seemed to have totally forgotten about the incident that had made me nuts. Despite a few random run-ins with her ruler, Sister Frances Mary and I got along fine. I wish kids today were taught phonics and basic grammar as well as she taught them to me. Once I came clean and got my secret out in the open, nothing was as bad as I thought it would be. Transparency solved my problem and that's been the case ever since.

That incident taught me a valuable lesson which guided my interest in openness and candor for years to come. Secrets can make you sick. Whenever I think about hiding things I think of my encounter with Sister Francis Mary. I really believe that incident taught me in some small way that openness and secrecy are ethical issues.

"GOODY TWO SHOES"

Rules were rules, and for many years I toed the line like a scared private in the Catholic School army. There would come a day when skating close to the edge of a pool of trouble was high fun and great challenge, but not in those early elementary years.

With each passing year, my goody-two-shoes reputation bugged me more. I was convinced I'd never be cool as long as I was viewed as too chicken, or too holy, to walk on the wild side. In the summer after seventh grade my friends Hackett, Fallon and I made plans to ride our bikes five or six miles into the country to visit Bill McDonald at his farm.

My cousin Hackett was just four months older. Part of Mike's charm is that altruism has always been a bit of an effort—but not when it came to me. Weeks before we started second grade, his mother Theo, my mother's cousin, told Mike to "watch out for Tim and help him if he needs it." Early that school year a huge rainstorm hit while we played at recess. I grabbed my crutches and Mike hoisted me on his shoulders for a piggy back ride through the rain.

Since that day he's been my close friend, protector and chief tempter. Throughout our grade school and high school years Mike sampled all of the forbidden fruits far ahead of me. By the time we were in college I taught him a few lessons in zaniness and debauchery, but in those early years Mike always seemed to feel a certain obligation to let me catch up to him in the vice department.

I believed Fallon was my match as a straight arrow. He was just two or three years from entering the seminary, an experiment in priestly life which did not take. McDonald was a big, rugged farm boy who knew hard work like I knew Bronc Burnett books. In seventh grade he intimidated every peer as well as some authority figures. His size, manner and experience gave him an adult aura I revered.

The long bike ride out to the farm was a major adventure for me. By seventh grade I was out of braces, and bike riding was as natural to me as prancing on crutches. But I had never traveled six miles. Hackett and Fallon had to wonder if I could keep up. Along the way we stopped at a convenience store for pop, lunch fixings and a pack of Kool cigarettes.

The rigid identification checks for the purchase of cigarettes were in the distant future and Hackett had no difficulty purchasing our illicit bounty. Had I tried to buy those smokes I would have melted into an unsightly puddle of fear. Not my man Mike. The swagger that would make him an All-State basketball player was always his trademark. He never blinked. It was his right, by God, to have those cigarettes, and he got them.

The McDonald dairy farm was an important area farm. Bill's dad and his brother were among the most successful farmers in a farming county. A gravel pit with the bluest water I can remember was the highlight of that farm for seventh graders. Our hike back to the water with our lunches and cigarettes was full of the promise of mischief. This was no accidental sin. There was no question we would have gone down on the premeditation count.

The day was like no other I had ever experienced. Even though it was a bit cool, we stripped off our clothes and with sweet abandon we skinny dipped in the gravel pit, ate huge amounts of snack food we didn't know was bad for us, and smoked cigarettes unburdened by a Surgeon General's warning.

For some reason, understood only by that motley collection of professional seventh-grade miscreants, Hackett and McDonald smoked eight cigarettes each and Fallon and I each smoked two. This may have been due to their prodigious size, their unquestioned ability to beat us to a pulp, their mischievous experience or the innate wimpiness of Fallon and me. I cannot be sure. I only know that I viewed that afternoon of skinny dipping and cigarettes as both emancipation and as a born-again experience in high naughtiness.

I had broken rules that had been only rumors for me but the devil did not snatch my soul on the bike ride back home. The disproportionate number of cigarettes proved I was not fully accepted as a lawbreaker by my friends Hackett and McDonald, but in my own eyes I had proved I could dance on the forbidden side and survive. In retrospect, it was a lesson I could have lived without, but for a young boy desperately battling to be accepted, that day of lawlessness was a necessary crucible.

With Sister Frances Mary's fearsomeness, Hackett's protective arm, and teachers' genuine respect for my intellect, Sacred Heart was a pleasant and healthy experience. High academic expectations and my parent's certainty I had to attend college were reinforced by good grades and showy scores on the Iowa Basic tests. It was about that time the parental refrain, "you'll never be able to dig ditches, you have to go to college," began. That admonition became a part of the air in the McGuire household and I breathed it constantly. I was college bound because psychical labor would always elude me.

Thanks to Hackett and others I steadily learned to roll with the occasional jibes at my stature and physical capabilities.

Sometime around fourth grade I learned the lesson that defined my life. I simply cannot recall the specific event that spawned my magic moment of understanding. I have a vague recollection that I was standing in the Sacred Heart hallway between classes, but I may be conflating events. I clearly remember having a stark realization that when I laughed and joked all the kids liked me. I knew intuitively at that moment that self-pity would chase friends away.

Laughing about life and at myself beat the hell out of crying. In a blinding flash, I discovered kids were more interested in hanging around with the class clown than the class pity master. If I had to be the butt of my own jokes, so be it. I know it sounds strange, but I made a vow that day I would laugh, and I wasn't ever going to cry over my fate or condition. For me, except for my marriage, it was the smartest and most rewarding pledge I ever made. Laughter has defined my life and friends say they can distinguish my laugh in a crowd. In mid-2013 a woman sought me out after a comedy concert to tell me how much she enjoyed that laugh.

A year or two later, I enjoyed one of my few summers without casts. I gloriously mastered swimming. Practically every afternoon I splashed and frolicked with my friends at the Island Park swimming pool. One of the group's favorite games was to dive deep and swim down to touch the grates on the bottom of the pool.

For some reason scientists and doctors would be hard-pressed to explain, this feat was my unattainable challenge. Invariably I would get to within a couple of feet of the bottom and then buoyantly pop back to the surface. The futility of my quest combined with my sudden, inexplicable pop back to the top prompted Hackett to give me a nickname which precisely defined the phenomenon—"Bobber butt!"

That nickname was an attention-getter, and soon that little kid who walked funny was known to all as "Bobber butt." There is no particular joy in being called such a name by your friends and strangers. Given a choice most 12-year-old boys would rather be ignored than carry such a moniker. I was not an ordinary 12-year-old boy. I knew that if I ran from a nickname like that I would be running away from acceptance and normalcy. That summer I made a choice I would make thousands of times in the future—call me any damn thing you want, just don't ignore me.

Just as I would in different ways over the years, I celebrated being "Bobber butt." I do not argue that was psychologically healthy. I simply proffer the thought that "Bobber butt" found it easier to be accepted than the quiet kid who might rail against mockery and find himself left alone.

SIXTH GRADE AND MY GREATEST GIFT

The story I have relished for more than 50 years occurred at the beginning of sixth grade. The summer chatter had warned us that the new sixth-grade teacher, Sister Ann Denise, was extremely strict. That year my class moved to the second floor of Sacred Heart for the first time. Elevators, like candies and sugar plums, were nowhere to be found. As usual, I arrived for the first day of class in casts and on crutches.

Classes adjourned about noon and with my friends I started toward the steps to make the trek downstairs. With the manner of a severely wounded and angry penguin, Sister Ann Denise waddled over to those stairs and barked to me, "Are you going to be able to handle these steps?" I was initially struck by the kindness and concern of this nun who must have been falsely maligned. I sweetly replied, "Well sure, sister, I have a lot of experience with these crutches."

"I'm just worried about what we'll do in a fire drill," this model of Christian charity shot back.

Hackett remembers that he and McDonald lifted me up by my armpits and carried me to the bottom of the steps just to prove a point to the nun.

I remember that my friends and I hooted about her callousness and prayed the year would end quickly. It gradually dawned on all of us that this was not a nice woman. When I tell that story some Catholic school veterans cringe at what they see as my mean-spirited willingness to tell it. Others wince at Sister Ann Denise's meanness, and they easily substitute some other religious name. The truth is most nuns I encountered in high school and college were kind and concerned but there were nuns such as Sister Ann Denise who created the legends surrounding so many teaching nuns.

That story has always stood on its own and always wins the cocktail party contests for meanest nun story, but I recently heard there was a sequel. My mother tells me that Sister Ann Denise's abuse continued through that year. Apparently her choice to pick on me became a popular gossip item. At one point, another mother called my mom to tell her that all the other mothers were fully aware of how "Ann Denise is picking on Tim and we all think it's downright terrible." The mother told Anita that if she wanted to make a case out of it all the other mothers would be behind her.

When my mom told my dad about the call his response was typical Jim. "Hell yes, they'll be behind you, way behind you. Forget it. Tim will deal with it." I apparently did because I do not remember it as a particularly difficult year; in fact, it is the source of one of my greatest memories.

That 6th grade year was a watershed year in many ways. Puberty was beginning. The boys at Sacred Heart Academy stood out on the playground admiring the developing young girls and talking about stuff that they really had no clue about whatsoever. I was in that group. I was well accepted, popular with my peers. I excelled in my studies. And my class was a close knit bunch. I valued their friendship deeply.

Suddenly in May those classmates, huddled in small groups, stopped talking when I walked up. People were in constant conversations where I was not welcome.

My popularity had seemingly disappeared. My closest friends were engaged in some mysterious activity from which I was totally excluded. I conjured the worst and fretted about it. I was so upset about being rejected I made myself ill.

These had been my friends. How could they leave me like this? Was it because I was different? Had I done something? Had I said something? How could I fix it?

Finally, on the last day of school I found out what all the secrecy was about. There was a party in my classroom—Sister Ann Denise's classroom. I was the guest of honor. My classmates knew that I was facing the biggest surgery of my life. Now when you have 13 surgeries before you are 16 years old, it may sound funny to separate the gravity of those surgeries. But this was going to involve both legs, and it was the surgery that was designed to free me from those hateful metal braces on my legs. It was also going to involve the first and only surgery on my wrist. I was facing a longer than normal hospital stay and a very long recuperation.

My classmates had been plotting to pool their dimes and quarters to buy me my first transistor radio to keep me company during that long tough summer.

Every time I read over that sentence I get emotional. It is without question the greatest gift I've ever received. As I lay in the hospital that year I listened to the rock and roll stations out of Flint. For some odd reason, I remember hearing Dick McAuliffe going to bat for my beloved Detroit Tigers. I always thought I heard his rookie debut on that radio, but a little research for this book proves me wrong. I do recall hiding that beautiful radio and my earpiece under the sheets when the nurses checked on me late at night.

That radio gave me tremendous enjoyment during my long days in the hospital. More importantly, in that package with the radio was all the friendship I was afraid I'd lost.

It meant a lot to the givers too. For my retirement from the Minneapolis Star Tribune in June of 2002 Fallon and Hackett gave me a replica of that transistor radio. Forty years after the sixth-grade celebration it was another beautiful reminder of the value of friendship.

CHAPTER 4

JASON'S EARLY YEARS

A friend of mine, Amy Silverman, writes a lively, touching blog called *Girl in a Party Hat* about her pre-teen Down syndrome daughter Sophie. A bright, animated woman you do not want to mess with, Amy told me recently "Every mother with an under-10 down syndrome child writes a blog!" Her rueful sarcasm was unmistakable. A lot of parents want to share their journey in one form or another.

When I reengaged with this book in 2012 I decided that my distance from the days of raising Jason was a gift and an advantage. I don't begrudge the writings of people who are going through the daily challenge of raising their Down syndrome child, but I am convinced our perspective of a somewhat finished journey gives Jean and me additional insight. I pretty much know how the story ends and people like Amy don't.

In fact, this book has forced some surprising and even shocking reflection about Jason's early years which were clearly the most difficult for us. Jean disclosed to me in the spring of 2014 that if our marriage could have ever fallen apart it was during those maddening, frustrating and sometimes hopeless early years.

Jean says that was the time of our life together she felt the most alone and isolated. Jason's inability to master what seemed like the simplest of tasks created a hopeless feeling that to this day makes Jean shiver. The word we often use to describe that period is relentless. For a time the progress came so slowly it was difficult to celebrate the baby steps forward. But I worked in a high pressure job that totally occupied me. I went to law school. I was an engaged dad but I was not a consumed dad. Jean had to be consumed.

Jason came home from the hospital to a jealous but attentive toddler sister, a mom who desperately wanted to believe he was like any other baby and a dad who secretly wanted him to be the best damned Down syndrome kid ever.

When Jason was a baby we played with him, touched him, exercised him, talked to him and played music for him. We did those things with our other kids too, but with Jason every developmental "victory" was a big deal. Stimulation was the magic word for Down syndrome children. We rolled him over and over until he could manage it on his own. We moved brightly colored objects back and forth in front of his face until he learned to "track" them, moving his whole head first and then just his eyes to keep them in sight.

We massaged his arms and legs, bending his knees and elbows, teaching him all the things his body could do. We propped him up on pillows, we encouraged him to hold up his head and we helped him sit in our laps.

Jason responded to that stimulation well and his developmental delays in those early months were small. He weaned from the bottle exactly the same time as his siblings—early. A specialist pronounced his sucking reflex decent when he was six weeks old and he never struggled with eating. All his teeth came in on the baby book schedules. He was a bit slow sitting up, but he ate solid foods from his high chair at a reasonable time. He started walking just before he turned two, but both his siblings started walking relatively late.

Infant and toddler Jason fooled us. We started to believe this Down syndrome gig wasn't all that bad. Hindsight is required to realize the developmental door closed gradually. Reflection reveals that with each passing month and year the gap between Jason and a normal development scale widened in small doses at first, but then ever more dramatically.

As Jason grew from a toddler into a little boy he was funny, frustrating, maddening and even mysterious. His sister seemed to intuitively sense Jason needed her. Tracy became the third caretaker in the family almost from the day Jason was born. When she was four she introduced herself to a visitor. Then she introduced Jason and told the disarmed adult, "Jason is down and I'm up."

By the time she was in kindergarten the teachers found it remarkable that even though Tracy was one of the younger children, she was the class caretaker. She rushed to aid any child in need. We will never know if that was a natural tendency or if Jason cultivated that behavior. It's a role she has played with Jason and, as a special education teacher, with other children to this day.

More than at any time in our parenting lives, Jason's early years, from 3-12, demanded we just put one foot in front of the other in a daily slog to do the right thing by our son and for our family. Daily letters back and forth to teachers and monthly evaluations attempted to capture the daily battles but the truth is the constant developmental fits and starts sucked the energy out of us. Jean remembers the scope of the drama but as these words forced her to focus on the details she admits it's as if she's hearing them for the first time. I think you would find most special needs parents in the early years are like us. You conquer the daily challenges and move another step forward. You pray you don't take more than a few steps backward. And even more importantly, you discover the good times are worth genuine celebration.

Jason's two or three year "running phase" and his somewhat deranged adventures with the barber will give you a taste of his maddening early exploits.

RUNNING JUST BECAUSE HE COULD

It was as if there was some distant call to post from the devil.

Jason pursed his lips. He intently surveyed the landscape for potential escape routes and enticing adventures. Then he looked into the eyes of his keeper with a crazed impishness, as if to say "I just can't help myself, this has to be done." Before your sophisticated adult mind could process all those gathering signals, before you could prepare for the great escape, the starting gun went off in Jason's brain. He bolted.

From the time he was about 5, until he was almost 9, Jason ran. Jason dashed through hotels, through neighbor's yards and houses, across busy streets, through shopping malls, into the stock departments of major department stores and even through china shops. He played the role of the bull.

Picture a family of five on vacation in a traditional Holiday Inn in Illinois with two floors, hallways open on the ends, a pool and a large parking lot. Now picture a thirty-something, overweight dad with a severe limp, chasing a wild six-year-old without a speck of judgment.

For 35 minutes we raced up and down those stairs and hurtled down the halls. We scrambled around that pool darting dangerously through the parking lot. Exercise and I have never been friends. Routine walks around an amusement park were not a strain. Thirty-five minute breakneck marathons were more problematic. Jason's occupational therapy in school was obviously wildly successful. Fed by a frenetic energy from some satanic well, he ran possessed while I gasped.

Between my huffs and my puffs I shouted, I threatened, I cajoled, but mostly I ran. I couldn't let this child maniac out of my sight for fear of the damage he might do to himself. I thought he was harmless to bystanders, but bystanders apparently didn't share that opinion. You would have thought Godzilla was on the loose for all the help I got. Grown men and women would actually step out of Jason's way rather than come to the aid of an obviously helpless dad. Whenever I saw someone I called for help only to be greeted by "can't get involved" shrugs. I was too busy chasing to deal with their callous insensitivity.

Our youngest son Jeffrey was only 15-months-old so Jean had to stay with him. Her role was advisor, cheerleader and assistant strategist. As a six-year-old Down syndrome kid made a fool of me my appreciation level for such contributions was small. Tracy was eight, but she was sane so she wasn't much help against a frenzied madman charging irrationally through an otherwise calm vacation motel. I tried to use her to block off escape routes, but Jason's deviousness dwarfed his cognitive disability. His awkwardness and recklessness fooled you into thinking he would wander into a trap. His boundless frenetic energy always made him the clear winner.

Finally, I exhorted a maid we had passed a couple of times to stop him. She calmly stepped in front of the tiny rascal. Jason struggled just a bit to escape, but he surrendered quite easily. He was never violent or mean during these episodes. Clearly the thrill of the chase drove his frenzy.

When I confronted him after one of these episodes he was always contrite. He *said* he knew it was wrong. He *said* he'd never do it again. I usually grabbed him by the shoulders to get his attention as I lectured him. This act always seemed to frighten the daylights out of him, but it was quite apparent I never really got his attention, at least not enough to make him change his trouble-making ways.

One warm spring day almost a year later all three kids were playing in our front yard when the demon seized Jason's spirit and set him aflight. As he scampered across the street and down the block, the already mature caretaker, Tracy, started chasing at the same time she barked orders to Jeffrey. "Go get Mommy."

That seemed rational except for the fact that Jeffrey really didn't talk that much or that well. On that day necessity was the mother of first sentences. Jeffrey found Jean and with a sophisticated frustration she remembers to this moment, he sputtered, "Jason runned away."

Meanwhile, Tracy struggled to keep her brotherly quarry in sight. Even at nine, Tracy was as much his "keeper" as mom and dad.

The rampaging Jason turned left at the end of the block, ran through some back yards, and ended up on the next street headed to a backyard deck, when Tracy lost the trail. She feared the little rogue had gone into a stranger's house.

Ever the polite young lady, Tracy rang the doorbell of the suspect residence. A harried middle-age woman answered the door and Tracy asked a rather amazing question, "Is there a little boy here?" The clearly rattled and apparently clueless woman meekly answered, "Yes, he's upstairs in my closet."

Why the woman did not prevent this little mischief-maker from his hostile occupation of her closet remains a McGuire family mystery. Not for the first time, nor for the last, the nine-year-old Tracy distinguished herself as the one rational adult in that house. She calmly walked up the stairs, fished her brother out of the closet, and marched him out of the house where she found her frantic mother searching the neighborhood.

We never understood why Jason ran. This strange compulsion seemed to be a unique quirk rather than a common Down syndrome symptom, although there do seem to be some other DS kids who do it. Now that Tracy is a special education teacher she says several special needs children do it because it gives them an easy, enjoyable thrill.

Jean always traced it to Jeffrey's birth. She believed it was the only way a non-verbal, low functioning Down syndrome child could seek the attention this newcomer was stealing. I had also started law school a year before Jeffrey was born, so my frequent absences could have been a factor.

Jean often wondered if Jason even knew what he was doing. The "possessed by a demon" argument was alluring to her. Tracy thinks he did it because it was fun. She regarded him as calculating about when and where he ran. She thinks he knew it was disruptive and that made for a hilarious adventure. I think Tracy is close. When Jason ran he was clearly in control. Disabled or normal, we all seek control. Racing into strange closets and through motels is a paltry price to pay to be king of the universe.

Whatever the reason, running became a way of life for Jason. Preventing it was the mission for the rest of us. Someone was always assigned to tightly hold his hand. Shopping malls were especially dangerous. At one point we even used one of those hateful child leashes. Despite our best defenses, our diabolical little enemy constantly outfoxed us.

On one vacation trip he escaped. I held my breath as he teetered precariously through the china department of a ritzy store. As our meager net worth flashed through my brain and the hateful glares of the store clerks pierced my ego, I gingerly piloted Jason through the precious china out into the mall. I couldn't catch him out there, but at least the college funds were safe from liability suits.

Every major department store in three different malls near our Minnesota house at one time or another pleaded with shoppers to be on the lookout for a lost little boy. Sometimes the announcer on the loudspeaker would even describe him as "special." After a time we discouraged such announcements when Jason was lost. We simply advised the manager to have the store's warehouse searched.

Jason simply could not resist a closed door. It was some sort of neon invitation. Whatever was beyond that door demanded to be explored. Usually it was a vast stock warehouse with scores of places to hide and run. Sometimes despite Jason's craftiness we could count on a stockroom worker returning with the scruff of Jason's neck firmly in his grasp. Other times, the thought of grabbing this miniature meteor crashing through their stock room reduced grown men to sniveling chicken-hearts. I was compelled to learn more about department store stockrooms than I ever wished to know.

Watching other people deal with this off-kilter little dervish was often as humorous as it was maddening. One of the key ways a parent of a special education child communicates with teachers is a notebook which describes activities and progress on the school front and at home. Jean made this entry in one of those notebooks during his running phase:

> We went to Chuck E. Cheese for lunch Saturday and lost him while we took our coats off. We found him creating a ruckus at the ball crawl. He'd gone straight back, taken his boots off and was trying to get in despite the best efforts of the attendant.

Jean remembers the attendant as valiant, but reluctant to exert any real control. That was totally the wrong approach for Jason. Raw power was often the only thing he recognized when he was in one of those crazed lathers.

The same agitation and frenzy that marked the runaway Jason distinguished "haircut Jason." A thousand crazed Klingons with monstrous weapons could not have been scarier for Jason than a barber with clippers and scissors. It may have been the tools or it could have been the invasion of his personal space, but hysterical seems such a weak word to describe Jason's reaction to getting his hair cut.

Unlike his runaway escapades the barber just ticked him off. He screamed and kicked and violently jerked his head away. Strangely, despite the shrieks, there were never real tears. Mom, Dad and an extra barber were the usual complement required to get a raging Jason anything resembling a decent haircut. One person needed to hold his arms, another person held his legs, and a third person was assigned to hold his head.

One children's specialty barbershop we frequented was in the basement of a major shopping mall near the base of an escalator. You could actually hear Jason's anguished yells from the top of that escalator. People stared and shook their heads either in disapproval or sympathy. We were way beyond making a scene. We were staging a three act dramatic extravaganza.

We tried all the best children's barbers in metropolitan Minneapolis and they assigned their best people to "the case." These people had all sorts of special training to handle troublesome children but gradually Jason forced them all to surrender.

Finally, my own neighborhood barber, Jerry, overheard me talking about the problem. Without hesitation or humility, he said, "Bring him in here. We won't have a problem." It was almost that simple. The first session was a bit rambunctious, but within a few months Jerry, with his gumballs and his M and M's, was Jason's favorite clippers-wielding friend. Jerry and Jason grew so close Jerry came to Jason's high school graduation party and he occupies a place of honor in the Jason Hall of Fame.

One of the biggest challenges I have faced with this book is when to tell the story chronologically and when to take a longer view. This is one of those chapters that require that longer view. The running escapades and the haircut hassles capture just a small part of the chaos of those years. From the time Jason was a toddler until he became a teenager, his life and his family's life was a tumultuous roller coaster of activity and emotion. Nothing about those years was neat and clean. Linear movement forward for a Down syndrome boy of moderate intelligence, such as Jason, is a sweet dream.

Jason's early years taught us five truths about that phase of the journey: Frustration and hilarity sleep together, childhood "phases" are eternities for children like Jason, discipline is essential, but not foolproof, there's a cycle of anger and acceptance, and families like ours convince themselves that if one thing were different, all would be a bowl of cherries.

YOU LAUGH AND YOU SCREAM

We learned quickly that frustration and hilarity sleep together. Even while we tried to cope with each frustrating escape or contrary behavior we ruefully laughed at the ridiculousness of it all. As we planned who was in charge of Jason at every point during a family outing we made jokes about his IQ or we reminded ourselves "some people even take them home." But we cried and yelled too. Our drifting and shifting between desperation and humor became instinctive and unworthy of special family notice.

At cocktail parties or family gatherings we milked the funniest, most ludicrous stories for laughs. Jason, the perpetrator of countless inexplicable acts, made for a great conversation starter. The lesson I learned in fourth grade that when you laugh everybody gathers around you, and when you cry you are alone, was intuitively true when raising a Down syndrome child with social savvy.

Whether it was because of the nature of his particular developmental disability, his upbringing in an upscale, intelligent, humorous household, his exposure to early childhood learning or his countless hours of television viewing, Jason's social IQ always dwarfed his intellectual one. He has always been remarkably savvy, especially compared to other Down syndrome children. From Sesame Street Live, to weekly movies, to trips to Disney World and other national hotspots, Jason was exposed to experiences that most adults would find stimulating. The cherry on top of the sundae was Jason's innate quirkiness. Jean has always believed that if Jason were normal he would have been our child with purple hair and nose rings.

Running was Jason's marquee weirdness but he had other tools of frustration and entertainment in his belt. Jean wrote this one in his school journal when he was four:

Jason has been slightly wacky this weekend. I spent most of Sunday dressing him. He goes into another room, strips to the skin and then brings me his clothes! I stopped counting after the fourth time.....Last night when we went to bed at 10:30 he was still awake and playing in his room–at 5.am. When Tim got up this morning Jason was sitting in our bathroom, apparently waiting for us to get up! Good luck today and don't be surprised at anything he does!"

The propensity for nakedness didn't end that day. There are a few old photos of Jason frolicking nude in our backyard. Modesty was an elusive concept.

When he was nine or so we were eating in a restaurant, as we did often. We never let Jason discourage us from eating in sit-down restaurants, such as this particular sports café called Champs, which we patronized often. By that time he went to the bathroom himself, but without intervention he would have stayed in there for thirty minutes or more. Jean believed a Down syndrome boy spending that kind of time in a public restroom was an unnecessary temptation for the city's deviates. So with alarming regularity I dutifully sauntered into restrooms searching for a lost boy. I challenge you to try looking cool with that job.

Champs sported one of those kitschy bathrooms with the sports page above the urinal and catchy advertisements everywhere. Jason occupied the only stall for sitters. I knew this for two reasons. The Jason babble emanating from the stall distinguished my first-born son from the steady stream of upscale young professionals parading in and out of the men's room. Men are more than a little self-conscious in a public restroom anyway, and eyebrows arched nervously at the incessant, incoherent jabber.

Just as striking to me, as I stared at the bottom of the stall, was the absence of one shoe from Jason's foot. Jason did not find it odd that he was engaged in an animated conversation into his shoe. His hero Maxwell Smart on the cartoon takeoff of the 1960s television series Get Smart, talked into his shoe, so Jason should too. Trying to explain to a Down syndrome nine-year-old boy that talking into his shoe in a restaurant's restroom violates acceptable standards of behavior is as farcical as it is fruitless. Stares and titters tend to shorten the conversation. The sense that everybody else is muttering to themselves "thank God, that kid's not mine" hung in the air like the bathroom stink. That is the same emotion my mom sensed when she brought me home.

We got the same looks when we took Jason and Tracy and their Michigan cousins to a Twin Cities amusement park shortly after Jeffrey was born. We survived the long lines for the log flume and started our journey peacefully. But as the wooden tube climbed the skinny rails, the astute Jason realized Galileo's truth: what goes up must come down.

As this decidedly unattractive verity slowly dawned on Jason he shouted "uh-oh!" Despite all the signs he could not read, he leaped from his seat. He was leaving. Again finding agility I didn't appreciate I had, and with my brother Marty's strong-armed help, I interrupted Jason's earnest effort to disembark at 30 feet.

Amusement park management and onlookers displayed looks of disapproval and we laughed. Jason actually discovered he enjoyed the diving sensation and the log flume became one of his favorites. And, every time a painfully obvious bad thing is about to happen, a McGuire will utter that immortal phrase, "uh-oh!"

Jason did not confine his hilarious, frustrating moments to public appearances. Christmas, 1988, was a sad one for us. Bandit, the part Alaskan husky, part fence jumper I gave to Jean for the first Christmas we were married, died a few days before the holiday. Jean had taken fourth-grader Tracy to choir practice early in the morning and returned home to find Bandit was not just sleeping in his favorite corner.

Jean cries in Hallmark stores, so she was a mess. Disposal of the body fell to me and Jean returned to pick up an unsuspecting Tracy with Jason and Jeff in tow. Jean's grief distracted her as Tracy opened the door to the suburbia-mandated mini-van.

Jason plunged into the conversational void with this greeting, "Tracy, remember Bandit? He's dead!" A profoundly sad moment in our family history will forever be remembered for Jason's cheerful bluntness.

That story wasn't complete and it offers a fascinating glimpse at the machinations of Jason's mind. About four years later we all were in church when Jason started quietly sobbing. A concerned Tracy ministered to him by asking, "What's the matter, buddy?" Without a trace of irony or sarcasm Jason sputtered, "Bandit died."

We all mourn in our own way. If you don't laugh, you'll cry.

DEVELOPMENTAL VICTORIES WERE TREASURES

Another huge lesson we've learned along the journey is that childhood "phases" are eternities for children like Jason.

Pull the baby development book off your shelf to remind yourself how children develop, regress and then grow again. It is seldom a seamless process, but crawling, walking, talking, learning adaptive skills and potty training usually occur quickly. If there's a regression there's often a good psychological or medical reason for it. Sound parenting can often overcome it.

Jason's early development didn't quite keep pace with Tracy's, but satis-faction outdistanced fear and disappointment as we watched our little boy develop.

He never walked but he "scooched" all over the house and he was an active baby who got into trouble just as any other baby would. An example of that is the time Jean was on the phone with a new Down syndrome parent when Jason was around two. We had volunteered to help other parents coping with newborn DS children. Jean was especially good at it.

As she counseled that distraught mother, Jason was getting into all manner of mischief. He repeatedly crawled behind the TV threatening to knock it over. Jean apologized repeatedly as she chased Jason around the living room. To Jean's shock, the mother suddenly burst out in laughter. She said, "This call has been wonderful therapy." She shared her fear that so many parents embrace, that their child would be lethargic and impassive. The woman told Jean: "Listening to you chasing your son around the room dispelled all my worst fears. I think we'll be okay now."

Jason's developmental delays in those early months were small but with each passing month and year the gap between Jason and a normal development scale widened in small doses at first, but then ever more dramatically.

Jason got his baby teeth right on time, but he never lost them. A surgical dentist intervened to pull every one of those baby teeth. He slowly learned to ride a tricycle but he never learned to ride a bike. He struggled for months, then years, and never did learn to tie his shoes. His guardian angel invented Velcro straps on shoes for him. Learning to zip and button takes most children a few days or a few weeks. For Jason those were eight and 10 year projects.

Jason started school when he was two at an innovative pre-school for special kids called Fraser. Development goals and fanciful dreams were often indistinguishable, but Jason started counting when he was three. By the time he was eight his count to 100 often sounded like this; "One, two three, four, mumble, mumble, ninety-eight, ninety-nine, 100." He usually declared the number 100 with an arrogant sense of accomplishment as if he actually believed you'd fall for the con. It took him many years to consistently count to nine. The alphabet experience was similar. He could recite many of the letters, unless you were a fixated stickler for the proper order.

When he was three or four, teachers started to teach him his phone number. We changed numbers once, but he never learned his phone number until he moved into a group home and started working at the age of 22. He learned it when he really needed it. The same thing happened with "monies." He could never distinguish a five dollar bill from a one, or a quarter from a dime, until as a teenager he was given the opportunity to buy his own Subway sandwiches.

In Minnesota special education students begin public school at two. Classes for children such as Jason, who are labeled as having moderate to severe cognitive disability, are organized around the individual student's abilities. The tools school districts use to track that individual performance according to the specific goals is called an IEP or an Individual Education Plan. Friends of ours often astutely commented how much better their child's public education would have been with the same individualized approach.

Students such as Jason do academic sorts of things even if they can't read or write. As my daughter Tracy, a special education teacher of children with abilities similar to Jason wrote me: "For some students it might be basic recognition of shapes, colors, numbers or letters. Some students might be working on following directions, or being able to sit at a table with a group. Some students work on eye contact and on how to play with toys."

Tracy pointed out that the starting point for all special education students is the teaching of functional academics, that is, things students need to function in the community. For Jason, even though he would never read, that meant teaching him how to recognize the letters in his name, his address, phone number and how to listen, communication strategies and alternatives. He even took numerous cooking classes which were a part of teaching him to be as functional as possible.

I have referred to journals and notebooks. Those five-by-seven notebooks were a crucial part of Jason's education. When my grandkids go to school they tell their parents about the high points of their day. To some parents' chagrin, children often tell teachers *everything*. Jason could not do that. The notebooks served as an essential communication tool between parents and teachers. With that notebook Jean and the teachers were able to stay plugged into Jason's accomplishments and failures. If he showed an interest in crayons at home Jean would tell the teachers that and they incorporated it into his lesson plan. Strategies for helping Jason were an essential function of those daily communications. Special education experts stress the importance of the entire team in raising a disabled child. Those notebooks made Jason's education team a unified, coherent unit.

Starting school at two allowed Jason to escape the separation anxiety phase which plagues so many toddlers, but his early entry into school may have exacerbated our difficulties with the most challenging of all of Jason's phases and the best example of teacher/parent communication—potty training.

There are more than 50 books listed on potty training and more than 5,000 child development books on Amazon. When you search potty training you get at least 16 million listings. Potty training is a watershed moment for toddlers. When it goes well the triumph is a really big deal but when it's a struggle it can incite some of the most anxious moments of childhood for many parents.

For Jason the process was our parenting Armageddon. We first saw him express an interest in training on January 18, 1982. Jean made this entry in his school diary. He was 33 months old, not a bad age to begin potty training. In a February 20, 1985 school evaluation, his teacher wrote this as one of his educational goals: *Demonstrate awareness of having dry, clean pants –Jason continues to be dry when schedule-trained. When he does have accidents he doesn't initiate to change clothes. We will continue to give him opportunities to initiate the need to toilet with subtle cues.*

That was three years after he first indicated an interest in the potty and two months before his sixth birthday. By that time his parents were way beyond the desire for subtle cues. Baseball bats or nuclear weapons seemed like much better options than "subtle cues." That evaluation had been the second consecutive one which indicated that not only was Jason still not trained; he refused to admit his failures by asking for a change of clothes. He finally achieved most of his goal in the fall of 1985.

My memories of the "long Jason phases" such as running and potty training are not fond. Yet, after reading three years of entries in school notebooks I am stunned at our patience with the roller-coaster of potty training success and failures. Those notes make the frustration we felt real and immediate. They also should serve as documentation for a move to nominate Jean and his teachers for sainthood.

Psychologists and urologists might argue for years about why it was so hard for Jason to master potty training. Power and control could be argued by some, but Jean is convinced he simply could not appreciate the signals his body sent to his brain. The pressure which sends us all to the toilet never seemed to register for Jason. For many years he could not translate the bladder or sphincter pressures into a recognition that they meant he had to head to a bathroom.

We had the same problem with vomiting. For many years Jason defined "projectile vomiting." He would sit up in his bed and spew without ever moving. It was as if he was surprised anew by the sensation every single time.

We often blamed all his "long phases" on what we called the synapse problem. Something that connects the physiological action like running, vomiting or peeing to the logical part of our minds is missing for Jason. Things that seem so obvious and coherent for us are a mysterious blur for him. At 35, Jason is obviously toilet trained but the projectile vomiting is still a part of his life.

ACCEPTANCE THEN ANGER AND THE CYCLE STARTS AGAIN

One of the most surprising lessons we stumbled upon was that there's a cycle of anger and acceptance in rearing developmentally challenged youngsters.

The toilet training issues ran well past Jason's sixth birthday. The running episodes were at their peak when he was seven and were not really solved until he was nine. When he was seven, Jason's maddening behaviors collided with our impatience and frustration. He was no longer a cuddly, madcap toddler whose development was within shouting distance of his age peers. Other seven year-olds were riding bicycles, understanding the difference between right and wrong and staying out of neighbor's closets.

We had an almost three-year-old son whose judgment we trusted far more than Jason's. Gradually, Jean and I realized, almost simultaneously, we were both mighty pissed off. Raising a Down syndrome kid was not the enjoyable lark it had first seemed. The pressures of disappointment, exhaustion and hopelessness started to suffocate us and we were surprised. Jean, the picture of peace and strength for so many years, was shaken as much as she was shocked. It would take us 15 more years before we realized that there is more or less a seven year cycle of anger and acceptance.

In the weeks following Jason's birth, Jean easily fell into mothering her special child and celebrating his 'babyness." She was constantly thrilled by his accomplishments. Eventually I joined her in those triumphs, but not before I struggled through an anger and blame episode a few weeks after his birth. It was one of those eight or nine "sinful" events in your life that haunts you to judgment day.

Fledgling support groups in Lakeland knew they needed to provide help and assistance, but vagueness surrounded their efforts. With a small group of other perplexed and overwhelmed parents of Down's children under two, we began attending weekly Wednesday night sessions we called our "Down's classes." That sort of irreverence had been born in the hospital and within weeks of Jason's birth it was our key survival mechanism. It remains so today even though some people are offended and even scandalized by it.

The class was taught and coordinated by a young woman who could have invented the term bubbly. Kathy DeWinkler was attractive, knowledgeable and one of God's great accomplishments in the "nice" department. About six weeks after Jason's birth she did, or said, something I can't remember that set me off. I bullied and browbeat her way out of proportion to the offense.

My only clear memory is of her quivering and trembling on the brink of tears, but finding the inner strength to blast me. She told me that I was not angry about the particular issue that set me off. Instead, she said, I was angry about Jason and I simply had not had the courage to admit it. Unsurprisingly, I blustered that she was wrong. The truth is her arrow scored a direct hit. Despite my vows in the hospital to avoid asking "why me" I was doing just that by allowing my anger to erupt inappropriately.

I never thanked Kathy DeWinkler for having the courage to set me straight. I never apologized for hurting her either. I have been unable to track her down so I pray she reads this book and accepts my apology and gratitude.

Right about that time, I was going through the same blame exercises Jim and Anita wallowed in shortly after my birth. I examined every beer I ever drank, every joint I ever smoked, and I tore apart the week Jason was conceived to figure out which sin I was being punished for by this terrible calamity. One of the couples in the support group dynamited me out of that self-pitying drill by pointing out the futility of blaming.

I regrouped. I shoved aside the anger and the blame, moving forward and leaving only one little obligation undone.

During my early newspaper career as the top editor in Ypsilanti, Michigan and Lakeland, Florida I worked diligently to establish a connection with the community. In both places I wrote very personal columns. Those columns allowed me to comment on important local news events but they also gave me an opportunity to humanize the paper and myself. In those days a lot of editors waltzed through small towns without becoming fully engaged. With the encouragement of my publishers, especially a man in Ypsilanti named Wayne Powell, I emphasized funny slices of life.

In Lakeland, I wrote a seemingly popular two-times-a-week column, first called, "Getting to Know Polk," and later, "My Polk World." I wrote countless columns about Tracy, including a heartfelt salute on her first birthday. Many of my "domestic" columns were about funny family scenes, such as trying to feed Tracy, or the stresses of Jean's pregnancy with Jason.

The column I didn't write was the obvious missive I owed readers when Jason was born. Readers knew about the pregnancy, but I dithered about how to write about Jason as I fought my emotional tumult.

Finally, a loyal reader caught me. A question to our newsroom forced me to confront all those emotions and I wrote this purgative piece which publicly set me on the course I would follow for years. This is a verbatim rendition of the column. I wish some of the language and the grammar were better but I resisted the temptation to edit because the thoughts are blessedly genuine and prove to me I have not engaged in revisionism.

The woman collects my columns, and she wanted to get the column I wrote about the birth of my little boy.

Our librarian knew I had written several columns about my daughter and about her birth, but she didn't remember a column about my son's birth. The woman insisted I must have written one and she missed it.

She was wrong.

I did not write a column about the birth of my son. I was afraid. I worried that anyone who did not know me well would not understand my emotions. I love my little boy dearly, and I have since he was born, but I didn't completely trust my ability to communicate the emotions surrounding the birth of a handicapped child to a handicapped father.

Jason McGuire was born with Down syndrome. That's the new fancy term. The term you remember from your childhood days is Mongolism. We all have 46 chromosomes in our genetic makeup; Jason has 47.

Years ago Jason would have been immediately institutionalized and unofficially registered as a non-person. There are still some Polk County doctors who think that's the best course, but scores of parents are rejecting that theory with more than a little bitterness. They are keeping their children at home, working with them, loving them. The result is the average IQs of Down's children is up some 30 or 40 points.

That improvement is not genetic. The difference is the investment of love.

I desperately wanted a little boy. A boy with whom I could share my love of sports, a boy who would be my friend and pal, a boy who could do all the athletic and adventuresome things I couldn't do as a boy because of a physical handicap.

When the doctor cried, "It's a boy," my heart almost beat out my chest, and I buried my joyful crying face in my wife's chest.

But the paranoia that follows a person who was born handicapped immediately took over. Jason's stomach looked funny, and there was something different about his face. I asked if he was all right. The nurse assured me that he was fine. She told me Jason looked just like his daddy.

Twenty-four hours later I was told Jason was a Down syndrome baby. I swore. I cursed my luck. I worried about my wife. I was so distraught I asked a close friend to drive me to the hospital in Winter Haven. I cried. And I hoped, but not too much. I knew there was no mistake.

My wife and I shared tears for another 24 hours. She was upset about me. She didn't think it was fair for a handicapped person to have a handicapped child. My friend felt the same way. He's an agnostic. And this experience did not bring him closer to God. He thought my God had shafted me. My parents were especially crushed because they had to live the heartache of 30 years ago all over again.

For a time Saturday night I started to feel guilty about making all my friends and relatives sad. The irony and inanity of that struck me hard. Suddenly I came to my senses and realized that I had been dealt a hand by God and I was going to have to play it. I vowed never to ask God why he chose me for this challenge. I knew it was because I had had every break in life and it was time for me to give a little back.

My resolve was strengthened the next day when we had Jason in my wife's room. He was just like our little girl. He was a baby, not a zombie. He reacted like any other baby to the warmth of his mother. From that moment on, my wife and I knew the world would be all right. We knew there'd be challenges and that our life would be a little different than most, but our lives had always been different.

Within days of Jason's birth some local parents were in touch with us, telling us about an active group of Downs' parents who meet each Wednesday at the Child Development Center. I called them my Downs' classes.

That parents group, we would come to find out, runs on grit. A dedicated and loving Child Development Center social worker named Kathy DeWinkler donates her time to counsel the group and feisty Downs parents like Doug and Jamie Bronson are out soliciting private donations to make Kathy a full-time counselor to parents of Down syndrome children.

The parents see themselves in a power play with the local offices of the Florida Department of Health and Rehabilitative Services. HRS has twice refused to fund the program, preferring instead to run the program itself. But most of the parents refuse to work with HRS. Some parents have such a fear of the government they'll have nothing to do with HRS. They want to control their own destiny and feel that's impossible with the government.

At this point there is a vacuum. HRS doesn't want to give away its responsibilities and parents don't want to give up the autonomy they feel they have with the Child Development Center.

Florida is not a good place to be handicapped. Florida is a low tax, low service state. The bottom line is that the Downs' children we've been exposed to in the last four months will not get the breaks Jason will get when we move to Minnesota with its high taxes and high service levels. Jason will get the best. The Florida Downs kids will have to depend on the bureaucratic success of dedicated people like Doug Bronson and the generosity of private foundations.

Jason is handicapped, but he will not be allowed to sit around reaping sympathy. He is going to work and study, and work some more. The goal is "mainstream."

We want Jason to go to school with his sister and the neighbor kids. We're willing to invest all the time and effort it takes to reach that goal. We

don't want to deny Jason's handicap. We simply want him to take his best
shot at beating it.

Perhaps it is a testament to spousal love or an example of how we blame ourselves before we give ourselves credit, but Jean does not remember my bout of anger with Kathy DeWinkler. But she does recall that shortly after my column ran the local agency funded the program. Jean has always credited my column. That positive contribution only flickers in my memory. Jean remembers it because "maybe, she thought, immodestly, Jason had achieved his first purpose."

For many years after I wrote that column and after that one foray into anger, Jean and I were enthusiastic Down syndrome parents. She was active with Downs' groups, especially the Fraser School parent groups. She used her formidable organizational skills to run several bazaars and other special activities for them. We were active in bringing parents together to talk about the challenges we all faced. We participated in the support programs for new parents of Down syndrome children.

In those early days in any conversation with me, if you didn't know I was the parent of a Down syndrome child by the time we got to pictures of our kids, you weren't paying attention. Down's parenting became a distinguishing element of our identity. We reveled in the fact that Jason was a toddler like all other toddlers. We told ourselves that while he was clearly developmentally delayed, there was so much to celebrate because he was fun-loving, affectionate and "getting better." We didn't obsess about his disability and we definitely didn't talk about it constantly. We lived life day to day and enjoyed watching our kids grow up.

When Jason was about 14 the family discovered the horrible truth about puberty, it does not spare mentally disabled people.

Once again we struggled with that eternal question that stymies all parents of special children: Is this particular behavior caused by the disability, by puberty or is my child by nature a hopeless and irrevocable jerk? There was a horrible moment somewhere around that age where we fought the terrible and irreverent realization that Jason had become "a big dumb kid" and not a little boy or an emerging teenager. He was not like everyone else's son.

The frustration gripped us again when Jason was about 21 and that episode prompted Jean to utter the most important and insightful words in

Jason's life; "It's time." It was time for Jason to move on and establish a more independent lifestyle. Both Jean and I found ourselves battling the frustration of realizing that many of the behaviors we were dealing with at 21 were behaviors that had driven us crazy when Jason was six.

Jean and I usually chose to laugh at Jason's hilarious antics and his cock-eyed view of the world, but a lifetime of insomnia and crazy tricks wears on you.

In many ways we created the environment which allowed us to get sucked in by the "improving Jason." His innate savvy fooled us. We never blinked at the prospect of integrating Jason into our active family's lifestyle. Remember, the deal at his birth was he would never negatively impact our family life.

Those efforts were not without their risks, such as the time toddler Jason's sudden grab for the President Nixon pardon document set off the alarm at the Gerald Ford Presidential Museum in Grand Rapids Michigan. That would have been a nice souvenir.

Jason benefited from this forced march to make him an important part of an active engaged family. It is also true he once almost killed himself by opening the car's back door on a Minneapolis freeway, 15 minutes into an automobile trip out west. His intimate encounters with Goofy and Donald Duck at Disney World, and his ride through Yellowstone Park at the height of their historic wildfires, made Jason a Down syndrome man of the world.

At an early age it became apparent he "got it." One teacher marveled at his ability to "get my jokes." This woman was a grizzled special education veteran. She kept herself sane by making wise-acre comments throughout the day, comments that flew across her students' heads like jet airplanes. But the jokes didn't soar past Jason. He laughed at her comments and cultivated a genuine relationship with her she found rare and amazing.

The discovery that Jason is socially savvier than his intellect emerged as a "Jason truth" when he was five or six and it remains a defining element of his personality today.

He moved from Fraser school into the public school system when he was four and he fooled the school folks too. His social adaptability made him seem "smarter' than he really was. Teachers placed him above his capabilities. For a few triumphant months, when he was six, Jason was "mainstreamed' which had been our earliest goal. That mainstreaming decision was fool's gold as he struggled to keep up. A diagnostic testing report was ordered, and it confirmed the fascinating Jason dichotomy.

The report listed his actual age as 6.6 years. His IQ was measured at 36 or "generalized moderate retardation" and his mental age was registered as 2.10 years. Yet, on what was called a Vineland Social Maturity scale, his attainment age was 5.9 years. That was just 7 months below his actual age. The diagnostician argued with those results supplied by the teacher and contended Jason was "more likely functioning between the three and four year level in social development." I personally buy the Vineland Scale. He was and is just that savvy.

Both the Vineland Scale and the diagnostician's skeptical assessment put Jason's social development way ahead of his cognitive mental age and explain why so many people were comfortable with Jason in social situations. The diagnostician wrote this:

> Jason is a very likable 6.6 year old Down syndrome boy....He may be considered primarily non-verbal, communicating mainly through gestures visual and verbal cuing.....Although he attempts speech in the form of one or two word phrases, it is often unintelligible especially for novel listeners. He is described by his teacher as very social, cooperative and alert and this may be attributed to a very supportive upbringing among family members and a well-structured educational environment..... During the individual assessment Jason was cooperative but distractible. He seems to have a very short attention span and requires constant redirection on tasks.......although he has substantial cognitive limitations and is developmentally immature in terms of socialization and communication; he seems much more functional in terms of adaptive behavior......."

Let me translate the psychological gobbledy-gook. Jason intuitively knows the chicken crossed the road to get to the other side but he can't effectively tell you about it and he won't pass any cognitive tests about the who, what, why and where of the chicken's action.

DISCIPLINE IS ESSENTIAL BUT......

One of the biggest reasons Jason was so socially adaptive was our firm belief that discipline is essential, but we learned it is not foolproof.

A parent cannot adjust the haunting, widespread eyes of a Down syndrome child, but when that omnipresent protruding tongue betrays his condition, a dedicated parent gently places his finger on it pushing it back into the infant's mouth. That telltale tongue marked our earliest encounter with discipline. It served as our first concrete lesson that high standards were fruitful. Constantly pushing that tongue back into Jason's mouth from the time he was a few months old paid big dividends.

In early 2013, Jean encountered a twenty-something DS man with a disturbing protruding tongue. It was an unsettling reminder that failure to discipline disabled folks early can make their life more difficult.

There were many times when it would have been much easier to leave our baby alone and keep our hands to ourselves, but we knew that a protruding tongue would mark him as hopelessly different. The overriding goal was always to allow him to successfully blend in with his peers. Rare is the picture of Jason which shows the protruding tongue. The constant repetition of having the tongue pushed back in made a difference for Jason and served as a metaphor for the way we dealt with him. If we made a behavioral problem a big enough deal, and hammered it relentlessly enough, we thought we could fix it.

Jean and I are both fairly strict disciplinarians with high expectations for all our children. We were both raised with high standards. Fortunately, both of us realized how important it was to our formation as strong, capable adults. We could even be accused of having precious little tolerance for parents who fail to discipline their kids. Jean has always joked she wanted to write a book she would title "Stupid Parent Tricks' to illustrate the boneheaded mistakes parents make in disciplining their children.

I sometimes tried to fix every other child I saw. One cloudy day as we vacationed in the Bahamas the three kids and I walked on the beach carrying ice cream cones. Two pre-teen kids were throwing mud balls on the beach unconcerned their mud was flying onto our ice cream. I launched into a lecture. In the background I could hear 11-year-old Jeffrey say to his sister, "Hi, meet Dad." His oft-repeated smart-alec comment has served as a reminder over the years that sometimes I need to mind my own business. I too often forget the reminder.

Tracy and Jeff knew the boundaries and always respected them, though not without occasional high-spirited challenge. Some parents are tempted to suspend those standards for "special" children. We resisted all those temptations. That discipline is a huge contributor to who Jason is today. He has succeeded to the extent he has, because we, particularly Jean, coached, disciplined and always had high expectations for him.

We frequently encounter Down syndrome people who seem to have a very poorly developed sense of right and wrong. They rudely interrupt conversations and are allowed to be the center of all attention. Jason dearly wants to be that center of attention, but he knows it's not socially acceptable, especially when Mom, Dad and/or Tracy are around.

Jason's manners and high level of respect always stand out even among peers who are more verbal and more accomplished. Yes, this is the same child who ran like a wild man through malls, motels and china shops. Discipline came hard and sometimes had its limits.

One day when he was three or four, in a rowdy round of play, Jason bit Tracy. Jean stepped in immediately to reassure Tracy that lawlessness would not be tolerated, as much to teach Jason right from wrong. She instinctively knew it was crucial that our other two kids appreciate there was only one standard of behavior and not two. The older Tracy and Jeff got the harder that became, but it was always our goal. Jean was convinced Jason was playing and the bite carried no malevolence. Jason didn't understand the consequences of applying his teeth to Tracy's skin.

Tracy had a far more difficult time coping with Jason tearing the heads off her dolls on an almost daily basis. When that kind of thing happened we always wondered if that was the behavior of a Down syndrome child or the typical behavior of a little brother. We never found the answer for that particular behavior or any other.

We always joke that when God handed out judgment Jason was sitting on the toilet for hours. Knowing that your target of discipline lacks judgment creates a burning need for creativity and focus. My favorite device was to grab his shoulders and square his body to mine and move within inches of his face. It was imperative to get that wandering mind attuned to the behavior at hand. It was not a task for wimps. A firm grasp and a tough voice were the only way to penetrate that fog.

My stern voice is legend in my family, and Tracy often talks about the power of Jean's "look." Corporal punishment was never our style. Observing Jason would give you a completely different impression. If I raise my voice and approach Jason, he reflexively pulls away in a defensive posture as if I beat him regularly. Jason respects and frets about any measure of disapproval from Dad or Mom. However, all reprimands are not created equal in Jason's mind. Dad's raised voice can reduce Jason to tears. He never wants anyone to be unhappy, especially me, yet figuring out that certain behaviors are what make us unhappy often escapes him.

A reprimand from either Jean or me often begets tears and a trembling, "I stilllllllll love you." No matter how much we tried it was always difficult to make Jason realize that discipline and expectations had nothing to do with how much we loved him.

Jason's nasty habit of smacking his food and eating with his mouth open was one example of the failure of firm discipline. Our nagging improved it to the point that we could tolerate it. However, that was the one social sin that caused him problems with other children. One particular time some intolerant kids, who obviously had issues of their own, mocked him and excluded him because his mastication habits didn't meet their standards. That sort of hassling seemed to befuddle Jason as much as it bothered him. He knew he was being treated differently and he didn't like it. Yet, the cause and effect synapse never seemed to click. The mocking never forced him to change his eating habits.

The most fascinating and perhaps wrongheaded discipline decision we ever made was our tacit creation of the world's greatest couch potato. When we failed to curb Jason's television viewing habits we failed on two fronts. We broke our basic rule about treating all three children the same and we failed to consider future consequences. It came back to bite us later.

We always had stringent rules about what Tracy and Jeff watched on television and when they watched. We insisted on reading, group play and independent play. We even banned Gameboys, and Jeff didn't get his first video game until he was 16 or so. We worried about a television addiction and we tried to use the learning aspects of television to our advantage. Time was precious to me in the evenings because I worked 12 hour days. I did not want the kids obsessed with TV at the expense of family time.

We abandoned those strict standards when it came to Jason. In this one case our fatalism and our irreverence clouded our judgment. We specifically said out loud, "What's going to happen if he watches too much TV? It's not like it's going to fry his brain." While that was irreverently funny, it regrettably missed the point.

Jason's obsession with TV exacerbated his solitary nature. It further disconnected him from reality and it allowed him to escape into an alternate universe he could control. As a person who appreciates her solitude, Jean argues he may have retreated inward even if he had been normal. I am convinced his lack of judgment made television an even more dangerous tool than it is for most kids.

Jason never slept well, and I frequently rose around 5 a.m. to find him watching Big Blue Marble or Saved by the Bell. In the early days he'd sit within inches of the TV. There, he would build a little nest of his shoes, socks and toys. He became one with the television and the "Jason" wall around the two of them was impenetrable. We nagged him to move farther and farther back until we finally ordered him to sit in a chair. That simply moved the nest to the chair. Now he had a throne from which to control his TV kingdom.

Jason became one of the first masters of the remote control. His channel-changing artistry dazzled as he flipped through channels with a motor dexterity we never witnessed in any other function. He seemed to intuitively know what shows were attractive and which ones to reject.

Our available alternatives to the TV were few because Jason could not read and his ability to amuse himself was limited. Yet, our acquiescence to Jason's TV excesses remains my great second-guess. It must be said Jason has been labeled a visual learner and you can argue TV has been his greatest teacher. But that judgment thing rears its ugly head when he ruefully announces a line from the movie Major League to his Mother, "Women, you can't live with them, and they can't pee standing up." At that uncomfortable moment, and scores like it, you realize the boy watches way too many movies and TV shows.

"Age appropriate" was always a big part of discipline. Teachers and experts hammered home the importance of trying to channel DS youngsters into age appropriate activities. We bought Jason a tricycle and other toys when we would have bought them for a normal child, but as he grew, his interests were decidedly juvenile. As he grew out of the toddler stage, Christmas shopping for him became a horror. The act of buying baby picture books for an 11 year-old was disheartening. Used together, the words Jason and Christmas sent Jean and I muttering to the liquor cabinet.

"Lovies" presented us with one of our biggest disciplinary challenges. Unlike our other two children, Jason never became attached to a blanket or any other sort of security anchor when he was a toddler. Gradually, as he held court in front of the television he developed a need for some diversion. He rolled his socks into a ball and to my disgust stuffed them into his mouth. Jason got the full ration of my wrath every time those socks approached his mouth.

The sock fetish evolved into a need for some sort of "lovey" around the TV. Eventually, Jason needed that object of affection wherever he went in the house.

The most exciting and long lasting attachment was a pink plastic hanger. The hanger displayed Jason's imagination because it could be anything from a person to talk to, to a gun, to a camera, to a microphone. He often would see a scene such as Mom and Dad kissing and his camera would start rolling. When he thought something needed a play-by-play announcer the hanger was a microphone. Since we never allowed guns in our house the hanger was the closest he ever came to playing with a six-shooter.

Once during a family visit, Jason walked by his Uncle David, my youngest brother. Anxious to share in the fantasy David enthusiastically asked, "What have you got there?" Jason slowly turned, looked at his hanger, and then looked at David as if he was the stupidest man God ever created, and said, "It's a hanger."

Mere mortals are not welcome into Jason's world.

At one time the item of attachment was a small stuffed Chihuahua dog. During another phase he was enormously attached to Tommy and Chucky dolls from the TV show Rugrats, which Jason always called "Baby Rats." Jason is often close, but seldom right on target.

His teachers in March of 1992 complained about his favorite activity which they described as "sitting in a chair and holding onto a favorite object which is often not age appropriate." He would talk to himself during such a reverie. Sometimes Jason's most energetic conversations were with himself. No amount of lecturing or hectoring could change Jason's obsession with his solitary fantasies. It took us years to realize that perhaps that creative play was disguising some serious intelligence of an off-kilter brand.

We did set up firm boundaries around the hanger and his toys—they were never allowed out of the house unless we were on a trip and then they had to be packed. We were convinced people in restaurants and other public events were not prepared to be shot at with a pink hanger.

Jason lacked a lot of tools to deal with adversity so just like his dear old dad did when he blasted Sister Frances Mary with his bike, Jason often feigned illness when the going got tough. As Jean always said when the R-word was still accepted, "The child is retarded not stupid." The simple equation that sickness meant staying home did not escape Jason. While he understood the cause and effect, his acting skills never reached Oscar quality. It was easy to spot the faker. Usually firmness solved the problem, but not always. And, sometimes the firmness needed to be applied to people other than Jason.

When Jason was 11 or so he declared himself "sick" practically every morning for more than a week. We pumped him for information on what was bothering him, but he either couldn't or wouldn't articulate the problem. We made all the correct inquiries at school and were told there were no problems. On a hunch, we decided he dreaded something on the bus trip to school. Teachers, administrators and the bus driver assured us there were no problems on the bus.

I didn't buy any of it. The problem was not going away, so I rode the bus. Within five minutes I discovered Jason being harassed by another youngster. Jason professed that the hassling didn't bother him, but he wasn't sick any more after I explained to the teachers and the bus driver that "good-natured needling" among special education children just does not work. Jason's new-found health was worth the resentment my intervention earned me with the bus driver.

"YOU'VE LOST MY SON"

Jason endured several other transportation indignities during those early years. We learned early that losing special kids will definitely go on your permanent record. The school district learned right along with us.

The most dramatic event came when Jason was seven or so. Jean got a call at home about an hour after the bus picked him up. His class teachers were on the phone asking why Jason stayed home. Jean was deeply concerned immediately. Jason was not home, she told the teachers, he had climbed on the bus as usual that morning.

Now lots of other people shared her concern. The teachers started checking other special education programs in the district and could not find him. Jean grew more agitated every time one of the schools inquiries came up empty. Finally, hysteria set in and she called me at the office.

My default position is usually to try to understand how an organization is managed. In a flash I decided losing any kid, especially a Special Education kid, was a profound management failure and I was not going to screw around with school principals. I knew the Superintendent of Schools and I called her.

As the managing editor of the Minneapolis Star Tribune newspaper I was always sensitive to charges of conflict of interest. Jean had been a journalist so we were very reluctant to ask for help just because I wielded some power. That sort of thing could easily erode credibility, but we both intuitively understood losing our special needs son was the time to use every available leverage point.

The secretary knew by my tone of voice and my disclosure of my position she needed to interrupt the superintendent. My clearest memory of that frantic, angry, consoling, panicked conversation is that it was clear to me the superintendent, a nice, competent woman, was thinking, "Of all the thousands of kids in this district why did we have to lose the child of the managing editor of the newspaper?" Her embarrassment was profound.

I stayed on the line while the superintendent got up to speed, barked orders and mobilized her staff to find Jason. As the horrible truth unfolded the superintendent's embarrassment turned to fury.

The emerging story was that Jason had gotten ill on the bus and either vomited or suffered diarrhea. Whatever the illness, he made a mess so the bus driver booted him off the bus at a junior high. Staff there took Jason under their wing and cared for him but none of them told anybody at district headquarters that they had a child they shouldn't have. Nobody thought to tell any central authority there was an uncommunicative child in a place he shouldn't have been. With the Superintendent on the case, people finally started to communicate and Jason's home school was told he was safe at the junior high.

A few years later Jason attended a summer program. To our bewilderment the district decided the best way to transport Jason to and from the program was by taxi. One day Jason was significantly late getting home, late enough that Jean called the school transportation department.

The resulting Keystone Cops behavior would have been hilarious to Jean if her son wasn't lost. She was on the phone to a dispatcher who patched Jean through to the taxi driver. The driver seemed hopelessly lost but Jean found both the dispatcher and the driver to be defensive jerks who insisted nobody was lost. Jean was totally uninterested in their prideful egos. She wanted her son back. Jean is like a Mama Bear, poke her kids and you are going to get poked back, hard.

It took her more than a half-hour to guide the driver through the Northwest suburbs of Minneapolis where we lived. She grew angrier as the driver's arrogance and defensiveness became insufferable. The only person who apparently enjoyed this little circus was Jason. He could hear Jean's voice on the driver's radio and he was apparently comforted by the fact his mommy was instructing the driver how to get home. He never panicked.

We always fought hard to get Jason on the "big bus." Comedians ridicule "short buses" all the time. The stereotypes that they are for special education students are mean and dangerous. We thought Jason might be better off on a big bus "just like the other kids." That decision led to arguably the most serious bus incident Jason ever had. It was certainly the most frightening bullying incident he ever encountered.

Jason hungered to be normal just as his father had years earlier. The way to be cool on the big bus was to sit in the back "with the other guys." On this day those normal kids turned into bullies. Two boys coached Jason to open the back emergency door while the bus was moving. They taunted and tantalized. Jason tried to resist but the attention from older boys was clearly attractive. A witness apparently believed Jason was succumbing to temptation and tipped Tracy at the front of the bus who notified the bus driver. He threw the boys off the bus, when it was stopped. We heard later the boys were suspended from school.

We never understood if those two bullies were simply seeking adventure or if they really wished Jason harm. Jean and I have searched our memories and that's the only clear example of bullying from mainstream kids we remember Jason facing. Tracy thinks Jason's friends from St. Joseph's parish and Tracy and Jeff's friends protected Jason. With deep pain, Tracy remembers another young special education student without a similar protective network who suffered unmerciful bullying.

I always attributed Jason's acceptance by normal people to one of Jean's most clever parenting strokes. The stereotype of DS kids hugging everybody they see is not necessarily an unfair one. Jean knew that hugging separated Down syndrome kids from others. As Jason neared middle school Jean taught him to extend high fives rather than hug the people he liked. For junior high and high school kids a "cool" high-fiving Down syndrome kid was easier to like and to protect than some hugging weird kid who made everybody uncomfortable.

OUR FAMILY'S "IF ONLY"

I have become convinced that most families with a special challenge convince themselves that if one thing were different all would be a bowl of cherries. No matter how sanguine we get about our obstacles, no matter how much we persuade ourselves we can deal with them, we harbor a deep belief that one thing could change the ballgame.

We always believed that if only Jason could speak more clearly his life and ours would be exponentially better. Episodes such as the bus hassling and the incessant running drove us to distraction because it was impossible for Jason to tell us what he was thinking. With a normal child you can sit down to explore feelings, frustrations and moods. A normal child could have prevented getting lost because he could have told authorities what was going on. Hundreds of times we wanted to shout, "Please just tell us what you're thinking!"

Body language, sentence fragments, intricate mimes and dramatic expressions were Jason's communication currency. Jason's true feelings and insights have always been imprisoned by his failure to adequately communicate. It is obvious much great wisdom and insight is crushed by his inability to speak clearly.

There was no stunning moment of clarity when we realized Jason would not be a verbal Down syndrome child. It was probably our earliest jealousy. We accepted the Down syndrome reality, but when other DS kids showed verbal potential we knew our verbal sled was in much deeper snow. Jason often woke us with his babbling in bed and we held out hope that someday intelligible words would rise from those scrambled sounds.

School records, when he was 10, show he was more successful in communicating with adults than peers. Jason was always a loner and the ugly truth is he didn't like other special education kids very much. Teachers observed that "he will take charge with a retarded person, but will acquiesce to an adult or normal person and expect them to do the (verbal) task."

Some days it was impossible to separate his inability to communicate from what we call the "ozone." At times he could be incredibly perceptive. At five and six he picked up on verbal and unspoken cues with the sophistication of a teenager. At other times he drifted into the "ozone" and the failure to articulate created a madcap atmosphere around the McGuire household.

In one of his school notebooks Jean tells the story of an evening Jason came home to find her busy. Later, Jean frantically looked for his lunchbox. She turned the house upside down, as Jason watched her frustration. Jean finally found the box neatly in place under his properly hung coat. Jason just never focused enough on the search to contribute that key piece of information. It simply never dawned on him.

By the time he was four it was clear he desperately wanted to communicate. His frustration was undisguised because he thought he was talking just as we were. The key to appreciating Jason's verbal abilities is to understand that he really believes he's saying words just like you are. He used to get very angry when I would correct him on the pronunciation of a word such as taco. He repeated distinctly and carefully, as if I were a particularly slow guy, Caco! "No, Jason, its Taco. He spit back, "I said Caco!" Oh.

We've never understood that speech phenomenon. I don't know if his brain hears the word correctly and his tongue simply can't pronounce it, or if there's a broken synapse somewhere between the brain and his tongue. Whatever it is, that inability to communicate clearly has shaped who Jason is and who we are. I truly believe that he has a special, though disabled mind. If he could speak more clearly his life would be fundamentally different.

JASON SOLVES HIS OWN PROBLEM

Experts our daughter Tracy has talked to say this is a developmental failure. Most toddlers say what they think they hear but as they mature their ability to match what they hear with what they say improves. Jason's never did.

The experts told Tracy that Jason hears our sounds just fine but the enunciation tools to repeat those sounds never evolved.

In 1989, when Jason was 10, a language expert at school divided his communication this way: Verbal only (intelligible)-37%; verbal clarified with gestures-28%; verbal only (unintelligible)-19%; gesture only-8%; verbal clarified with pictures-5%; verbal clarified with formal sign language-3%.

By the time he was 25, his verbal clarified with gestures had increased significantly. The family practically always gets Jason's broad message even if they don't understand every individual word. I have more difficulty because, even though I should know better, I often try to engage Jason in "real" conversation. This is sometimes akin to my conversation in France with a taxi driver who couldn't understand my request to go to the racetrack. I communicated with hand signals and he gave me a confirmation by whinnying. Jason has become very good at just that sort of mime.

The older Jason got the better he became at alternative communication. When he was in his early teens he tried to discuss an afternoon host on the Nickelodeon TV network with Tracy and his mother. The character's name was Stick Stickly, but neither Tracy nor Jean had a clue. He said TV and then started miming the licking of a Popsicle. Tracy understood the word Popsicle and said so. Jason then said stick. In the context of Popsicle, Tracy then understood the word stick and proudly shouted, Stick Stickly! Jason was just as pleased as Tracy that they had effectively communicated.

The amazing fact about his miming capability is that it was Jason's solution. It is intricate, personal and unique to Jason's moods and high spirit. One of the first mimes I remember, and perhaps my all-time favorite, despite its political incorrectness, is "tonese." Tonese is Jason's word for Chinese and is always accompanied by a folding of the hands and a bow. Without that stereotype we would probably never have figured out the word. Like so many of his mimes, that one is based largely on his television viewing.

That miming success did not come easily and the first temptation when he was learning to speak was to quit. Frustration almost won in those early years. Mom and teachers had to cajole and even get tough to urge him to sign or use one of the other flavor-of-the-month solutions the specialists recommended.

His early school notebooks capture the excitement Jean felt when nearly three-year-old Jason made the sign for bus and sauntered over to where we kept his lunchbox. A few weeks later teachers reported that Jason pointed to a paper snowman he had created and he made the sign for "cold' which was the signal to sing Frosty the Snowman. A few months later he learned to say the word "boot" and Jean reported that he was so proud of the word he constantly searched for his boot and took it to Jean just so he could work it into the conversation.

There was real cause for hope the day this note came home from Fraser School:

"Jason had a good day today. He is very comfortable in his new room and he enjoys our routine. Only problem—we can't let Amanda and Jason lay next to each other at naptime. We heard good speech sounds and the interaction between them was very appropriate—however they were keeping everyone else awake."

But even with those occasional victories there were notes from Jean to school explaining that his favorite new word, courtesy of his dad, was "buddy." But the teachers probably wouldn't be able to understand it. The more Jason actually spoke, the more obvious it became that he was going to be unintelligible to strangers who hadn't invested daily effort in understanding him.

And there were odd mental glitches too. At one point teachers reported that "Jason labels blue correctly. The only problem is he calls all other colors blue too."

During another school exercise teachers would ask him to walk to various objects such as door, sink and table. Every time, Jason would first respond with "Huh?" And then he'd do the task. Sometimes it seemed as if he was buying time so he could process what he heard.

Confusion and Jason were close friends. When I shaved off my beard when he was 3 or 4, he reacted badly. He simply didn't know me at first. He was wary until all those mental pieces clicked in, oh so slowly.

Yet, Jean contends that the "huh" he always uttered at the teacher's commands, could have been Jason's expression of "boy that's a dumb thing to do. Why would I want to waste time walking over to that table?" Jason's savvy sometimes makes you wonder if he isn't laughing at us.

We tried several communication solutions through the years, but we never found much success. Jason dabbled in formal sign language at Fraser school, but as he learned sign language he stopped speaking altogether. Teachers and parents quickly decided that even with his imperfect speech, that was not a good tradeoff.

In elementary school we again tried sign language, but Jason's poor fine motor skills prevented him from effectively forming letters. He learned some macro signs such as work, same and different, which he still uses fairly frequently.

Late in elementary school and junior high school, an imaginative communications coach decided Jason should use a wallet filled with pictures of his favorite restaurants, foods, essential life issues such as restrooms and pictures of his favorite people. Jason was supposed to go into fast food or sit-down restaurants and use his wallet to convey what he wanted. The wallet was clumsy and tested his patience and the patience of merchants and fast food service folk. It made Jason seem odd and out of place. Lord, we can't have that! The wallet slipped into extinction without protest from any interested party.

As early as 1991, teachers began praising Jason's "clarification strategies." That's the clinical term for what I call miming. They were especially proud of his clarification of a word they heard as "Bahball." He dramatically moved into a full pitchers windup to explain the word baseball. When he couldn't say Santa Claus, he said ho-ho-ho.

Those are the kind of victories parents of a Down syndrome child celebrate during the early years. You constantly find ways to cope with everyday challenges such as painting "eyes" on his shoes and explaining that if they point at each other he had his shoes on the correct feet.

As Jason careened toward adolescence his parents collided hard with the realization that there would always be a substantial amount of the five-year-old in Jason. Running madman phases and clueless potty training were in the past, but frustrating communication, childish attachment to "baby" objects, horrible fears of the dark and of thunderstorms, along with the see-saw emotions of a mature toddler were clearly a permanent part of his life.

For Jason's siblings his early years were full of impact but they largely lacked the drama that was to come. Tracy definitely grew up faster because of Jason. She felt responsibility for him as early as four and that shaped her personality. In kindergarten her teacher marveled at how Tracy was always the one to comfort a classmate with a skinned knee or a damaged psyche.

She was on her way to developing a "broken bird," care-giving personality. If a child was in trouble Tracy would be there, especially when Jason was involved. She just assumed responsibility. Seamlessly and with little notice, she guided him to the right places and coached proper behavior. In retrospect she was a clearly a budding special education teacher.

As a preteen, Tracy always the caretaker displayed no resentment toward Jason and she remembers none. Jason was her little brother and he demanded more vigilance than other little brothers. That was just the way it was.

Jeffrey's early interaction with Jason was different because they started out as buddies. Jason was four when Jeff was born. For the first five or six years they were partners in crime. They laughed, squealed and found mischief together. Jason did not know the cookies were up there. Jeffrey did but he couldn't reach them. The duo quickly learned by pooling Jeffrey's smarts and Jason's brawn they could have a lot more fun and eat more cookies. They amused each other constantly.

On one trip to the badlands and Mt. Rushmore, when Jeff was about three, we left an amusement area and encountered heavy traffic. An oncoming driver obviously lost patience and attempted to pass four or five cars only to find the McGuire family in his sights. He was certain to hit us but my defensive actions were limited because there was a steep ravine on our right. With fate on my side, I turned the wheel hard right to avoid the oncoming car. As we precariously skidded on the edge of that ravine I jerked the wheel back hard left to avoid guaranteed tragedy.

I had just saved my family from one of our scariest encounters ever, and probable death, when my two little boys simultaneously and gleefully shouted "Wheeeeeeeeeee." Not the kind of acclaim I expected for my life-saving maneuver.

The two boys stayed friends and collaborators, but by the time Jeff was five or six it became obvious we trusted him more than Jason. He started to get responsibility and Jason did not. Jason didn't react much to that during those early years but later, as a teenager, he came to resent it. Jason's early years were filled with all sorts of similar battles, but despite his day-to day-difficulties and big overwhelming challenges we know we are profoundly lucky.

I remember taking Jason to a movie several years ago. A gravely mentally disabled and physically disabled boy, whose age was indeterminable, sat a few rows in front of us. He continuously roared unintelligible sounds of approval. His behavior was out of control. His father looked incredibly beleaguered. Poignantly for me, the father looked as if he wanted to cut and run. I didn't blame him. It was just one of a thousand moments I have experienced that remind me how lucky we are to have Jason.

I have found this to be a common theme among parents of a disabled child. They can usually find some reason their child is better off than another child they meet. Jean and I think brain injuries are the cruelest afflictions because the range of behaviors is so dramatic. We've always been sympathetic to parents whose child is mentally challenged and nobody knows why. At least the diagnosis of Down syndrome staked out some boundaries and expectations. Diagnoses of autism or "brain damage" create a mystery about potential and expectations that is sometimes never solved.

As childhood started to fade for Jason his body started to change from that of a skinny, thin-faced little boy to the more typical chunky Down syndrome frame. His reckless childish abandon started to change as well. The raging teen hormones captured Jason just as they do any adolescent. A funnier, quirkier, sometimes angrier and often more frustrating Jason began to emerge. The hard work was just beginning.

CHAPTER 5

TIM'S COMING OF AGE

My adolescence was hard. What part of that involved hormones and a developing frontal lobe, and what part was dealing with a disability that I thought made me different, will always remain the great mystery. I realize now just how dominant "being normal" was to me as a youth.

Through high school and college there were often two Tims. One was a solid, but not sensational student, a state championship level debater and a professional reporter at 17. The other Tim was a rowdy partier who made a lot of bad decisions and earned a mighty questionable reputation, especially in college.

Late in 1969, my sophomore year, nine girls crammed into the tiny dorm room in Regina Hall, the only girl's dorm on the Aquinas College campus. Bodies sprawled across beds and huddled on the floor. The gossip ping-ponged through the room until it landed on an attractive, quiet, brainy young woman. The graduating senior may have been an outstanding student, but her friends felt she just didn't get it.

The girls needed to set her straight on her boyfriend, the Rodent, my well-earned nickname. Passion and venom spiced the vocabulary of some of the girls. Others were more matter of fact, but just as certain. Only one friend of both the woman and the Rodent refrained from the gang beating. The tenor was clear five minutes into the harangue, but the lecture raged on. One of the most passionate girls made sure there was no mistaking the message: "Tim McGuire is a bum, and he'll never be anything but a bum. Drop him and drop him now!" I do not contend I was wronged in that debate.

At that point in college there would have been a lot of hearty laughs if one of those girls had predicted I would one day become the editor of the 14th largest newspaper in the country and the president of a major editor's group. Most would have thought the chip on my shoulder built during high school and the resulting crazy college behavior would have disqualified me from any significant achievement. I didn't believe that for a minute. Without much justification I always had very high ambitions.

When I was 15, I had the last of my 13 major surgeries. The cutting for this one had been severe. The pain was monstrous. It was so bad my doctor prescribed morphine to relieve the pain, but he did not prescribe morphine for me after I left the hospital.

That meant for 3 or 4 days I went through the most excruciating pain I can remember in my life. It was a defining pain, a 10 on the pain scale, and every pain since has been compared to it in my mind. But a fascinating thing happened on the third day of that horrible test. I would like to say I found a tremendous spiritual grace or that I made a profound religious commitment. I did not.

I vividly remember lying on that temporary hospital bed in the dining room of our house on Lansing Street and saying to myself, "Tim, for the rest of your life you must avoid pain. You must avoid discomfort. That's why you have to succeed in life."

When I tell that story, some people look at me and question whether I really thought those things at the age of 15. But I did. I didn't know the specific manifestation, but as I lay there in pain, I knew that it was crucial that I get an education and succeed in life because I despised discomfort so much. That memory has been another driving force in my life. I believe to my core it was that painful torment that kept me from completely going off the deep end in college. Success was required, not optional.

Within a year of that solemn, motivating promise one of the most important events of my youth occurred, even though classmates and family don't seem to remember it. One day we had an all-school assembly. As part of the program the principal introduced a Sacred Heart graduate who was probably around 50. The man was some sort of an engineer who was a part of an important business in California. All the details are vague in my memory but it was very clear to me the man had graduated from my small Catholic high school and gone on to success. He left Mt. Pleasant and now he was so famous and important we were honoring him at a school assembly.

I vividly remember where I was sitting in that high school gym and I remember forming a transformational thought. "That is going to be me someday. I am going to leave Mt. Pleasant and I will come back to Sacred Heart as a triumphant hero."

It was an inspirational day for me and that aspiration became a driving mantra. Years later, the school instituted an annual award to honor successful alumni and I was the first recipient. The recognition fulfilled a dream I really had no business dreaming when I was a misbehaving adolescent.

Nobody in the early years of my puberty would have marked me as a potential crazed college student.

I was raised to follow the rules. The little guy who learned to walk in casts and found that it pleased people wanted to keep pleasing people. The wild side was still foreign territory only to be visited occasionally. I distinctly remember being mocked for not swearing at an eighth grade class picnic. I remember a sense of being left behind at that picnic. Boys were experimenting with Cokes and aspirin and I felt I was on the fringe, a feeling I despised.

Some of my skills were already emerging but they were separating me from other students. Vatican II took effect in the Catholic Church that year and lay people proclaimed scripture at Mass. I performed those scripture readings at school masses and it emerged pretty quickly that one of the most sought after "readers" in the entire parish, including adults, was the little crippled eighth-grader.

I was often pulled out of class to read for funerals when the families had made no other arrangements. I was viewed as holy and good to the point that with some urging from nuns I even considered seriously going into the seminary. Then a pivotal thing happened that would mold me for years to come.

I don't remember the specific details, but some people made some inquiries about whether I would be accepted to the seminary with my crippled legs and hands. In those conservative days when Vatican II was creating intense controversy somebody observed that holding the chalice for consecration would be too difficult. Suddenly, from the ether it seemed, it emerged that I would not be welcome in the seminary. A couple of years later the parish pastor told my mother, "Boy, the seminary sure made a mistake when they didn't take Tim." So somebody, somewhere, made an affirmative decision to exclude me.

That seminary denial in the early 60's did a lot of things. Significantly, it seriously ticked off my mother. At that time she was pretty subservient to the power of the church, but that church had just rejected her son. Most Catholic moms wanted a priest son, and her church had said that was not going to happen. That was a big deal.

It angered me for a lot of the same reasons. My parents had been coaching me all my life that I was just like anybody else and that I could do anything I wanted to do. Now my church was one of the first institutions telling me that wasn't true. I really was different if my church wouldn't accept me as a priest. The unknown seminary official who made that decision built the chip on my shoulder even larger.

The effects were gradual, but the goody two shoes image became even more burdensome and so did my need to show the world I could achieve anything I wanted to achieve, no matter what the seminary said.

My reputation as "the good kid" often exceeded my actual performance. I had been a nominal part of our State Championship debate team, I was a good student, responsible and an accomplished lector and public speaker. At the annual awards day ceremony at the end of my sophomore year I was awarded the student of the year prize for my class. The prize was a beautiful, carved wood statue of the Blessed Mother. I still have it.

The next year at the same ceremony, I was helping as an usher and an organizer. One of my friends showed up at the back of the gym. Certain I would not win the award again, we violated all the rules and walked off campus to a downtown drugstore for my favorite, a cherry phosphate.

Upon our stealthy return I reentered the gym only to encounter one of the nuns who informed me that "while you were running errands in the school you won the outstanding student award again." She automatically assumed I was off doing the Lord's work. She never considered I was violating school rules.

But to some in authority I just didn't fit. I was developing an independent, contentious mind which was not viewed as a good thing in a Catholic school in the 1960s.

One day I was sick at home when an elderly English teacher handed back papers. I had written a three-page "masterpiece" on "What is nothing?" I explored the age-old question, is nothing something or is it nothing? I thought it was hilarious and wonderfully existential. The nun found it something else entirely.

When she came to my paper, she said aloud to the class "that Mr. McGuire is so queer." She had no idea there were two meanings to that word in 1966, but it was clear that such an autonomous, freewheeling mind was not the nun's idea of a model student.

That may have been the beginning of the realization that Sacred Heart and Mt. Pleasant were not very tolerant places. I was starting to feel some genuine confidence in my abilities to speak, think and provoke. It was becoming painfully clear this small town was not the perfect place for me.

HIGH SCHOOL WAS HARD

I shout from mountaintops that my life has been blessed and idyllic but I admit high school was hard.

For most of those years I carried a very unfortunate nickname. For reasons I never really understood a neighbor girl who went to Sacred Heart took to calling me "Sex." I don't know if she thought I used bad language or if it was like calling a big guy Tiny. Or, perhaps my lack of a dating life intrigued her. Other students thought it was hilarious and the nickname stuck.

Being taken seriously had become a big issue for me, especially with girls and that nickname didn't help. I was short and hopelessly skinny. I weighed less than 100 pounds when I graduated from high school. Even though I didn't wear braces on my legs anymore, I walked with a profound limp. My butt stuck out noticeably, and my right arm was merely decorative. I could not even lift a glass to my lips.

My first love was a delightful Candy Striper volunteer during that last stay at the hospital when I was 15. She was a year older but she came to my room often when she was on duty during my two week hospital stay. We really enjoyed each other's company. By this time I was starting to grow into the class clown persona and she loved to laugh with me. I was genuinely smitten and for the first time I could remember she seemed to share the feeling.

We wrote to each other faithfully for the rest of the summer and we made plans to meet when I went to Saginaw for a football game in the fall. She did not go to the high school we were playing so she made a special trip to see me. Our encounter was not the stuff of which dreams were made.

When I was lying in that hospital bed neither of us fully appreciated that she was at least six inches taller than I was. She was very attractive and it became apparent in seconds that she had not fully understood the shape of my body. Conversation suddenly did not come as easily as it had in the hospital or in our letters. That love affair crashed before it took off. For me, it was one more example of girls not taking me seriously because of my stature and my disability.

Sometimes it felt as if I were incredibly insignificant. I could have had halitosis, but in my mind it was my disability that kept me from being treated like other guys. One popular girl didn't have a date for homecoming one year so I decided to ask her. When she heard my intentions on the grapevine she literally ran from me in the school halls until someone else asked her.

I was largely unabashed. In the summer my friends and I often drove some 50 miles north to Houghton Lake, a big recreational area, for dances at a teen spot called The Box. While my friends usually danced with every girl they asked, I faced an uphill challenge. I got turned down a lot. One night I decided to count my turndowns, probably for the same perverse reason I counted the number of times I fell on my bike when I was seven.

To my friends' horror and amazement some 90 girls turned me down at The Box that night. I didn't usually count but that number seemed pretty normal to me. One friend, Jim Cotter, just didn't understand how I could keep asking when the odds were that stacked against me. He admitted his own self-esteem would have been crushed.

For me, falling off my bike was the same as getting turned down by 90 young women in one night at a teenage dance. When you fall down or get knocked down, you pick yourself up. You never show weakness and you never give up. You keep plugging, believing good things will happen. I learned my parents' lessons better than they could have ever imagined.

Obviously, some anger built up and I always had a need to be reaffirmed. That large chip on my shoulder kept getting bigger. One of the most shameful manifestations of that came during a phase in which I started picking fights at public dances.

My friends and I would be at a local dance place when I'd brush up against somebody and with my smart mouth it quickly escalated into a confrontation that was headed outside. Before we got outside the word would fly through the dance hall that "McGuire has a fight." When it got to "put up the dukes" time I would be backed by a score or more of friends who made it clear that if McGuire had a fight they all had a fight. The prospect of battling a crowd discouraged every fighter I encountered.

That phase was blessedly short because my friends effectively impressed upon me that if I picked any more fights *they* would kick my ass. It doesn't take Freud to figure out that in a place that was so hostile for me because so many girls turned me down for dances, I needed to know I had friends who would defend me.

PARTY PROBLEMS AND I WASN'T EVEN THERE

Midway through my junior year of high school a big, problematic event occurred. A close friend of mine had two parties and I didn't attend either.

Things went terribly wrong at the second party, and it became public. SHA officials staged an inquisition. Several students were brought to justice with suspensions from sports and extra-curricular activities. I felt really bad for my friends who were in big trouble, but that should have been the extent of my involvement.

Pretty soon there developed a theory that school officials knew way too much about the goings on at the party. It was decided there was a snitch who told the parish pastor chapter and verse specifics about who did what.

Then, incredibly, the rumor started that I was the snitch. I quickly protested that was impossible because I hadn't attended the party. The rumor was an incredible falsehood but the basic idea that Tim McGuire was the snitch even when I wasn't there became accepted.

Everything changed. I was under such suspicion that my presumed chance to be elected Student Council president was derailed and many people made their suspicions obvious when they passed me in the hallway.

My core group of friends stuck by me, but I pulled back from seeking recognition and I specifically refused to run for class president which the runner-up in the Student Council election usually did. I was enraged at the injustice. For almost 40 years I blamed one person for spreading that rumor.

Those false accusations made that chip on my shoulder into a mountain. I am certain it shaped my college behavior because it became even more imperative to prove I was "one of the guys." That whole incident made me a more skeptical person. I have always been paranoid about being falsely accused. I used to make my wife Jean take baby sitters home for fear of being falsely accused. To this day I keep my office door open when young coeds seek my counsel.

It was unusual I didn't go to that first party because I usually provided the wheels. A car was always a crucial part of my high school career. The day I turned 16, my great Aunt Mayme gave me a brown and tan 1953 Chevy. With that simple act I had mobility, freedom and a ticket to cementing friendships. I was usually the driver for my buddies, and it made me a necessary part of our group.

My friend Mike Hackett admitted a few years ago he always thought that car was a brilliant maneuver by my parents to increase my acceptance. It was not planned at all, but it is clear that my distinctive set of wheels was a key to my inclusion.

But more than my car, my skills turned out to be the best way to be taken seriously in high school—a profound lesson there.

DEBATE MOLDED ME

In my freshman year I joined the legendary Sacred Heart debate team. A tremendous high school debater named John Johnson had just graduated. John, his sister Janet and a girl named Kathleen Gallagher had won two or three state championships. However, there was a new rule that four people had to debate in the district tournament.

So when I tried out for the team there was an obvious place for me. There was another senior, John Tope, who debated for the first time. With Janet and Kathleen doing the heavy lifting we skated through the district contests. Tope and I stepped aside and Janet and Kathleen won another state title.

When the publicity started, John and I were included, so the record shows I won a state debate championship. I have never really claimed much credit for that. It was not my championship. In fact that team was invited to be grand marshals for the homecoming parade in 2013. I declined the invitation, telling the organizer of that event, "I was little more than decoration."

That did not stop me from spending the rest of my high school debate career trying to duplicate the feat.

In my sophomore and junior years I debated with a brilliant young man, Tom Plachta, who was a master of public policy and creative ideas. He brought a level of sophistication to our debate arguments that astounded me. He was both a challenge and inspiration to me intellectually. He also shared my deep competitive spirit. Most high school debaters were more egghead than athlete. I was a frustrated middle linebacker who had never made it onto a high school athletic field.

In my senior year the team was younger and the increased responsibility improved my performance. Judges were effusive in their praise and my confidence increased dramatically.

We came very close to winning the state championship, losing in the finals. I later finished sixth in the state individual debate contest. Those finishes taught me an important life lesson:

I was really good but there are always people who are better. Always.

I don't want to give short shrift to the role debate played in my life. Debate taught me to think on my feet with both creativity and coherence. The research on deep public policy matters expanded my limited small town sophistication. The confidence I gained to express my thoughts quickly and effectively shaped my newspaper career and my teaching.

Critical thinking is the spine of scholastic debate and I hope of my career. I think teaching students how to think critically is the most important thing I do.

THE ORIGINS OF A CAREER

A skills issue that was more important to my life, and to my senior year, actually unfolded late in my junior year. One weekend I placed highly in a state forensics contest and that same weekend I won a state editorial writing contest for my work on the school newspaper. Somebody decided that was a big deal and invited the local newspaper to do a feature story on me.

I don't remember much about the story and the picture except that I told the interviewer I dreamed of one day being Eric Sevareid, who was an opinion commentator on the CBS Evening News.

I basked in the glory of that feature story for a while but moved forward with little indication that it was a genuine life changer. It was.

Late that summer, before my senior year, I got an important phone call from the publisher and owner of the local paper, Richard Milliman. He talked about the story that had appeared in his paper a few months earlier and then he asked me if I would like to cover Sacred Heart Academy sports teams for the princely sum of $10 a week plus mileage. I jumped at the chance without ever considering the difficulties of reporting on my friends. I never doubted for a minute that I was ready to write professionally.

I covered the football team on Friday night, my story appeared in the Saturday paper and Saturday night I hung with my classmates as if that were absolutely natural. That conflict of interest would have sent me screaming many years later but the arrangement worked for the paper and for me. And, I might have fired somebody years later for how I handled expenses. Even then $10 bucks a week wasn't much but the job became a good deal if you charged the paper for mileage and then took the school bus to the games.

By the end of the football season I was not only covering Sacred Heart, I was also helping to take scores and write brief game summaries for regional games. Writing newspaper stories came naturally to me. During second semester I was scheduled for study hall until 10:30 a.m. With permission, I worked at the newspaper from 7:30 to 10 writing police briefs, obits and other basic newspaper writing tasks.

By that spring I also worked routinely on Tuesday and Friday nights until early in the morning taking basketball scores from around the area. I learned that this journalism thing was fun and profitable.

Covering the Sacred Heart basketball team, however, was growing complicated. The team was one of the best Class C teams in the state. There was a lot of statewide attention and a few of the players were heading to bigger and better things. So the amount of coverage I gave them mattered. My friend Hackett told people many years later that my work helped him win all-state honors. I think that's baloney, but I have been told that some players thought I cheated them out of coverage in favor of friends.

I knew that everything I wrote wasn't pleasing everyone but that was the beginning of my journalism education. I started to understand I could not please all the people all the time. I couldn't fret about it. I had the pen and the accompanying power. I had to use my responsibility honestly and fairly, but if I did my best to do the right thing, they could all go to hell. That attitude served me well for 40 years. A journalist must be independent.

Sacred Heart kept on winning and it was clear they had a great shot at the Class C State Championship. On March 17, SHA played a tough team from Wakefield Michigan in the Upper Peninsula, one of the few teams in the state as physically imposing as Sacred Heart.

The game was everything cliché-ridden sports writers would dream a game could be. Close throughout, controversial calls, and then with a few ticks on the clock a Sacred Heart junior named Mike Funnell shot an awkward shot from the side and slightly behind the basket to win the game.

The lead paragraph on my story focused on that unlikely, last second dramatic shot. The publisher, Richard Milliman, came to the newspaper that night to supervise coverage of the local school winning the championship. He was incredulous when he read my lead. He seemed to think that the fact the Fighting Irish of SHA won such a crucial game on St. Patrick's Day, with more than a bit of luck, was a pretty big story.

Milliman artfully inserted the luck of the Irish allusion into my lead about the last-second shot. He saved my bacon that night, and he is one of the most important people in my newspaper career, even if reluctantly so. Milliman gave me two more jobs before I was out of college but constantly advised me to go into law. He actively discouraged me from the newspaper business and I actively ignored him. I encountered him a few times later in my career and despite my success I think he still had some regrets I chose newspapers, even though he gave me my start.

My debate and forensics success and my "grown up" work at the news-paper writing sports gave me genuine bona fides. And yet, I will never forget a comment Hackett made that year when we were competing for a community club's Mt. Pleasant Student of the Year award. He won the award and said prophetically, "I knew they'd never choose a debater and writer over an athlete."

But my road to the graduation ceremony was not smooth. Two other fellows and I routinely skipped religion class to walk the neighborhoods smoking cigarettes. This malfeasance was discovered days before gradua- . tion. The three of us were suspended from school and there were threats we would not be allowed to formally graduate.

That would have meant that the class would have a top nine rather than a top 10 since I was ninth in the class. Thanks to that fact, along with the intercessions of the priest who taught the class, we survived that little escapade and I was set to go to Aquinas with a mixed bag of experiences.

CHOOSING A COLLEGE

Even though Central Michigan University was 10 blocks away from my house in Mt. Pleasant, there was never any question whether I would go away to college. My parents believed I needed to get out in the world and there was a vague sense that my mother and I were too closely attached. At that point, my independence was still a primary goal for my parents: "Tim has to stand on his own; he can't remain sheltered at home."

My primary dream had always been to go to Notre Dame. I loved the football team and as a Catholic high school student in the 1960s Notre Dame was Shangri-La. That idea got kicked off the table quickly for finan-cial reasons. There was no way my family could have afforded the Golden Dome. The truth is, I probably couldn't have met the math requirement either. I don't do well in math.

I was going to need financial help to go to school. My dad sold cars at that time and my mother was an admitting clerk at a hospital. There was a tuition program for Michigan disabled students that I thought would help me to go Michigan State, by then my first choice. It was some 70 miles down US 27, south of Mt. Pleasant. I had attended summer programs for debate and radio-television there. I loved the campus even though I never considered its vastness. At that point in my life, I would have bristled at a suggestion that the campus was too big for me to get around. I never thought in term of limitations. My defiance over that giant campus may have been the primary attraction of Michigan State.

It seemed like an adventurous place to me with lots of academic options and exciting opportunities. My parents wanted me to be independent, but not too independent. They were afraid if I went to MSU I would become a "drug crazed hippie." As I've told people for years, "I showed them, I went to Aquinas and became a drunk." That always elicits a laugh but it was not untrue.

Aquinas was a small Catholic school founded by the Grand Rapids Dominicans. That was the same order of nuns that taught in my grade school and high school. In fact, during my time at Aquinas more than a few nuns I had encountered at Sacred Heart taught at Aquinas.

Grand Rapids was an hour and 45 minutes from Mt. Pleasant over small country and state roads. Aquinas was a collection of six or seven handsome buildings on the East side of Grand Rapids nestled in among trees, a pretty pond and handsome hilly walkways. It was compact and fairly easy to navigate. That made it a Mecca for disabled students. At the time there were about 1,200 students. It was not particularly distinguished academically but my academic record wasn't that special either. I just don't remember academics being as powerful a draw in those days as it is now.

I probably paid a price for my college selection. The Aquinas academic credential was never a big boon to my career. More than once I am certain it hurt me as I competed with Harvard and Northwestern graduates. Despite that I am convinced Aquinas was the right choice for me as I was testing boundaries, searching for my identity and trying to prove I was as good as any non-disabled person.

I was still palpably bitter about being falsely accused over The Party but I had enjoyed some academic success, a lot of debate success and, after a summer of newspaper work, I had real journalism experience. I was ready for Aquinas even if it wasn't ready for me.

I became a well-known freshman fast. The current President of Aquinas, Dr. Juan Olivares, was a contemporary and a good friend in college. He recently told me, "I always considered you a four-year senior. You seemed to fall in with the upper classmen the day you got to campus."

My nickname was bestowed in the early days of freshman year when a sophomore looked at my small stature and twisted body and said "you're the rodent."

Full acceptance into the party crowd came one night in Mike Ferguson's room. "Fergie" was another upperclassman and highly regarded as the campus wit. The two of us started insulting each other in front of a crowd.

In those days, in that place, you earned your stripes by insulting better and faster than the other guy. It was called "pimping" and my quick wit enabled me to play the mean, often cruel, game at a high level. Naturally my size and my disability were put in play the more I insulted the other guy's intelligence and appearance. I ended that night's bout when my opponent moved in for the kill with a brutal insult about my twisted limbs. I feigned deep hurt. With high drama I snapped back, "Let's not talk about my Vietnam injuries now!" Silence engulfed the room as I stared hard and straight. Suddenly my opponent realized he'd been had. Fergie slapped me on the back and said, "Rodent, you're okay." I was in.

Within weeks, Fergie, a dismal athlete, invited me to join him as the core of an intramural basketball team to be called "The Bosstown Celtics." His stated goal was to assemble the 10 or 12 worst athletes in the school. He succeeded beyond his own twisted imagination. Joining that team was signing on for humiliation and ridicule—and maximum attention.

I leaped at the chance to join the ragtag bunch. I was one of the top two or three players. Not to put too fine a point on things, I was awful.

I delighted in our first game when we were demolished 67-4 by the Animal House team. Many of the key players on that team lived in a house called the Animal House years before the movie stole the name. They were the most infamous group of partiers on campus. There were also several pretty good athletes on the team.

I accounted for all four of the Bosstown Celtics points, demonstrating how bad we were. My score on a 12-foot jump shot was a thrill, but the second basket scored by the Bosstown Celtics was the legend maker. As I charged in for a lay-up—as if I have ever *charged* in my life—a 6-4, 250-pound giant, a fun-loving "Animal" named Joe Rumler, snatched me up by the waist, and I instinctively dunked the ball through the hoop.

The big crowd, for an intramural game, went crazy. Players laughed and fans cheered wildly. However, observers say that's when the varsity head basketball coach and Athletic Director stomped out of the gym in disgust, muttering something about the Celtics being a disgrace to basketball. We were so proud.

The Rodent legend grew from there. My antics, and the fact that I was different from the other "gimps" as I called them, made me stand out. Aquinas was a magnet for disabled students. Some quirks in the Michigan private college funding law and its compact, friendly campus attracted scores of limps, crutches, wheelchairs and wounded limbs. Most disabled kids blended into the woodwork. I never blended well.

Only one other disabled student, Dennis Leiber, who had a malformed arm, was well-known on campus. He was an outstanding actor, an exceptional student, beloved by faculty and popular among upperclassmen. Leiber is now a successful Circuit Court Judge in Kent County, Michigan.

I was a pretty good actor too. And, I could debate politics and culture with the best of Aquinas. I was also crazy. I had great friends and plenty of detractors. My power to polarize which would become so obvious later was starting to show.

Throughout my freshman year I made friends and my outgoing, partying personality earned me substantial attention. I had never dated much, but as my infamy spread toward the end of that freshman year, my confidence started to bloom. In the last nine days of the semester I had 12 dates. Two dates in one day constituted a real coming out party and pretty much buried any pretext of shyness. Throughout that period my head was pretty much stuck in a barrel of beer. My flair for excess was on full display in both departments.

My freshman popularity, which got me elected to the student senate and made me a candidate for homecoming king, quickly morphed into notoriety. Everybody knew who the Rodent was. Just spell the name right. I reveled in my status as a "party guy" who was "pretty damn smart." My clear college mission was to screw around as much as possible and still bring home a three point grade average. My zaniness was always tempered just a bit by a basic sense of responsibility and on some days, but not all, by an ethical base. My early forays into college debate and forensics withered as I gained admittance to upper classmen parties. I was a good debater, but I was a great partier. I celebrated the shaking heads and knowing grins which came when people found out I was "The Rodent."

The fellow who gave me the Rodent nickname took me aside at the beginning of my sophomore year and warned me that people viewed me as "changed." He said people had elected me to the Student Senate and nominated me for Homecoming representative because of my likable humility. He implied I was reveling too much in my new status.

We could debate about what the guy said, but what I *heard* was my cockiness and confidence were not acceptable traits for a disabled person. I *heard* that it was okay for "normal" people to be rowdy and brash, but not my kind. I have no idea if the guy meant that, but it was what I heard. Not surprisingly, I replied with a popular campus epithet rhyming with Fire Truck U. That put my defiance on the record. I had convinced myself that partying, fun and notoriety defined the "real Tim."

SUPER RODENT FLIES

The "Rodent legend" gathered steam at a school-sponsored Halloween party at the beginning of that sophomore year in college. As I mulled over an appropriate costume for the dance it made consummate sense that I go as "Super Rodent." I dressed up in a cape and a tee shirt with an "R" on it. I became Super Rodent. As was my wont in those days, I prepared for the dance with five 16-ounce malt liquors. I weighed about 115 pounds at the time. This made for a very inebriated little fellow.

At the dance, several of my buddies and I were in the restroom when, stirred by the malt liquor in my bones, I raced across the restroom and leaped in the air shouting, "I'm Super Rodent!" I landed on the sink. I broke it clean off the pipes. Gushing water sprayed everywhere. About 10 of us raced out of the student union, scared as hell, laughing hysterically and marveling at the powers of Super Rodent.

Every student on campus knew the story by the next morning. I simply bided my time until the hammer of Aquinas discipline slammed me in the head. For some reason there were never any repercussions for that particular transgression. I have been an aggressive giver to Aquinas over the years. I've always contended I am still paying for that sink.

One spring day, during my sophomore year, I needed to conduct some business in Mt. Pleasant on a weekday. I skipped a class or two and traveled to my home town from Grand Rapids in my 1960 Corvair when that notorious car performed to its reputation. As I approached a utility truck too quickly I moved toward the shoulder to try to get around the truck. As it happened with thousands of Corvairs, the front wheels caught and the car flipped. I rolled about three times without a seat belt.

After opening my eyes and not seeing God or Satan, I counted my limbs. Satisfied I had survived, I scrambled out of the car and met the utility truck driver racing down the hill to help me. As he approached, he became wide-eyed as he looked at the body God had given me. "Your arm, your leg," he shouted. Believing this wreck had done incalculable damage, he was frantic. I barked some rendition of "screw it, I've been like this all my life. Get me to the hospital." That confirmed to my friends Rodent would say anything, especially if it was self-deprecating and funny.

Unfortunately, most of the attention I received revolved around alcohol. My frequent appearances at local bars were facilitated by a horrible piece of false identification. My long-time friend, Hackett, who played basketball at Central Michigan University, had found a CMU identification card underneath some bleachers. His conniving, charitable mind immediately recognized the picture looked ever-so-faintly like McGuire. The date of birth would magically make McGuire legal to drink.

That ID card would never pass muster these days, but it made me a regular at bars throughout Grand Rapids. It earned me treasured access to upperclassmen of legal drinking age. One of the more popular emporiums in town was the Back Room Saloon, a peanuts-on-the-floor, mug-of-beer hangout in the basement of the legendary Pantlind Hotel. One night I walked out of the Pantlind with one of their treasured distinctive mugs under my coat.

As my sophomore year drew to a close, a Friday night party at one of the off-campus houses was the place to be. Parked cars clogged traffic on East Grand Rapids streets as 100 or more kids streamed into the four-bedroom house. Aquinas parties were raucous, but this one set a new standard. I happily guzzled beer from my prized beer mug purloined from the Back Room Saloon and dedicated myself to the task of being the most enthusiastic reveler at the party.

As the evening wore down and I headed to the door, I found my roommate, Bill Cheevers, immersed in conversation with a stranger named Al. Al asked me where I got the great beer mug and with shameless pride I announced I had stolen it from the Back Room saloon. He seemed to think that was pretty cool and we all wandered outside.

Cheevers continued his energetic conversation, but paused by a tree to answer nature's call. That's when the badge appeared. Al informed Cheevers and me we were under arrest. At that moment a horde of gendarmes descended on the house and took the entire party crowd into custody. As it became clear to my intoxicated mind that our new friend was not really our friend, I blurted out, "Hey this mug? I didn't really steal it from the Back room Saloon." Months later the incident was memorialized, without my name, as a hilarious college student caper in a Saturday morning bits and pieces column in the local newspaper.

Cheevers and I were the first two people arrested so we got tossed into a police car. As scores of students were rounded up, we were the specimens in the fish tank and thus the stars of the show. Everyone at the party saw us sitting in that police car. I was petrified about what my parents would say. I had danced on the edge for a few years, but it was the first time I ran afoul of the law. I was going to at the least be charged as a minor in possession of alcohol and maybe even charged as an accomplice to peeing on a tree. For all my bravado I was still just a scared little kid who believed in authority.

At that fretful moment, the siren and lights in that cop car mysteriously and inexplicably began to wail and flash. I swear to this moment I never touched a thing. And, I don't remember Cheevers touching anything. An angry cop marched back to the car with a menacing glare convinced one of us had set off that siren. He muttered a warning that made my pants faintly brown, but by that time the crowd of arrested students was murmuring with excitement about what "Rodent just did."

The assumption that I somehow manipulated that siren and lights was rampant that night and in stories told years later. It remains intriguing that Cheevers was never anyone's suspect, but while Cheevers was considered a bit wild, he was not the crazy Rodent. Despite my loud and frequent protestations, few ever doubted I was the miscreant.

The hosts of the party and a few others were separated at the police station from the scores of party goers. Seven people were quickly singled out as major offenders. Everyone else was ordered to give their name and address and they would be allowed to go. Somehow Cheevers and I managed to disappear into that second group. As we surreptitiously sidled to the door, Al saw us and screamed, "Stop them, they're two of the prime perpetrators!" Ah, I was a prime perpetrator at my tender age.

We were *that* close to getting away with our transgressions, but the select seven quickly became the notorious nine. We all got bailed out by the

Aquinas chaplain, a popular Irishman and a Dominican priest, who hired us the best defense lawyer in Grand Rapids. Within weeks we all pled nolo contendere, which meant we didn't have a record, and the night from hell became the stuff of legends rather than serious legal difficulty. At the height of the plea negotiations I asked the good priest if I should tell my parents about the arrest and adjudication. He became my favorite priest of all time when he advised me that such news would simply upset them and it was probably best to keep the information to myself. And I did, until now.

There was never anything formal, but two of my close friends and I were given strong indications we were not invited to live in the Aquinas dorm for our junior year. The three of us joined another friend in searching for an off-campus house. We all had cars and not much money so we drifted a little farther off campus than most. Jim Ward, who became the business manager of the group, found us a great house in what was viewed as a "changing neighborhood." The house was on Watkins Street and for the next two years "Watkins Street" as it was called, took its place in the Hall of Infamy of great Aquinas party houses.

While I was hell bent on proving I wasn't "one of the handicapped" kids in a lot of errant ways, it was also crucial to me to be to be regarded as one of the smart ones. I was respected enough among political science students that I had the credibility to call frequent "study sessions." Routinely, I had not read the material, but from class notes I knew just enough to orchestrate great discussion sessions.

One of my gifts has always been the ability to catalyze discussion and stimulate learning. Discussion and debate constituted my best learning strategy so I was usually the big winner in those sessions. Only my best friend, Frank Hughes, also a political science major, knew that I had seldom read a lick of the material we were discussing. It always ticked him off when I got the same "A" on tests that he did.

I also earned considerable campus respect from my job. Providentially, when I arrived on the Aquinas campus the student who served as Sports Information Director (SID) was a senior named Jim. My background as a sports writer emerged pretty quickly and Jim took a genuine interest in me. Without much fanfare I was more or less anointed as the next student Sports Information Director. That's the way things worked at a small Catholic college.

The job carried considerable prestige and some important perks, such as early registration to insure I got classes that facilitated my work hours. The assignment paid good money for a student position. It gave me access to the top echelons of the college and the local sports scene.

The post also gave me an opportunity to work for the full-time director of information, Marcia Clapp. Clapp, a widow, personified the old-time, chain-smoking, pragmatic journalist. She knew how Grand Rapids worked and she taught me some ugly but important truths about the corruption of newspaper sports departments at the time. When I complained we weren't getting coverage in certain newspapers, she bluntly replied, "Of course, you're not, we're not paying them."

I was shocked and more than a little disillusioned. I later learned that sports department was one of the last corrupt ones but the lessons increased my vigilance and shaped my management and teaching of ethical lessons.

A RADIO CAREER DIES

One other campus job put my disability squarely in play and, to a large extent, dictated my career.

Many people argued I had an excellent radio voice. It was already obvious I had a face for radio and not television. A famous monsignor named Behan preached on a local weekly TV program and he ran the diocesan radio station based in Aquinas facilities.

The station programmed classical music which was not my favorite. In fact, as much as Behan liked me, he chewed me out now and then for playing too many classical renditions of the Beatles. As a DJ on that station I played the music, identified the songs and did the news. My voice won me raves from the boss, but there were more important and difficult issues.

Radio has come a long way in the last 45 years. Today a DJ comfortably controls everything from a computer. That was not the case circa 1969. I vividly recall the horror of the day my radio career ended.

I was sitting facing the control board. I had to spin a record with my weak right hand, and control a tape deck on my left while I reached back to my right to control a reel-to-reel tape. I must have looked like a mangled pretzel.

As I sat there, twisted into an inhuman knot and exhausting my cuss word vocabulary, that moment is still quite vivid in my mind. To no one in particular I yelled, "Bullshit, writing stories for the newspaper doesn't make me do acrobatic tricks! I'm a newspaper guy!" And with that flourish I quit my radio career. For perhaps the only time in my life, my disability won. I can't think of a single other decision that was based on my physical inability to do something. The reality is newspapers were far better for me and to me than radio could ever have been.

My college career was a two-headed sort of monster. On one hand I tried to impress people with my skills and talents and succeeded. The other head of the monster was a crazy partier and drinker. My intent was to make the perception of a disabled Tim an afterthought.

There were some tangible consequences for my crazy antics, but not that many. The most significant came at the end of my junior year in the political science department. My life might well have gone a very different direction if my zany reputation had not intervened.

It was 1970 and Gerald Ford, a powerful person in the House of Representatives was from Grand Rapids. He would become President and a lightning rod because he pardoned Nixon, but at that point he was just a powerful congressman who asked Aquinas to send a talented political science student to his office for the summer.

I immediately applied and visions of sugar plums obsessed me. I should have had a great chance to win that position. I was smart. I was a fine public speaker. I was a good student in the Political Science department and my oft-stated dream of becoming Eric Sevareid would only be enhanced by congressional experience.

One professor named Blake, looked quite approvingly on my application. I thought he gave me subtle indications I was a clear favorite. I waited with confidence for an announcement that eventually came with the name of a serious-minded young woman who was a great student. Naively, I was miffed, surprised and hurt.

I approached Professor Blake for an explanation. The professor fit the stereotype of an easily distracted, tentative academic. He hemmed and hawed and made it clear he thought I was an excellent candidate for the position. He gradually found his footing and began to discuss how surprised he was to hear that many of my professors found me less than totally dedicated to academic excellence. He even mentioned reports that I was "quite wild."

I feigned horror at those accusations but I knew that for the first time at Aquinas I had been seriously unveiled. I bragged to my friends that my craziness had kept me from going to Congress. I wore it as another badge of how "normal" and "cool" I was.

Yet, fundamentally I knew the school had chosen the better candidate and for the first time I started to consider the impact of the persona I had chosen for myself. After all, I really wanted to go to Washington and it was pretty obvious my bad behavior had helped bring me low. That decision gave me some serious pause. The choices I was making had an impact on how I was perceived and perhaps even on what I was going to become. I can't say I considered the issue so much that I changed overnight, but that rejection probably started the process.

There was another incident a year or so earlier that made a small impact on me at the time, but a much greater one as I matured.

Sister Mary Frederic was a relatively young nun who taught American History. I remember her as an energetic and engaged teacher. She had an odd assignment in her syllabus that I recall challenging in class. We were expected to write a daily journal. The entries could be poetry, random thoughts, or essays.

I remember asking Sister what this had to do with history. I think I recollect her stated pedagogical intent was to have us observe daily the history that was developing around us. I found that pretty strange and more than a bit of a reach. I also found the assignment, which required contemporaneous daily entries, to be far more time-consuming than my party schedule would allow.

As was quite typical, I delayed the chore until the night before it was due. Only then did I attack the project with a genuine vengeance. The truth is I remember enjoying the task immensely because there were few things I savored more than writing.

I pretended these had been contemporaneous journal entries and I used all sorts of rhetorical tricks and high-minded profundity. I worried the entries were too truncated and that they looked rushed. I knew I could write effectively, but I wondered what kind of grade my slap-dash effort was going to produce.

Sister passed out all the papers and she still had mine in her hand. Thoughts of certain doom hurtled through my guilty mind when Sister put down my paper and prepared for a speech to the class that was as inexplicable to me then as it is now.

The exact words she used are hazy but she told the class that they were in the presence of a very special writer. She said someday Tim McGuire was going to distinguish himself as a writer and you will be able to say you knew him. She piled on with specific praise and stunning effusiveness for some of the pieces I had written.

At the time her words definitely puffed me up, but as the years went by I found Sister Frederic's words nagging me whenever I didn't put out my very best effort. I don't know if that was her intent, but it worked.

REFLECTING ON COMING OF AGE

When I tell people the outrageous stories of my college days, more than a few men respond that they went through the same thing. They argue my crazy days had nothing to do with being disabled. Their contention is it's a natural testing of boundaries that young men go through as those frontal lobes are forming and as they enjoy their first real taste of freedom from mom and dad.

I don't debate that theory to argue that I was "badder" than the next guy but I am afraid that my antics were marked more by pathology than psychology. I did way too many things that I regret, things that simply were inconsistent with the values I developed later. So many of those things were done without consideration of values, but rather to impress other people that I was "just like any other guy." I bent the rules and expectations so far that I am afraid I became a caricature.

Aquinas gave me some cover and discipline. Even if I was outrageous, people cared. At a Michigan State I might well have quickly become a drop-out statistic that nobody noticed.

Despite my regrets and despite people who might protest, I am convinced my unruly college experiences were a necessary step toward becoming the man I'd eventually become. I stretched the boundaries, found my personal limits and then thoughtfully retreated. That's probably the way it is supposed to work.

I needed all those experiences, good and bad. I certainly abused my freedom and I pushed past all reasonable boundaries. On the other hand, I actually survived "bumness" and by the time I graduated I had about three years of journalism experience, thanks to a semester of work at a daily newspaper during my senior year. With my resume, my degree and countless hard-earned lessons about who I really was, I was ready for the world.

And interestingly, not everyone thought those years were a waste.

In 2002 a psychologist named Dave Chadderdon sent me a letter from Kalamazoo, Michigan. He said we had gone to Aquinas together and he had kept an eye on my career. He complimented me on my success but he also congratulated me on my college career.

He wrote this:

I wanted to share with you that you were one of those who left a strong and lasting positive memory. ....I have been a psychologist for over 25 years now and in the course of my work I occasionally have the opportunity to help out a kid with what they consider to be insurmountable challenges. As I remember, you considered all challenges mountable. I am confessing to you I have been telling "Rodent" stories for years....I want you to know you inspired me and I like to think that hearing of your irrepressible optimism has helped a few others over the years.

CHAPTER 6

JASON'S COMING OF AGE

*J*ason will go into a group home when Jeffrey goes to college. That simple statement had been a mantra in our house from the time Jason was four, about the time Jeffrey was born in 1983. People scoff at us and give us questioning looks that imply we are engaging in revisionist history. But we made that decision about Jason in the hospital as Jean recuperated from Jeff's birth.

Giddiness and reality were in a mortal struggle in those days after Jeff's birth. Triumph, prayerful thanks and relief overwhelmed us because Thomas Jeffrey McGuire was normal. For parents of a disabled child that glorious six letter word, normal, was the Holy Grail, the 49ers gold and the Lost Dutchman treasure all wrapped into one 6 pound 11 ounce package. The stress over having another disabled child had been profound. We had just started our long battle of toilet training Jason and while he had brought us great joy and we loved him dearly, another mentally disabled child would have been an incredibly depressing blow. And yet, we never sought amniocentesis, a test that would have told us if Jeffrey had Down syndrome, because we were not prepared to abort.

As we reflected in the hospital on our good fortune and chattered about how Jeffrey would fit into our family, we reaffirmed the promise we'd made in a different hospital when Jason was born. As long as Jason didn't disrupt our family he would stay with us until he was around college age.

Family strategy with a cognitively disabled child in the mix is improvisational at best. But we felt strongly that a boundary was as necessary with Jason as with our other children, if not more so. Our decision was largely influenced by Frank Wright, a kind, gentle man I worked with at the Star Tribune. He was my co-managing editor and we talked often about our family situations. By the time of Jeffrey's birth, Frank's mentally disabled brother was almost 50 years old and he still lived at home with his parents. His parents were in their seventies and Frank worried about what would happen to his brother when they died. That story profoundly bothered me. The situation struck me as exceptionally unfair to the disabled man, Frank and the parents. My memory is Frank also disapproved of his parents' choice.

We had heard similar stories from others and those tales frightened us. The Jean and Tim relationship remained the center of our attention. Six years of parenting taught us our relationship needed tender loving care. We knew of too many parents of disabled kids whose marriages had faded into nothingness. The statistics are overwhelming. Some studies say 80 or 90 percent of marriages with special needs children end in divorce. That was not going to happen to us—ever.

None of our kids were going to commandeer our relationship. If Jason stayed with us until we were 70 or 75 he would do exactly that. We would not be able to travel or become the spoiled snowbirds we aspired to be. Jason was a snowbird wing clipper if there ever was one. If he lived with us forever our lives would inevitably revolve around Jason and not us. And that would do him no good when we would become too old to care for him or even pass on ourselves. We had no idea then what it would feel like to have Jason sleep under another roof, much less any of our children. And we had no idea what it would be like to convince Jason the wisdom of moving on. We all had to get a lot wiser than we were then.

***

Years later we found ourselves sailing down Olson Highway in Minneapolis at 55 mph on a clear, sunny July day, but my mind and soul were slogging through a foggy swamp of confused emotions—fear, sadness, frustration, concern and anger. And, worst of all, I was clueless.

I turned to Jean and said, "I have no idea what I'm about to say or do. How about you?"

"I have none," was the even more frightening reply. Jean always knows what to do when it comes to Jason.

It was 8:25 in the morning, July 10, 2002. Jason, 22, moved into a group home with three other developmentally disabled young men just 12 days earlier. At 8:10 that morning his job coach called and told us Jason complained of feeling ill and upset. He wanted to see his parents.

Jason had been in the home only 12 days. But getting ready to get him there, both for us and for him, had begun shortly after Jeff's birth. This group home decision was basic to our entire life plan. It had to go smoothly. If Jason didn't fit in the home, or if he was terribly unhappy, years of planning, of dreams and hopes would explode.

DRAMA

In retrospect it is obvious that drama represented the defining phenomenon of Jason's life. He is simultaneously 5 and his chronological age. On that July day Jason was experiencing the emotions of a 5-year-old wrenched away from his parents even though the 22-year-old knew that going into a group home was a good idea.

Jean and I are often at odds about whether Jason operates at a four-year-old level or a five-year-old level. Jean's eloquent argument that he acts four is based on her contention that five-year-olds understand the world is rule-based. She argues that while Jason knows there are rules he is far more into instant gratification than he is into considering consequences, so she thinks he's kind of stuck between four and five. That works for me to a certain extent but I have chosen to use five in this book because a four-year-old would not solve problems as quickly or imaginatively as Jason does.

Examine this exchange with his 16-year-old sister, Tracy, when she was trying to teach him honorifics. Jason was about 14.

Tracy: "What's your brother Jeffrey?"

Jason: "Mr. McGuire."

Tracy: "Who am I?"

Jason: "Miss McGuire!"

Tracy: "Very good, what's Mom?"

Jason: "Mrs. McGuire."

Tracy: "Great, what's Daddy?"

Jason said without any hesitation "The King!"

We laughed hard that day and I've captivated dinner audiences with that story for years. Consider though, the flash of insight and the deep sense of perspective communicated by Jason's rapid-fire response. Despite his serious cognitive difficulties he sometimes has a keen sense of irony and can speak deep truths.

There was the time when he was 18 or so and I was sitting at the computer doing some writing. Jason was sitting on a couch a few feet away. He was positioned so I could not see his feet. I wanted him to go out to my car in the garage and fetch something for me. But did I make that simple request? No, I had to make it complicated and ask, "What do you have on your feet?" The response was immediate. "Toes." He was not being a smart mouth. The answer was obvious to him. Savor that response for a few moments and you realize the line between being utterly profound and not having a clue is very thin.

His movie and TV habits are probably the best example of Jason seamlessly moving back and forth between his chronological and mental ages. He is a big fan of the decidedly adult daytime soap opera "Days of Our Lives." I could probably start a huge national argument by theorizing whether that show appealed to the five-year-old Jason or the older Jason. Soap operas were not a part of Jean's lifestyle so we were always surprised that he is such a fan of over-the-top drama. His obsession with the show often got him in trouble at his workplaces because he just couldn't take his eyes from it.

Jason always had a murky sense of what is age appropriate even though he sometimes drew bright lines. He always enjoyed animated shows and juvenile shows such as *Rugrats* (which he called "Babyrats") and *Sesame Street*. But he was reluctant to let on because that might ruin his self-image.

He often snapped in frustration when I offered him something that he deemed too childish. "Daddy, I'm 18!" At that age he didn't take candy from Jerry, his longtime barber, because only kids take candy. About the same time, he stopped taking balloons from one of our favorite restaurants because "I'm too big." The five-year-old wanted the balloons and candy, but the 18-year-old was "too big."

As he moved farther into his teen years we concentrated on giving him "age appropriate" gifts but it was incredibly difficult, bordering on impossible. He did not like most things an 18-year-old would want and yet you risked embarrassing him with gifts he saw as too childish, no matter how much he might have liked them.

When he was 18 we finally wised up and recognized the 5 and 18 phenomenon. That Christmas he got an expensive air hockey game and "baby rat" dolls. However, when his mother told him to pick up his dolls, he patiently and with a bit of condescension said, "They're not dolls, they're Tommy and Chuckie." He intuitively knew an 18-year-old should not play with dolls but conversing with the people, Tommy and Chuckie, is quite another thing. And converse he did. As he held the two dolls, he often conducted long, imaginary conversations. He was usually oblivious to observers.

One of Jason's many mysteries, especially during his teen years, was his vast TV and movie knowledge and his almost total lack of cognitive learning ability. Some days he could count to 20 and others days he got lost in the jungle of the high teens. In the same way on some days recitation of the alphabet was a breeze and on other days the Phoenicians themselves would be confused by Jason's version. Yet every time you asked, Jason was able to tell you at least four of Danny DeVito's movies or tell you that Kel, of the TV duo Keenan and Kel, was in Mighty Ducks II.

During one of my attempts to have a serious conversation with him I told him, "Jason, I never lie to you. I always tell you the truth." His only way to respond was, "The truth, you can't handle the truth!" You often don't know if you are talking to Jason or some theatrical figure such as Jack Nicholson.

And yet Jason was often the arbiter of what was real and what wasn't. One morning when he was 18 or so he came downstairs for breakfast. I greeted him with "Hey Little Buddy." Jason was not amused. "I'm not little buddy, I'm a grown up." I said, "Well Jase, the captain on Gilligan's island calls Gilligan "little buddy" and Gilligan is a grown up." "Dad," came the exasperated reply, "That's TV, this is real life!"

At various times in Jason's life, I was convinced that this complete mastery of television and movies meant that he's a visual learner. Teachers often humored me to no avail. Jason does not seem to grasp cognitive skills any better when he learns them visually.

In recent years I have come to believe that it is the human element that congeals in that funny little brain of Jason's. Characters such as Keenan and Kel, Danny DeVito, Lucy Ricardo and the characters from "Days of Our Lives" are actually real people to him. In the same way he has warm feelings about his cousins from Michigan, or a family friend from years ago, the characters in movies and TV shows become wonderful memories. It is the characters' humanness which allows him to fondly recall their antics with a vividness few of us normal folk could muster.

He often seems to have difficulty separating reality from fiction. Jason loved to recount the particularly zany activities of certain characters at the dinner table which dragged down otherwise important conversations in a hurry. I used to tell him, "We are talking about real stuff here, Jason. TV is only pretend. He would look at me with total seriousness and say, "TV is my life."

PUNK AND SUCKER

Actually Jason never really said, "TV is my life." He said something that sounds more like, "TV eh my wife." Jason's articulation did not improve as he got older but his grasp of ideas and concepts did, so communication became even more troublesome and even isolating.

Waitpersons always figured out when he wanted a Coke and they usually understood that he wanted ranch dressing on his salad. But if he ordered something such as beef enchiladas the waitperson's eyes darted to me or his mother in a desperate plea for help. I admit I tend to judge the character of waitpersons based on their patience with Jason's ordering ability. More than one has found a 30% tip just because they took the time to make Jason feel like a human being.

During his teenaged and early adult years I comprehended about 40% of what Jason said. I'd say his mother understood 60%, his sister Tracy got

75%, his younger brother Jeff understood about 90% when he lived with him. But, when I asked each of them in 1999 how much they understood, each said they comprehended 90% of what he says. I was incredulous and I was convinced they all must have believed in the tooth fairy.

When I asked Tracy's boyfriend and future husband, Ben, how much he actually understood, he said "less than half." At last, an honest man.

Actually there is a probably an explanation for the different perceptions. Jean usually understood the *gist* of most of what Jason said. That was usually enough, particularly because she was often focused on his primary needs, food, hygiene, recreation, and similar crucial daily activities.

By the time he was 18 Jason had gotten quite clever in alternative communication. I remember one night in particular when Jason was in high school. I gamely asked him how his school day had been. He launched into a soliloquy that would have made Hamlet proud. There was one small problem. Nobody had any idea what he had said. The only thing anybody grasped was that some exciting thing had happened at school.

Jason said key phrases over and over again, but we were all lost. He was on the verge of giving up, which is always a temptation that we all try hard to avoid. Suddenly, like some sort of madman, he leaped out of his chair and put his hand on the wall. He immediately withdrew his hand and said "hot!" One of the kids immediately said fire. With that, Tracy triumphantly said, "fire drill."

When you think about it, finding out your kid had a fire drill at school is not a very big deal. If Jeff's school had such a drill it probably wouldn't have been mentioned. But it truly was a big deal when we could engage Jason in a real conversation and overcome huge comprehension gaps. Everybody puffed with pride for a few moments especially when he'd been particularly clever with his mimes or signs as he was with the "hot" wall.

Some of Jason's mispronunciations have become an important part of the family life. "Wait just a mimmit" and "Aabbee, aabee not" are the way most of us say wait a minute or maybe, maybe not.

We make fun because we all know language is Jason's biggest separator. Joking makes it easier to handle the heartbreak of realizing if Jason could speak as well as many of his Down syndrome peers he'd be exceptional. His social adaptability, his ability to grasp subtlety and humor and his high spirits would make him an absolute star.

Jason's language difficulties almost resulted in suspension from high school. A teacher called Jean to report that Jason had been thrown out of swimming class for calling another student the "F" word.

The teacher was distraught and kept telling Jean, "This just doesn't sound like Jason."

Jean was just as convinced that didn't sound like Jason but it took her several hours to figure out the puzzle. One of Jason's best friends among adults was the Junior High youth coordinator at St. Joseph's Parish. Larry and Jason loved to rough house and insult each other. They often stood and yelled "punk" and "sucker" at each other. They both found this hilarious and it formed a genuine bond between them.

Some bold stroke came to Jean after she fretted for a while and she realized that the Catholic Youth coordinator was actually the cause of Jason's problem. The swimming instructor could not distinguish "sucker" from the more unsavory appellation. Jason was cleared of wrongdoing with the poor enunciation defense.

St. Joseph parish was one of the most important factors in Jason's development. Right about middle school the parish abandoned a special needs religion class and mainstreamed all the developmentally disabled children. Many parents were bitterly opposed to the idea. They supported continued separation while Jean and I were thrilled that Jason would attend religion classes with regular kids. That camaraderie saved him from a lot of bullying and made him feel like he was one of the guys.

Jason's participation in that program was never about the theology. He understood very little. When he was younger he called Father Blaine Barr "God." He never called other priests that, which says something about Father Barr. Jason made his first communion with Jeffrey, and while Jeffrey was a perfect seven-year-old gentleman Jason celebrated his by leaping flat-footed off the altar. The congregation was more than amused.

Jason also was confirmed but it was about this time that his failure to grasp theology became quite apparent. He despises thunder and lightning. It frightens him to death. One night Tracy picked him up from religion class in a driving rainstorm. This conversation ensued:

Jason: "Tracy, does God like thunder and lightning?"

Tracy: "Well Jason, God made thunder and lightning and God loves everything he made, so yeah, I guess God likes thunder and lightning."

Jason: "God's nuts!"

I have always admired Tracy's efforts that night to be theologically correct, but how many of us have believed at one time or another that Jason is correct? Most of us have sometimes wondered if God is nuts. Jason often thinks very grown-up thoughts.

And yet there always seemed to be a battle between fantasy and reality going on in Jason's head. My close friend and managing editor at The Star Tribune, Pam Fine, ran the paper on a daily basis, but among her more minor duties was managing our weather pages. The use of symbols on that page along with Jason's obsession with thunderstorms made the weather pages Jason's favorite. One day under question, I disclosed to Jason Pam's weather page responsibility. From that day to this, he believes that Pam controls the weather. He frequently blamed her for weather he did not like even years after she left the newspaper.

FATHER AND SON

Jason was always funny but he emerged as more of a smart-alec during his teenage years. One time he saw Jean talking to my boss. He looked at me and said, "It's over for you."

Playing around and teasing each other is the core of the Jason/Tim bond. We punch and push each other like kids and we constantly "jerk each other's chains." Jason has developed a deep, loving suspicion of my "tricks." That bond really took hold in his teen years.

One time he was "reading" the comics and wouldn't give them to me until he finished. He can't read so he was just trying to get a rise out of me. Another time he had gotten up early and was standing in the kitchen watching the clock waiting for the appointed time for the bus. He routinely stood there for 10 minutes. One day I said, "Sit down, you drive me nuts when you do that." He slowly turned and said, "Don't look."

My favorite story actually occurred a few years ago. Jason and I were in my car when we came to a street sign that read, "Dip." "Look Jase" they knew you were coming. You're a dip!" Without hesitation he shot back, "Where's stick for you?" I was confused and asked "What?" "You know, dip-stick," he said, immensely proud he'd one-upped me.

The teenage Jason struggled with ethics and morality in the same way any five-year-old would. When he played his new air hockey game with his brother Jeff, he pretended his stomach hurt. When Jeff showed concern,

Jason scored. He routinely tried to score when Jeff or I paused to change the score. His histrionic celebration after scoring a goal was almost worth his trickery. But later, he said, "I kinda cheat." He knew he had done wrong but he enjoyed the experience so much he didn't stop.

Jason often justified bad behavior on an alternate personality. He would tell us the mean Jason took candy from a dish in the living room. Apparently in his mind he was without guilt because good Jason hadn't done anything wrong.

Another time his Mom told him not to take orange juice upstairs with the admonishment, "You'll spill it." When he said he wouldn't spill it, his mom said, "Well somebody does, do you have an evil twin?" Jason was either clever or clueless when he answered, "Yes, he's nasty Jason. I am clean Jason."

When Jason got caught dead to rights doing something wrong, like sticking out his tongue at someone, he was never accountable. "Oops it slipped," was the explanation. The tongue must have countered Jason's wishes.

Whenever you got extremely frustrated with the teenage Jason he would deal with it with a smart-mouthed remark that, again, you were never sure if it was clever or clueless. I would often say, "Jason, Jason, Jason what am I going to do with you?"

"Take me to a movie?"

When I tell that story to friends, even today, they find it uproarious. Yet, I have to admit I don't know if Jason was attempting to be funny or if he thought he was providing a serious answer to a serious question.

While movies are Jason's passion, he is not a discerning critic. He rates every movie he sees as "awesome" or "too scary." Scary can usually be translated as sad or raunchy. Jason despises sadness and he usually declines to go to R movies because he is discomfited by sexual situations.

Sex perplexes Jason more than anything else. It led to his greatest moral quandaries. The teenager and the five-year old engaged in dazed conflict between what he thought a young stud was supposed to do and what the little boy in him really wanted to do.

Tracy's friends were the most frequent victims of Jason's sex muddle. I have a vague recollection of him getting in trouble at school for patting a student or a teacher on the butt while he followed her up stairs, but his "moves" on Tracy's friends provided our biggest embarrassments.

Usually he would simply sit down next to one of Tracy's friends and stretch out his arm as if he was yawning and put it around a young woman's shoulder. Obviously learned from television, this silly "move" was usually handled with a wink and everybody viewed it as a joke.

But one time one of Tracy's sleep-over friends was in the bathroom when Jason walked in and closed the door behind him. Again, obviously stealing a line from TV or a movie, he told the girl, "It's you and me, babe." To her everlasting credit the girl calmly said, "I don't think so," and walked out of the bathroom.

Jeff and Jason were talking one day when Jeff wisely commented, "We're both adults." Jason didn't miss a beat. "Adults get married but not me. I don't want to get married because making out scares me." Then out of the blue, Jason said, "I'm a virgin." Jeff changed the subject quickly. Another time Jason told Jeff that he considers sex "icky." Jason still talks occasionally about wanting to get married and he still brings sex into conversations, usually totally out of context. Before Jeff and Jason left home Jeff had left a picture of his attractive girlfriend on the kitchen counter. Jason saw the pictures and murmured, "Wow." Jeff said, "She's pretty isn't she Jason?" Jason said, "Yes, she's beautiful." Then Jason put his hand on Jeff's shoulder and said, "Don't worry, Jeffrey, I won't steal your girlfriend." Jeff still tells that story with genuine fondness.

JASON, MAN ABOUT TOWN

One of the more remarkable aspects of Jason's teen years was his presence in the community.

One day he was shuffling through Dayton's department store in his semi-oblivious way without ever really lifting his feet. As usual, he was following me by six or eight feet when a stunning young lady behind the counter in the Men's Department shouted, "Hey Jason, how are you?"

Jason beamed at the young salesclerk. She asked, "Do you remember me from last year?"

Jason nodded and cried, "Annie! "

Annie was particularly pleased Jason remembered her. They had a brief conversation about his summer and about the fact that Annie worked with him in school two years ago. Annie couldn't have understood more than

50 percent of what Jason said, but she engaged with enthusiasm. As Jason departed, it was obvious both were a little bit richer for the exchange. Yet, if you examined the content or the depth of the conversation objectively there was really not much there. What mattered was the connection.

That very night Jason and I were in a takeout line at a popular barbecue restaurant when a perky middle-aged woman stormed out of the waiting line shouting, "Jason, how are you?" Again, Dad had no idea who this strange woman was, but Jason was obviously pleased to see her. Apparently, she was one of his teachers two years before. They talked only briefly, but the woman somehow seemed proud to have seen Jason and to have interacted with him. Her smile was broad as she rejoined her group. Jason was just as pleased by the encounter.

Movie theaters, restaurants and department stores are all places where someone will see Jason and either shout a greeting or slap him a high-five. He seldom spots these people first. He's too busy navigating or daydreaming, but when the encounter comes he's always proud and will often say, smugly, "I have a lot of friends."

We lived in the Minneapolis suburb of Plymouth from 1989 to 2002. Jason was active in our church's mainstream Christian youth development program and won a lot of friends there. He was not mainstreamed in high school, but there was a mentor program in which students got volunteer credits for working with special education students.

One of my favorite encounters came at one of Jeff's high school awards events. He was getting some sort of student award and the family attended in support. One of the major honorees was a former Armstrong High School hockey player, Jordan Leopold, who had just won college hockey's Hobey Baker Award and had been drafted into the NHL.

This local hero was a very big deal and crowds of people wanted to touch him and get his autograph. Leopold was gracious to the crowd but he stopped suddenly and purposefully. To my complete shock he moved a few feet from the crowd to embrace and greet his buddy Jason. Apparently Leopold knew Jason from a mentor program several years before and he obviously had great affection for our son. Jason didn't understand the hockey player's stardom but he was savvy enough to figure out that the star of the show had taken time for him. He glowed.

We always regretted that Jason was not cognitively strong enough for mainstreaming but every exposure to normal kids was crucial to him.

That's why we jumped at the chance to allow Jason to "walk" at graduation. There was only a certificate of attendance waiting for him, but he was incredibly proud to wear what he called his "red dress" and sit with the regular students. A big party with friends and family, just as we threw for our other kids, was planned.

But then the hammer came down. A few weeks before the ceremony we were notified Jason was not going to be able to "walk" because he had an overdue library book. That didn't stun us, but the book he was accused of failing to return was astonishing: "American Imperialism in 1898." Maybe the kid has been holding out on us. More likely, some smart-alec took advantage of him. The librarian quickly backed down.

Those regular moments such as graduation kept Jason in the game, because there were darker moments.

Jason was a happy guy when he was interacting with family, friends and teachers but the adolescent Jason was far different from the 11 and 12 year-old Jason. As a little kid he was an innocent. Things changed as he developed physically but stayed exactly the same mentally. Puberty did this man-child no favors. He was lonely, often bored and never just hung out with friends. I can't ever remember him going to a friend's house or having a friend visit.

Jason often bordered on compulsive. He fretted about what was coming next and wished things were more orderly. During his teenage years Jean or Tracy started advising him to "go with the flow." That anxiousness about what's next is still one of Jason's most serious challenges.

Jason's coming of age naturally coincided with our other two children's maturity but he affected them both differently. And the difference in their relationships with Jason led to considerable tension between the two of them. Tracy was the caretaker and third parent, Jeff was Jason's friend. Both of them were convinced their approach was correct and the other's approach was wrong-headed.

Tracy worried about what Jason ate, how he dressed, how he behaved and his manners. She cut him little slack. Jeff resented her bossiness and thought Jason needed more space to "just be a guy." Tracy believed Jeff coddled Jason and that he should hold him to higher standards. Tracy admits she often got her nose out of joint at Jason during their teen years. She worried about Jason embarrassing her. Yet, Tracy says Jason has made her a deeper, more understanding person. Jeff mourns the fact that he never had a big brother. He says, "As little kids we were not only brothers, but we were friends. As I grew older, though, I started to feel more responsibility for Jason. I had to take care of him more and this is when the relationship became more difficult. He knew I was his younger brother yet I was in charge. That didn't always make sense to him."

I am positive Jason is more social, savvier and more mature because of the different approaches taken by his siblings. The third parent/friend dichotomy definitely enriched him.

The most maddening stereotype for me is that all Down syndrome people are happy, loving and contented. The fact is Down syndrome people have the same range of emotions all of us do. They can be happy and contented but they can also be angry, bitter and ticked off at their fate. I always said Jason was no Corky on the TV show "Life Goes On," but I am no Einstein either. Abilities vary in all people, disabled or not, a fact too few people seem to appreciate.

Our first exposure to the reality that Jason struggled with bitterness about his fate came a few months after his 16th birthday. He was in a McDonalds with Tracy when she pointed out a Down syndrome woman at another table. Tracy said, "Jason look, she's the same as you, she has Down syndrome."

The reaction shook Tracy and revealed a truth none of us were ready to deal with.

Jason violently shook his head and exclaimed, "Tracy, I quit being Down syndrome! I'm sixteen now!"

Our first flip reaction was "if only it was that easy." Slowly though the tragedy of the statement grew on us. At 18 and then again at 22 Jason expressed similar sentiments. At major milestones he apparently sincerely believed that he would "grow out it."

We hadn't even realized how much Jason actually focused on his disability. We never had a detailed talk about Jason's disability. At Jean's instigation we seldom told him he couldn't do something. When he made noises about driving Jean never told him he couldn't drive. Instead, she said, "You can drive when you learn to read." When he talked about getting married, she simply told him he could get married if he could find someone who wanted to marry him. That approach seemed to make sense to him.

IRREVERENCE AND EVOLUTION

We were quite aware that Jason never liked other developmentally disabled people very much. He would always choose to hang around with normal kids or adults than be with mentally disabled people. Shortly after he expressed frustration at being retarded I told him that he was acting retarded and he had to stop talking to a particular toy if he didn't want to be considered retarded. His tart-tongued reply was, "Dad, I am retarded."

Notice, I just used the R-word. I know that many parents of cognitively disabled children hate the word and after a long soul-searching journey I have come to agree with those parents.

Throughout the book I have struggled with the correctness of language. To make a point, that was the first time I have used the word outside of historical context, quotes and paraphrases. The words developmentally disabled or cognitively disabled simply didn't exist in the first 20 or so years of Jason's life. Remember, Jason was born when the term "mongolism" was common. We thought it was a big victory in the early 1980s when we were part of the movement which made that word unacceptable. The R word was quite accepted.

Since shortly after Jason's birth Jean and I have dealt with Jason's disability with deprecation and sometimes coarse flippancy. I'm sure some people would label it cruelty, but making fun of Jason's affliction and my own disability has been essential to our survival.

Early on we were told Jason's IQ was 36. That was later changed to 52. In those early days we often referred to him as ol' 36. Jason, of course, had no concept of what we're talking about. The expression BDK also escapes him. That stands for Big Dumb Kid. If Jason did something particularly frustrating, Jean or I would mutter "damn, some people even take them home." Mocking the doctor who told us about Jason's disability is a great way to relieve stress and put the situation in perspective.

My ungainly walk, my lack of handyman skills and my legendary clumsiness are all fair game in the family. Irreverence is the byword. Sanity is the result. That is the way we chose to deal with words in the early part of our journey.

I understand the recent move to make language around disability more sensitive. I do think language matters, and I dislike it intensely when people decry political correctness. I think what some people call political correctness is simply sensitivity.

But I think the real problem with the R-word has developed because of abuse of its original meaning.

Jason and I have experienced deep insensitivity. When Jason was 19 or 20 we attended a San Francisco Giants Spring baseball game. A twentyish woman sat behind us with friends, gossiping constantly, paying little attention to the game. She repeatedly referred to various friends as "retards." After she hit double figures with those rude references I angrily turned and motioned toward Jason. I vehemently barked, "Are you the most insensitive person on the planet or are you just an idiot?" She seemed mortified and was very quiet for the rest of the game. I may be kidding myself, but I think I had a profound effect on that young woman's life. Jean is convinced the woman is probably still an insensitive lout.

Using the word as a pejorative has reached almost crisis proportions. Some people frequently say, "That is so retarded." Jean and I used to have coffee with a guy who used that phrase all the time. He stopped because Jean jumped on him so often. He also stopped coming to coffee but I think that was more about our political disagreements.

Even the New York Times ethicist Chuck Klosterman had to repent for using the word three times as pejorative. The final straw for me came last year when a fairly famous commentator on journalism issues, who I actually know, referred to newspaper publishers as "retards." I was dumbstruck that such a sophisticated man could be so insulting and dismissive. Pejorative uses of retard or retarded are indeed demeaning and wrong. They must be stopped. That's the real problem on which we need to focus. While I still think the dictionary definition of retarded, "slow or limited in intellectual, emotional or academic progress," describes Jason's situation better than cognitively disabled, I have become convinced the word is so subject to abuse, we have to stop using it completely.

GETTING INTO THE SYSTEM

Shortly after Jason entered the public school system at the age of four, social workers from Hennepin County showed up at our door to check up on him and us. They did a bunch of tests to be sure Jason was being treated well and then disappeared. We didn't demand anything, and they were apparently satisfied Jason was in good hands so we fell off the radar.

We intentionally stayed out of the system. We never needed anything. And, as managing editor and later editor of the local newspaper I was happiest if I didn't use county services. That way I avoided arguments and potential conflicts of interest.

That's why it was such a big deal for us when, at 18, it was time to get Jason ready to enter a group home. Even though he wasn't going until around 2002 we knew we had to get him into the county social system and sign him up for Social Security. We also had to apply for guardianship and our unfamiliarity with the bureaucracy boggled our minds. Fortunately, there were advisers you could hire to help you with the process.

We were referred to a wonderful grandfatherly type named Arnie Grutzmacher. That meeting was seminal in several ways. He helped us get a social worker, sign up for social security, arrange for court hearings to achieve guardianship and to get on a waiting list for a group home. But the major contribution Grutzmacher made was around financial issues and he put us a bit more at ease on the most difficult issue we faced.

I made excellent money at the Star Tribune. A year before the conversation with Grutzmacher the newspaper had been sold to the McClatchy Company for a huge sum. It was one of the last big sales of a newspaper company before the value of newspapers began a steep decline. I had a modest amount of stock in the grand scheme of things, but it gave us security we never had before.

I have always had an almost pathological aversion to being viewed as a freeloader. Jean and I walked into Grutzmacher's office wondering if Jason really had to get Social Security and personal support from the county. I knew that people who didn't like the Star Tribune or me might try to make an issue of Jason getting federal and local assistance.

We pushed Grutzmacher hard and specifically proposed that we take on the entire financial burden of supporting Jason in a group home.

The kindly old gentleman was incredulous. He told us he didn't care how much money we had, we would have none by the time we were done. "The state and county would get every dime you have," he said. Grutzmacher was nice, but he implied we would be crazy to take on that burden. He told us "it's just not done."

That made us more comfortable but Jean and I were correct. We did get grief for the decision. Several years later when I wrote a commentary about Sarah Palin and Down syndrome I was criticized by a commenter for allowing the SSI system and the county to pay for Jason's care.

The encounter with Grutzmacher was typical Jean and Tim. We laughed and joked and enthusiastically displayed our characteristic irreverence. As we wrapped up the meeting we were sincerely grateful for the advice we had received and we said so.

Grutzmacher then shocked us by growing serious. He told us he owed *us* the thank you. He said this meeting had been unlike any meeting he had ever experienced and it was great pleasure for him.

Probably the gracious thing to do would have been to accept the thank you and move on. But I couldn't leave that alone. I asked Grutzmacher what made the meeting so unusual.

He shuffled his papers, he played with his glasses and then he said something like this:

> *Ninety-eight percent of the people who walk through that door walk in with the attitude that something bad has happened and by God somebody has to pay! Most people are intent on extracting revenge in some way, shape or form. They are angry and they really are not very particular about who they punish. That's what makes you two so refreshing. You are not bitter, you are not looking for a handout or revenge. You just want what's best for your son. That is so damned refreshing, it's made my year.*

Nobody had ever told us that we were that different. Jean and I were both pleased that Grutzmacher had captured our basic beliefs and saw those beliefs in our behavior. Yet we were stunned and even saddened that approach made us so unique.

THE GUIDING CONVERSATION

About the same time while visiting relatives in Florida over Christmas, 1998, Jean and I settled on the beginnings of our plan. With all the kids off at the beach, we stopped at a franchise pancake joint for breakfast. Humble fare, but we had one of those blessed conversations—the kind that flow, build and contain nuggets of wisdom you know you won't find again for months or years.

We decided, for a lot of sound reasons, I was going to retire from the Star Tribune in 2002, four years later. We also decided we would buy a second home in a warm clime that eventually turned out to be Scottsdale, Arizona. Jean was ready to retire too. She was an outstanding journalist when we married and had planned to return to the workplace. Jason changed those plans and after fighting the same battles for 22 years she was ready to slow down. The rigors of caring for a five-year-old all that time had clearly worn on her.

Most importantly, we decided that Jason would go into a group home in Minnesota because Tracy would always be a Minnesotan. From the time she was four, Tracy had been the logical and obvious choice as the person to succeed us as the overseer in Jason's life. We never doubted that for a minute. Despite all the adventures Tracy has been exposed to she is a homebody at heart. She gets nervous if she is away from her own pillow for more than a couple of nights. She was born in Florida but she considers herself a native Minnesotan.

We knew it would be unfair to move Jason around like a snowbird and that if he was with us, he would have to start all over back in Minnesota when we died. Moreover, the original idea that Jason would go into a group home when Jeff left for college still seemed like a good one.

That Christmas 1998 affirmation of our long-time belief became an article of faith in our house. Jean and I knew it. Tracy and Jeff knew it. We promised both kids as they reached adolescence and then adulthood that they would not be saddled with taking care of Jason in their homes. We were convinced that the way to keep their love for Jason alive was to make sure he was a brother of value and not a burden they might come to resent. The both heartily agreed with our choice. They both loved and valued Jason but neither saw themselves as daily caretakers.

The one person who didn't regard Jason moving into a group home as an article of faith was Jason. Oops!

We weren't being malicious or surreptitious in not talking to Jason. We simply felt that the idea of going to a group home "in three or four years" was too abstract a concept for him to grasp and we had never broached it. This was a man who got "esscited" about Christmas in July. Time was a cryptic concept for him.

But after our meeting with Grutzmacher Jean and I became convinced that our secrecy was a mistake. We became intent on preparing Jason for the possibility of a group home even if it was three or four years down the road. So we sat him down for a "talk." That's always an adventure. You need to get his focused attention in that kind of situation, but the ominous implications of a "talk" frighten Jason.

We gently explained that as all the kids got older they would be moving out and before too long he would also move. He would move into a group home with other people.

"No I don't have to do that," Jason said with reassuring affection.

"Yes, you do Jason. Tracy and Jeff will move and so will you."

"No, I don't have to. I'll stay with you guys."

We had to laugh. We were not being taken seriously and our efforts were slamming up against that brick wall that is so often Jason's mind. We decided to pull back and fight another day.

But sure enough, our worst fears were realized a few months later. In early October, Tracy asked Jason if he was excited about going to Scottsdale for Thanksgiving. We had just bought a second home in Arizona and the whole family was going there to celebrate what Jason calls "Turkey Day."

Somberly, but without histrionics, Jason replied, "No I can't go. I'm going to the group home." Just as we anticipated, his inability to abstract the concept of "in three or four years" made the group home a looming and inevitable event in his mind. And it obviously was some sort of a prison he would never leave.

We scrambled to take the immediacy out of the prospect and made sure Jason understood that not only was he part of our Thanksgiving plans in 1999, he would always be a part of our family celebrations no matter where he lived.

From that point on we treated Jason going into a group home the same way we treated Jeff going to college. It's going to happen. Every now and then we would get a little pushback along the line of "no, I don't have to do that." That was always said in a non-contentious way as if he were saying 'no, you just don't have to go to all that trouble."

THE SUMMER OF 2002

Few families have experienced a summer like ours of 2002. The wheels of family change moved rapidly with little intentional design.

Emboldened and somewhat enriched by the sale of Cowles Newspapers to McClatchy in 1998, I announced soon after the sale that I would retire in 2002 at the age of 53.

In 2001, Tracy and Ben Moll announced they would get married in 2002 after Tracy graduated from St. Cloud State with a degree in Special Education teaching.

Since junior high, teachers have always described Tracy as "the perky one." She is cute, bouncy and always wears a smile. Tracy has always been obsessively drawn to people. She must have friends around her and if they need her care and attention all the better. From the time she was a toddler she has always been kind, attentive and concerned with others.

Tracy and school were not compatible for many years. She wasn't interested and she regarded herself as a poor student. She forged on because Jean and I made it clear if she wasn't pursuing an education she'd be on her own. Career goals ranged from murky to non-existent until one night when she was 21. She came into our bedroom for one of the family's frequent sessions on the end of Mom and Dad's king bed and announced she was going to be a special education teacher.

It seemed so logical and natural for the young woman who always hungered to help people to eventually teach people such as her brother. Actually, Tracy's experience with Jason was the one thing that bothered us about her career choice. Jean gently counseled that not all the kids she taught would be like Jason. Some would be much worse behaved, undisciplined and sometimes violent. Tracy convinced us Jason was not her model, but she did allow that she thought her interactions with Jason gave her a huge head start.

Tracy and Jeff both acknowledge that a litmus test for friends was their acceptance and tolerance of Jason. Tracy managed to fall in love with the perfect man for Jason. Ben and his family have always enthusiastically embraced Jason and Ben considers him such a buddy and so important to the family that he asked him to be a groomsman in the wedding.

As much as Tracy and Ben love Jason they never wanted to have daily responsibility for him, much less house him. They both enthusiastically supported the group home idea. Like Jean and me they both recognized that Jason had stopped maturing and developing and that he would basically be a five-year-old forever. For two young people with plans for children of their own that was not a stimulating prospect.

We never gave a thought to Jeff taking responsibility for Jason. Most parents will resonate to the fact that Tracy and Jeff are two totally different people. Like practically every parent we talk to we are often stunned they came from the same gene pool and lived in the same home environment.

Jeff was mature at six. At that age he refused to hang out with two neighbor kids because he perceived them as bad kids. That same year he begged us to take him out of a class because, while he was the teacher's pet, she treated other kids badly.

He was a fine student, usually did the right and wise thing and really was a model son. One night when a rebellious 16-year-old Tracy stalked out of the house, slamming the door, 10 year-old Jeff made an announcement: "Mom, Dad, I will never be like that." He never was.

It was obvious to everyone that Jeff would be the traveler in the family. While Tracy hated her one trip to Europe, Jeff had been there four times before high school graduation. Jeff fell in love with the mountains and sun in Arizona and never applied to any school other than Arizona State University where we owned a second home.

None of us ever considered that Jeff would be a major player in Jason's life because we always had the sense he would seek a career somewhere other than Minnesota. He's now a producer at ESPN in Bristol, Connecticut. So, we made the right call. While Jeff's investment in the group home decision was relatively small he always cared about one thing when it came to his brother. Were the rest of us treating him like a "guy?" He despised it when we or his sister treated Jason like a little boy even though that was his mental age. Jeff wanted Jason treated like a "dude."

So here was the state of our family in 2002: I was scheduled to retire in June, Tracy was getting married on Aug. 3 and Jeff was scheduled to start at ASU in late August.

The window for sending Jason to a group home was starting to sharpen. But other subtler things were also happening. Jean vacationed in Scottsdale by herself in the fall of 2001 for two weeks. Things went poorly at home.

"IT'S TIME"

Jason got sick with a two-day bug. Tracy was student teaching and she couldn't help. Jeff was in high school and my work schedule was hectic. Jean sat helpless in Arizona, unable to get a quick flight back to Minnesota. She was so helpless she began to cry. Her homemaker status had always meant an easy solution to this sort of problem but now mountains had to be moved, friends had to be imposed upon, and we even had to call a hospital day care service.

Amid her tears in Arizona Jean muttered another burgeoning mantra. She announced it to me that night on the phone. "It's time. It's time Jason moved to a place where all his needs can be met all the time." That phrase "it's time" became the catchphrase that described all the dramatic change in our household.

"It's time" also began to signify something much deeper. Jason was increasingly pushing everybody's buttons. Jean was becoming frustrated quicker when Jason wouldn't shave or brush his teeth. His inconsistency was driving me nuts and Tracy and Jeff were getting incredibly discouraged because they were juggling their schedules so they could "baby-sit" for a 22 year-old man whenever Mom and Dad had other things to do.

We started to use county services to find him a companion but we were feeling guilty more often because we were finding "the big guy" a burden. Yet, Jason wasn't being well served either. We knew his capabilities too well and probably didn't allow him enough room to try new things. And our diverging busy lives made it very difficult to continue to make Jason the center of everything. He needed more attention than we could offer.

As I've said many times in these pages the most dispiriting thing about a mentally disabled child is the painfully slow rate of growth or the complete absence of growth. In 2002, Jean was correcting Jason for the same behaviors he displayed in 1992. In some ways Jason grew and developed beautifully. In other ways he never changed.

Call that disappointing, maddening, or a strain on our collective patience, but it was starting to take its toll. It was a big reason "it was time." But that realization carried considerable guilt. Were we being selfish? Had we lost our patience to the encroachment of our "mature years? We always made room for Jason in our lives and we were always rewarded with love, wisdom and laughs. Should we stop now?

I've tried not to be heavy-handed about God's role in our life with Jason. God has not been heavy-handed with us. Little bits of wisdom here, nice little breaks there, gentle feelings of guilt when I screwed up, all made the journey easier, but the heavens seldom opened up with lightning bolts of good fortune.

This time we got our lightning bolt. Jason decided he wanted to go to a group home.

One day I got home from work and Jean had one of those cartoonish, you're-not-going-to-believe-what-one-of-our-kids-did-today smiles on her face.

"Jason has done a big switch on group homes," she said. "Apparently somebody at work has convinced him they do fun stuff in group homes."

Jason works through a daily jobs program called Choice. It is a jobs site that matches developmentally disabled people with employers in the community. He works off-site four days a week and volunteers at a nursing home the fifth day. Jean hadn't pushed Jason for a lot of detail so we staged one of our frequent semi-scripted, spontaneous dinner conversations to probe how this remarkable transformation from reluctant participant to group home enthusiast had occurred.

Jason always had trouble getting a lot of conversation time at dinner. When it came to a choice between hearing about Jeff's theatrical play or Tracy's student teaching and Jason's TV schedule for that night, Jason usually lost. So whenever Jason had legitimate conversation fodder we all paid particular attention and he reveled in it.

I ham-handedly steered the conversation by asking if people talked about group homes at work. He started with his typical conversation killers—"yep" and "nope"—but he eventually told us that group homes are fun because they "go places and do stuff."

Jason was increasingly finding his parents "boring" and as his siblings built their own busy lives they had less time to entertain him. And he clearly wanted to do "more fun stuff." Fellow workers who lived in group homes had started telling him about "going places and doing stuff." That simple concept ended his apathy and his antipathy toward a group home.

Overnight, Jason had his own reason for moving into a group home. He now controlled his own destiny and we seized on it. We endorsed his worldview and vowed right then that it would be true. He would go places and do stuff in a group home that he couldn't do at home. Jason's enthusiasm and interest cast "it's time" in new and positive light.

From tales we have heard from other parents of special needs children, finding the right home might have been an entire chapter in this book but once again the entire group home process seemed magically blessed. The fact is we had put the process off way too long, but this time our guardian angel was a Hennepin County Social worker named Carolyn Jasperson.

Actually, we were turned off by Carolyn the first time we met her because she seemed to take Jason so seriously. He told her he wanted to live alone in an apartment in the city and that he wanted to work for the police. None of those things was going to happen and every time he brought up working for the police we broke into laughter. He often told Tracy he aspired to be a "plumber-cop" with Tracy's future husband, Ben. We never had any idea what a plumber-cop was and Ben claims he didn't know either.

Carolyn sat through all that and nodded encouragingly which bothered us. Gradually though we learned that first meeting was just an example of her care, concern and dedication. Carolyn turned out to be our Pied Piper and a full partner in finding the best possible living arrangement for Jason. We would follow her anywhere.

Just before Christmas of 2001 Carolyn told us she had found the right group home owner for us and she even had three other young men lined up. Early in January we met with Nick Thomley, the young man who was establishing the group home. He seemed like a great young guy and his parents had been in the group home business.

When we met the other three candidates for the home we had more than a few concerns. We were concerned about Jason's reaction to them because of his past attitudes about cognitively disabled classmates. We were on the lookout for negative vibes from Jason which never appeared.

None of the other young men had Down syndrome. While they all had cognitive disabilities they seemed significantly more advanced than Jason. That became apparent when the boys met at a go-kart track. The other three navigated the race course with a cool poise. Jason couldn't go 15 feet without colliding with something.

We became more sanguine about the mix of boys, when rather than mock and taunt Jason for his driving failures they all seemed to pitch in to help him. We found that a positive, endearing sign. And, as always, Jason's own social savvy and his irrepressible happiness made it easier for the other three to connect with him. The deal to provide a home for these four men came together in a few weeks.

MAKING THE MOVE

The tension around the actual move taxed everyone. It was obvious Jason was nervous and tentative. This moving away from Mommy and Daddy thing had seemed better in theory. His brother Jeff and Jeff's buddy, Andy, did a lot of the heavy lifting and soon-to-be brother-in-law Ben took care of the mechanical hook-ups while Mom and Dad tried to feign normalcy.

For Jean and me this was the first of three such separations that summer. We were rapidly emptying our nest and this was our neediest bird.

I've always thought Jason's fears were the same as ours—we were losing our sense of what Jason called "the fambly." Our tight-knit little group wouldn't gather at the foot of Mom and Dad's bed anymore. Nightly family dinners where we tried to get Jason to address reality rather than the fantasies of television would no longer be a staple.

All of us seek a sense of "belonging" but Jason didn't "belong" in other communities. Jason's greatest sense of belonging came from his "fambly." That was his prized jewel. His inherent inability to see things in the abstract inhibited his ability to see that he would build a new family with new traditions at the group home. For him he was truly jumping into an abyss with little hope to recreate his most important possession—"fambly."

As all the physical tasks of moving were accomplished Tracy and Ben drove away and so did Jeff and his buddy. Jean and I stood in the driveway of the four bedroom suburban house where Jason was going to start his new life.

Jean clearly remembers internally chanting her mantra for the day: "Do not cry, Do not cry, Do not cry." Her brave front wasn't mere protocol. She knew that if she cried, Jason's brave front would collapse too. He stood there with his lip trembling and with sad somewhat panicked eyes. Jean also knew that if Jason started sobbing it would be impossible to leave her special baby in that driveway just as she could never leave him alone in the hospital.

We desperately needed him to know that we loved him but his pained look made us feel as if he doubted us.

Jean's most distinct memory of that day is that as our car got to the street and out of Jason's sights she burst into a torrent of tears. It was hard to shake the guilty feelings of leaving behind our special needs child. No matter how much this move had been planned and no matter how essential it was to our future plans, and to Jason, the feeling we were abandoning him stuck in our guts like a huge rock.

A few days later we spent July 4 with Jason to celebrate the holiday. It was pretty clear he was not his normal, enthusiastic self.

And that brought us to this seminal meeting 12 days after he moved into his group home. Jean's mind immediately went to abuse. Was someone taking advantage of her baby? Tracy worried that Jason was having a difficult time assimilating with the other young men. We fretted the whole way there.

We picked up Jason at his workplace to take him to a Starbucks near his work site where he could enjoy his favorite berry smoothie. The short trip was tense. We tried to make small talk but Jason was obviously worried he was in trouble. As he did often when he felt we were upset with him he plaintively cried "I stillllllllll love you." We assured him we loved him too but made it clear we'd talk when we got to the Starbucks.

We had seen him only a few days earlier so we were surprised at this sudden drama. As we listened and sorted through things we discovered that much of this was about the drama. Jason loves drama. It didn't take long in the conversation to realize the job coach had fallen for it. Certainly Jason was upset. He cried a little bit and told us he was really homesick and we teared up a little as we told him again how much we loved him. But we held the line. We needed to make it clear that nothing was going to change. He was staying in the group home.

Through tentative questions and tearful answers we satisfied ourselves that the problem was just old-fashioned homesickness and nothing more serious. It was glaringly obvious that we were dealing with the five-year-old Jason. He was having a painfully difficult time appreciating that we loved him but left him at a home where he could not see us every day.

The other thing that emerged was a fear most of us share. He seemed petrified that we were all having a fantastic time in his absence. Tracy and

Jeff were still in the house for a few months and he seemed convinced we were having wild parties and incredible fun in his absence.

We still see signs of that attitude 12 years later. His failure to abstract things simply can't process that we simply go about our daily lives when he's not at home.

Just as was the case when we initially dropped him off at the home our rational selves were locked in mortal battle with our emotions. We knew we were doing the right thing and so it was crucial that we show confidence and love. At the same time Jean and I were both on the edge of tears and worked hard to resist sobs and hugs.

When we dropped him off back at the group home, I vaguely remember him saying that this was his home now. It was a long time before he became convinced of that.

WEDDING TRAUMA

Things remained tense for the rest of the summer. At the group home he was assigned chores and the staff worked hard at accommodating Jason's efforts to settle in a routine. That did not come without some boundary testing. In the early days when staff asked him to do something Jason would frequently ask, "Can you make me?"

The weird thing about that question is that group homes struggle with that issue more than any other. Because of the history of mental health abuse staff *really can't* make Jason do anything. Jean and I found that silly. If Jason could be trusted to make his own decisions he wouldn't have to be in the bleeping group home.

We solved that problem the old-fashioned way. We made it clear to Jason that we *could* make him do things and the staff would let us know if he didn't. That worked only in the short term.

In the first several weeks of living in the group home Jason was reluctant to stay at our house on weekend visits. When we pressed him on that he told us he didn't want to stay because "it makes me miss you more." We never genuinely understood that special sort of Jason logic but we tried to respect it.

On August 2, it was imperative that Jason stay at our house. The next day his big sister was getting married. Ben invited both Jason and Jeff to be groomsmen. Jason was incredibly "esscited" to be in the wedding.

But that night the stress of the wedding, his still fresh anxiety over the move, his legendary gluttony at the groom's dinner and his natural difficulty sleeping, led to a disaster. Around 4 a.m. Jason got sick. He was throwing up every 10 minutes. The illness did not pass quickly.

The wedding was scheduled for 2 pm. Mom had plenty of pre-wedding details to handle and Jeff was her assigned helper. That meant Jason and Dad were attached at the hip because Jason does not do sick independently.

Jason was fully decked out in his tuxedo as he barfed frequently and violently. I would hold his head out away from his duds and constantly try to guide him to a polite place he could lose his cookies.

As I watched the clock he did not improve. By 11 a.m. our families and everybody close to the wedding started to worry. Would Jason be able to go through with the wedding? His illness and a bridesmaid's dissatisfaction with her hairdresser became the two major sources of tension for everyone.

The bridesmaid got there about 1 p.m. and that made it picture time. Just before Jason was to be called for pictures we went outside and he lost it again. I carefully put my hands on his shoulders and looked deeply into his eyes as I asked him if he could go through with the wedding. He knew by my tone that this was decision time. He looked back at me determinedly and said he could do it.

The decision was mine. Understanding the risk if Jason got sick during the ceremony, I decided we'd all regret it forever if we cut Jason out of this wedding. This was his chance to be normal. More than most dads, I understood what that meant to him.

In the pictures Jason looks decidedly peaked, but by wedding time he looked fit. That night at the reception nobody danced longer and harder. The anticipation almost killed him, but he was a champ during the actual event.

Tracy's wedding and Jeff's departure for college three weeks later seemed to settle Jason down significantly. We had promised him that he would go into the group home when Jeff and Tracy left the house and until that happened, Jason's stress was obviously high.

Within several weeks we got a report that Jason was "doing great and everybody likes him."

That was rewarding but the real prize came about a year later. We were eating out with Jason and without any warning he turned to us with a rare, serious look on his face and said, "Thanks Mom and Dad for *making* me go to the group home." He was sincere and genuinely grateful because he loved his new-found independence.

Jason had grown up.

CHAPTER 7

THE ADULT TIM

I n early 2013, Michael Branson, a physical rehabilitation specialist, kneaded my back muscles while he explained my recent back injury to his young intern in technical terms.

I knew Branson well and he knew my body even better. He had helped me through other injuries in the past. As he lectured the somewhat glassy-eyed student he referred to my "history." I raised my head off the table and explained, "I have a congenital birth defect called Arthrogryposis Multicongenita."

"But, he's lived a life most of us would kill for," Branson shot back.

Some people see my disability and Jason's Down syndrome and they think I have had it tough. Not true at all. I have strolled through a charmed life with a fantastic family, many treasured friends, two careers I truly consider "callings" and experiences most people can't begin to appreciate. I owe much of it to the newspaper business. Newspapers gave me a purpose, an opportunity to lead and a front row seat to observe the world, locally, nationally and internationally. A newspaper editor of a large newspaper has the opportunity to meet people, visits places and hobnobs with power in ways most Americans cannot. For a small-town boy born with crippled limbs, that good fortune was both treasure and blessing.

Take a little tour of the pictures on my walls.

There I am at a barbecue with Nelson Mandela six months after he got out of prison. That three-hour barbeque followed a festive, mind-blowing two-hour Catholic Mass in Soweto. It was easily one of the best days of my life.

There's a picture of me with Fidel Castro and several with President Bill Clinton. One snapshot captures me with my friend, the late Senator Paul Wellstone, who long before that warm picture was taken, once threatened "to go down to the Star Tribune and kick Tim McGuire's ass."

There are several signed syndicated cartoons on the wall, including a Peanuts comic strip signed by Charles Shultz. In my bathroom, the only appropriate place, there's a hilarious x-rated cartoon drawn for me personally by the Pulitzer Prize winning editorial cartoonist Pat Oliphant. There are pictures of me with Lady Bird Johnson, Vice-President Al Gore, and the president of Mexico. And, equally as important, are the images of me with dear friends from the newspaper industry, and of my beloved college buddies from the Watkins Street house. Thinking about the loyalty and affection I have with several friends from high school, college and the newspaper business makes me emotional. And, I glow when I look at all the family pictures on those walls.

I have broken bread with sports figures such as George Steinbrenner, Don Mattingly, Sparky Anderson, Carl Yastrzemski, Howard Cosell and Hank Stram.

I have parried phone calls and sometimes contentious visits from Dear Abby, Ann Landers, Jesse Ventura and Jesse Jackson. I have been a guest speaker in Europe and I traveled through Africa. I was a Pulitzer Prize jurist six times. I was a part of a Pulitzer Prize winning team when I was managing editor of the Minneapolis Star Tribune. In 2001-2002, I was President of the organization of newspaper editors, The American Society of Newspaper Editors.

It all speaks of a rich life that, as Branson said, most people would covet.

But it is a life that would have been denied me had I followed my original instincts and pursued law or something more mundane in the political science field. Editing a large newspaper brought me a strong sense of service, a bit of power tempered by huge responsibility, and the constant knowledge you cannot serve all masters.

TWO HALVES OF OUR LIVES

Richard Rohr, my favorite Christian writer, is a Franciscan priest. His book, Falling Upward discusses two halves of our lives and nicely personifies my bumpy journey. Rohr writes that the preoccupations of the first half of one's life include "establishing their personal (or superior) identity, creating personal boundary markers for themselves, seeking security, and perhaps linking to what seem like significant people or projects."

When I graduated from college, as one wag said, "McGuire got purposeful." I earnestly set about establishing who I was. Being really successful was a crucial part of that desired identity. I never forgot that promise I made to myself on that bed when I was 15 and suffering in pain. I had to succeed and erase the memories of discomfort I felt as a teenager.

But making a difference was always a driving force for me. My parents had instilled a strong sense of obligation to my fellow man. I never forgot those suffering twins in the hospital and I wanted to make the world better. I discovered early on that my ability with words could make that difference.

I had worked for about eight months at the Dowagiac Daily News in the first semester of my senior year at Aquinas. After graduation, with 33 rejection letters from newspapers all over the country and bruised hopes, I reluctantly returned to Dowagiac. A few months later I went to an upscale weekly newspaper in Birmingham, Michigan, eccentrically named The Birmingham Eccentric. My plan was to go to law school part-time at one of several Detroit law schools. At that point I was simply not committed to newspapers as the best path to fame and fortune.

That Birmingham stint was rocky. My direct supervisor almost immediately decided I was an idiot. She truly viewed me as incompetent. I was facing dismissal when she left on her vacation which turned out to be the most fortuitous vacation of my life. Her boss took over the city desk and at the end of that week he pronounced me "just fine." With my career saved, my productivity soared. I quickly fast-tracked to a supervisor position at another Eccentric newspaper before my old boss from Dowagiac called.

He had been named the top editor in Ypsilanti, Michigan, an 18,000 circulation newspaper. Fran Reidelberger was a character of the first order. He drank too much, his humor was zany, and he was an excellent editor. He had a great eye for a story and he could convey the essence of a story succinctly. I learned a lot about newspapering from him. He called in a panic one day in 1972 and told me he desperately needed a city editor who shared his values.

It was a move up with a boss I really liked, so I grabbed the opportunity. For several months we did very good work and hired some fine people until Fran got into an impetuous row with the publisher. In early 1973, Fran quit his job in a huff over an issue that should have been easily resolved. The interim top editor job fell to me.

When the publisher asked me to take the interim spot he made it clear I was not a candidate for the permanent job. I told him that was fine because I didn't want the job. But circumstances can change.

For three months the publisher marched potential candidates through the small 22-person newsroom. With each passing month I got more confident in my ability to do the job and less impressed with the candidates he found.

Finally, in May of 1973, I applied for the top editor's job with a letter that I personally walked upstairs to the publisher's office. I handed him the letter and announced I was applying for the job. His response was instant: "You little shit, I wasn't sure I could outwait you."

There was one minor, funny snag. When I wrote the press announcement of my appointment it included my age, 24. The publisher sheepishly inquired if we could instead say, "Approaching 30?" I emphatically told him that was not ethical because I was approaching 30 much too slowly.

The newspaper could not afford to pay the salaries the big Detroit papers offered their top reporters, but I quickly figured out I could match the starting salaries the big boys offered. That allowed me to hire some of the best young talent from Michigan colleges even though I could only keep them for a couple of years. That tactic, the skill and aggressiveness of the staff and the fact that Ypsilanti produced some good news stories made our little paper the most prize-winning small newspaper in the state.

From the first days in Ypsilanti I noticed one of the female reporters.

At the first staff party I attended in 1973 that attractive woman seemed to watch me closely but disapprovingly.

I eventually overcame her disapproval and after a two-year friendship, cemented over way too many nightly drinks at the local watering hole, and a secret whirlwind courtship, Jean Fannin, became my greatest gift in life, Jean Fannin McGuire. Nepotism rules forced Jean to resign as assistant managing editor when we got married. There's a good possibility the best journalist in the McGuire family left journalism at that point.

The summer of 1975 in Ypsilanti was as stunning a time for newsgathering as you could possibly imagine in any town.

On July 11, a bank, a block from the newspaper office, was robbed in broad daylight. A policeman and a robber were killed. Even now I remember the dead robber's face when we raced to the scene. We covered the hell out of that story. Then a couple of weeks later Jimmy Hoffa was kidnapped. There were rumors his body had been dumped near Ypsilanti so that became another big story for the paper.

The breakthrough story came a few weeks later. A tremendously talented reporter named Donna Leff had arrived a few months before because her husband was interning at an Ann Arbor hospital. I considered her a pro's pro. As I remember it, one night she was calling funeral homes when a mortician innocently said, "Boy, they're dropping like flies at the Veterans Hospital."

That random comment combined with some hush-hush doctor conversations she had overheard at home, sent Leff into full investigative mode. Soon, the little paper that could was printing stories about murders at the local Veterans hospital. Our competitor, The Ann Arbor News denied the stories for days. The reputations of the newspaper, the reporter and me were hanging out there in serious jeopardy until the Detroit Free Press came to town and confirmed our reporting. That case exploded into a huge national story. Wikipedia reminds me that two Filipino nurses were charged, convicted of poisoning 10 hospital patients. Those convictions were eventually overturned and the charges dropped.

All that happened long after Harte-Hanks newspapers, which owned the Ypsilanti Press, and Gregory Favre, the new editor at their Corpus Christi newspaper, decided to hire me as managing editor of the Corpus Christi paper. Law school was on hold now because I was making good money and this newspaper thing was looking like a career.

Once again my boss got crossways with management and left. After I stabilized a contentious newsroom, management informed me I was going to be the top editor of the paper but they would not formally name me editor because I was too young.

My reaction was unsurprising, at least to me. I was too headstrong and full of myself to swallow what I saw as a silly, capricious decision based on age. If I was good enough to do the job the publishers should have given me the title and the money that went with it. Anything else was baloney, and I told them that in more vulgar terms. I resigned, but only after I had secured a job in Lakeland, Florida with a huge assist by new friend, mentor and top cheerleader, Gregory Favre.

In Lakeland, with the invaluable help of Will Corbin, we tore apart a newsroom. I thought it needed rebuilding and we put together a top-notch young staff. We converted the afternoon newspaper to morning publication, only the second newspaper in the country to undertake a conversion that later became commonplace in the industry because of changing consumer behavior.

More positive attention came and so did our two oldest children, Tracy and Jason. Jean and I both loved Florida but Jason was born right about the time the colorful and controversial new editor of the Minneapolis Star, Steve Isaacs, started courting me. Isaacs made a big splash with his efforts to save an afternoon newspaper. He was a big man with bigger ideas.

The decision to go to The Star was not as easy as many would imagine. It was a metropolitan newspaper, but it was another afternoon paper and the vultures were already circling that endangered species. Plus, we were being asked to leave Florida, a place Jean and I really enjoyed. Jean was born and raised in West Texas. Michigan and Minnesota were hard duty for her weather-wise. Isaacs eloquently called Lakeland and my set-up as the top editor "a verdant Nirvana."

Three things drove the decision to take the leap north. Taking the managing editor's job at a major newspaper, even if it was an afternoon paper, stoked my ego, and Minneapolis had always seemed like an exciting big city and an amazing place to make a career and a life. Isaacs' bold ideas were empowering. He told me no idea that might save the paper was too crazy. Nothing was off limits. That was heady stuff for a guy who prided himself on creativity.

Jean understood that and while she was not excited about the cold and snow she was intrigued by the big city. This was a woman who left a small West Texas town to find a big new world. Minneapolis perfectly fit that goal.

JASON DOMINATED THE DISCUSSION

But every discussion we had about relocating to Minneapolis wound back to Jason. He was only about four months old so his future was a mystery. We were pretty ignorant about education and health for Down syndrome kids. Fear drove our thoughts more than information.

I thought the Winter Haven pediatrician's clumsy behavior when he told us about Jason's condition had offered important indicators about the state of health for mentally impaired people in Florida. To make matters worse, the other parents of Down syndrome children told us that early childhood special education was terrible in the state. They also painted an ugly picture of the resources the local school system invested in special education. Many years later we learned Jason would have made a 45-minute one-way trip to the only school for special education in Polk County. Imagine Jason and his personal trouble with school transportation on that long trip.

On the other hand, we knew Minneapolis was known for its dedication to education. It was a high tax, high service state. That was a fine approach in my mind.

More importantly for us, a young woman named Vicky Solomonson had been born in Minnesota in 1960. She had Down syndrome and the doctors suggested institutionalizing her. The family refused. Not a particularly surprising story there, but Vicky Solomonson had a profound effect on policymaking. That's because Vicky had a very important grandpa, Sen. Hubert Humphrey. Humphrey and his wife Muriel became major dynamic advocates for more spending on special education and for equal rights for mentally disabled kids.

The Twin Cities and Fraser School benefitted greatly from the Humphreys' advocacy. Isaacs arranged for a tour of Fraser for Jean as he interviewed me. A Cowles executive had a son who had used Fraser's resources. Jean was still in the dark about special education but she knew she had found the light when she saw Fraser. They were forward thinking with a positive, individual approach. They believed in establishing aggressive expectations for each child. At that point Jean and I needed that. Jason still did not have obvious physical problems, but the Twin Cities' brilliant reputation as a medical center sealed the deal.

It seemed to me that my age was a bigger issue than my disability when I arrived in Minneapolis. I was 30. That was young by any industry standard. There were lots of jokes about my youth. Staffers were asking if the new guy would be "wearing knickers." Would there be recess during the middle of the day?

But there were also jokes about my disability. My profound waddle captured everybody's attention. Behind our backs, my boss, Isaacs, a huge man, was called Whale and I was called Flipper because of my odd gait.

I had been in Minneapolis for three or four years when a production supervisor told me that story in a bar one night. A friend of mine from the newsroom was with me, and he was horrified that I heard that reference. He confessed later he had heard it many times, but he never wanted me to hear it.

Stories like that hurt, of course. I was always amazed when adults could be as cruel and juvenile as kids on a third grade playground. Mostly, that kind of put down just strengthened my resolve to not be disabled.

My disability was not going to be an issue, just as it had not been an issue in high school, or college, or during my early newspaper career. If I had to drink more than anybody else to show them I wasn't disabled, I would. If I had to swear and sound tougher than anybody else to show them I was not disabled, I would do that. If I had to work longer hours and come up with a million creative ideas to show them I was not disabled I would do that too.

My actions clearly fit into Richard Rohr's fascinating analysis of the first half of life. Too much of the first half for me was about becoming well-known and successful. I did not spend much time on the bigger issues of newspapering and spirituality. I loved the action of newspapering but I simply did not spend very much time on purpose and meaning during that phase of my life. I was single-minded about my goals. Rohr argues the attempts to find security, stature and identity are worthwhile even if they are flawed. He writes, "We grow spiritually much more by doing it wrong than by doing it right."

I did a lot of things wrong. I had never had any formal management training and running newsrooms at smaller papers had not fully prepared me for the political daggers of a large newsroom. I did have great intuition and instincts but I learned a lot by making countless mistakes and trying to grow from them. Eventually I became passionate about management and leadership and how to get newspaper staffs to serve readers, but it was an intellectual, emotional and spiritual journey.

My biggest test came when, two and half years after I arrived in Minneapolis, the Star folded, just as many afternoon papers around the country did. My boss and loyal advocate, Steve Isaacs, was fired. The publisher wanted me to stay even though the editor of the morning paper, and now the merged paper, did not want me at all. At the direction of the publisher, I was made managing editor for features. The editor handled that easily. He told my assistants to ignore me.

I was essentially exiled. I still had influence with the people who had worked for me at the Star and by the force of my personality, but my formal authority at the new merged paper was negligible. My career had smashed into a most troublesome wall. The editor was active in his hostility toward me. He prepared a list of his potential successors. He placed me eighth on the list but I believe I was only that high so the publisher wouldn't laugh at the list. The editor seemed to think copy boys were more qualified than I was. I have never attempted to ascribe motives to him. He seemed to simply believe I was not a good editor.

With my career demise staring me in my face, and running the features department without any power boring the hell out of me, I frantically searched for alternatives. I was pretty sure my time in the newspaper industry was winding down. But I was smart enough to make two commitments: Don't do anything rash, but do something.

I didn't quit in a huff. The publisher of the paper apparently saw potential in me and he wanted me to stay. So I did. And, 12 years after I moved to the Detroit area with the intention of going to law school, I finally made the plunge.

BACK ON TRACK

The William Mitchell School of Law in St. Paul and its evening program was perfect for me. My entire first year at law school was made much easier by the fact that I wasn't being particularly challenged at work. At the end of that year, when I'd done the really hard work of legal writing and legal research and got my bearings, two incredibly wonderful things happened.

The most important was that Jean, despite having only one ovary after a tumor was removed, gave birth to the perfectly normal son we wanted so desperately. Jeff was the answer to our prayers. At that point Jean and I had what we irreverently described as "all three flavors, a girl, a boy and a Down syndrome."

Almost as remarkable, the editor resigned in a huff over a dispute about manpower in the newsroom. Joel Kramer, the new editor of the paper was wicked smart. He was not a schmoozer like me, but he recognized its value in leading newsrooms. He was only 11 months older than I was. The Harvard grad was laser focused on making the Star Tribune a better newspaper. He was not at all hung up on who had worked at the morning Tribune or at the afternoon Star before the merger. I correctly saw Kramer as my get-out-of-jail-free card and I worked like hell to impress him by developing new ideas for the paper.

After a few months I was urged by friends to apply for a pretty good job out west. I told Kramer out of courtesy. Two days later he invited me to breakfast and made me the sole managing editor of the paper.

I was still young and I could not do anything about that. I was still disabled, but I was determined not to be thought of that way. I would not even consider a handicapped sticker for my car. I pugnaciously and actively denied I was different. I was convinced that people who considered me disabled often resented that I did not fit into their preconceived set of expectations they had for the disabled. And I was just as aware that many people never even considered me disabled. When a long-time friend, Terrie Robbins, heard about this book she says she was pulled up short because she never thought of me as disabled.

I clearly dedicated most of my early adulthood to avoiding stereotype or categorization, of being thought of as the quiet crippled kid in the corner. I always laughed at Jason's decision to "quit being handicapped," but during my early adult years I pretty much did the same thing, deciding to act in every way counter to the expectations of the disabled.

Many disabled people make fairly clear choices about avoiding or seeking the limelight. I had to have it.

I had gotten married in a yellow leisure suit. One of my college friends argued I looked like a wounded banana. I wore loud ties and whimsical socks. Peanuts and Disney characters on both earned maximum attention.

I honored the maxim: I don't care what you call me, just spell my name right. I was outspoken, and blunt, often-times too blunt.

My temper was notorious in my early years in journalism. One of my tantrums in Ypsilanti produced a hole in the wall I am told was there until the day the newspaper closed in the 1990s. I was a big pencil thrower in my early days.

That behavior subsided more than a little with age, and though some people would argue the point, I became more tolerant and less controlling as I grew older. Still, the chip on my shoulder got reinforced often.

My 5-3 height and my excessive weight combined with my obviously crippled gait always drew stares, even in important professional settings. Sometimes I'd accommodate the gawking, and other times I'd stare back or return rudeness with confrontation. I was especially conscious of the quizzical looks Jason and I would get when we were out together. I am certain many people looked at us and deduced "the boys from the home were out for the day."

That was one reason I bought expensive luxury cars. People would think twice about categorizing the "poor handicapped man" if he was driving a Mercedes or a Cadillac. I specifically remember a McDonald's employee who complimented my car, saw both Jason and me and then said, "Wow, it's a really nice car." It seemed obvious to me the young man was thinking "it's an even nicer car for you two."

For a long time Jean wondered if I was imagining these slights and especially the "two boys from the home" impression. Three or four years ago we were in Minneapolis at a movie theater. A man clearly patronized Jason and me and deferred to Jean as if she were our keeper. As we walked away, a stunned and shaken Jean said, "That was incredible. He thinks I'm the guardian for you two!" I could not resist an "I told you so."

Those callous categorizations were infuriating and hurtful for a major newspaper executive but professionals were often demeaning to me as well, even if they didn't get it. I can't tell you the number of times people in First Class on Northwest Airlines would find out my occupation and remark "Well, good for you." In my mind they do not respond to other editors of major newspapers that way. They have whole bodies.

Interestingly "others," such as women and my Latino friend Rick

Rodriguez, a former top editor at the Sacramento Bee, report similar reactions from executive level people.

It mattered none that most of those slights carried little or no spite, they still wounded, separating me from being what I viewed as normal.

"SECOND HALF OF LIFE"

The early 1990s were seminal for me as I matured into the "second half of my life." I became the editor of the newspaper in 1992 when my mentor and biggest supporter, Joel Kramer, became publisher. Becoming editor was a big deal for me. I never thirsted to take the step to being a publisher. I would have taken it had it been offered, but it was not crucial to establishing my identity. Being an editor was, and that sense of genuine accomplishment probably opened my mind and heart for some major changes in my life. I began to think more about purpose and meaning in my professional and spiritual lives. In retrospect I think there was a pretty clear trigger for that change.

Year after year the form came around to every employee. It was voluntary, optional and all the other caveats the lawyers could think of, but they wanted to know if you thought you were a member of a racial minority. I was not. It asked your gender and I was able to confidently check the *male* box. Then the form asked if you were disabled.

For the first twenty or so years of my career, with all the energy and anger that kept me riding that bike when I was seven, I checked the "no" box with defiance. The chip on my shoulder did not crumble easily. I could do anything anybody else could do, so there was no way in hell I was disabled. Jason desperately wanted to "stop being handicapped." I never wanted to start. I was unwilling to give an inch.

Shortly after I became editor of the newspaper the form came around again. I was still male. I was still not a racial minority.

That time, for some inexplicable reason, my hand paused above the disability box. I cannot tell you what had changed. Perhaps I felt a greater sense of responsibility to diversity as editor. Perhaps my gradually aging body spoke truth to me. Perhaps I was tired of carrying around that chip on my shoulder. Perhaps I was beginning to face the hard questions of identity, of discovering who I really was.

In Richard Rohr's book he argues that a key to growing into the second half of life is "coming home." He writes, "Somehow the end is in the beginning and the beginning points toward the end." He adds this about the call home. "All I know is that it will not be ignored. It calls us both backward and forward to our foundation and to our future."

I didn't understand why I had changed. I simply knew I was ready to own up to a basic truth about who I was and needed to be. Pleasing all the people who watched me take my first steps, repeatedly tumbling off my bike, the loneliness of the hospital and my rage at the taunting second graders formed my foundation. Those experiences were my core. They defined me at least as much as my newspaper success and important titles. I think I was also recognizing the truth of what I told my brother Marty 30 years before when he was ready to blast the little bully: "I *am* handicapped."

I didn't know it at that moment but checking the disabled box signaled a seismic change in my life. In retrospect it opened me up to who I really am and allowed me to approach the second half of my life with greater purpose. Call it spirituality. Call it acceptance. Call it the beginning of my journey "home." A close friend of mine compares it to her decision to announce she was gay. I don't think it was as big as that courageous move, but it was seminal for me.

Several spiritual things happened around the time I checked the disabled box.

In late 1992, I joined a prayer group of Catholics in high stress, high responsibility jobs. I had known Father John Forliti when he served as a visiting priest in my home parish. When he became the pastor of the downtown Catholic parish, St. Olaf's, he invited me to become a part of a group he viewed as a crucial element of his emerging ministry.

I often attended Lenten daily mass at St. Olaf's, and I had hungered for an opportunity to share my faith with like-minded people. Every foray I had made into such groups broke apart because my work and status were so different. In this group I found a police chief, a female judge, a county supervisor, two prominent businessmen and, later, a former U.S. Senator. We all shared similar responsibilities and stresses.

The group morphed a bit over the years, but it played a profound role in growing my spirituality.

Just as important was an invitation to become a lay preacher in the Catholic Church. That fit perfectly with my speaking skills but it also forced me to open up about my spiritual self. That was crucial in facilitating my "second-half" development.

My spiritual journey has always been a bumbling one. I like to call myself a "Sermon on the Mount Catholic." To me, that means I am deeply interested in Christ's message that we take care of the least of our brethren. I am far less interested in the hierarchical church. The Church's misadventures with pedophile priests and the mean-spirited attacks on women, gays and gay marriage have challenged my participation considerably.

When Jean went through cancer surgery and chemotherapy a good friend told me how impressed he was with the way I had handled that difficult time. "All of us are so impressed by your faith."

I didn't argue with my friend, but he was talking in terms of my Catholic faith. That is not the faith that gets me through trials. The faith I have is not that some magical god will fix everything for me. I do not believe God is a micromanager. Rather, I have a powerful sense that a powerful unearthly force, call him or her God if you wish, loves me, infuses me with strength and guides me. My God does not guarantee me an earthly outcome that I want, but gives me the strength I need no matter what happens.

Another crucial event occurred that changed the way I defined myself.

It was a day in 1993 or '94, I can't remember the season, but the sun was shining over my right shoulder and into the eyes of the workplace consultant attempting to counsel me. I was bitterly complaining about some negative behavior of staff members. In the next 30 minutes that consultant said many important, provocative things that deeply affected my work and my management style.

The most important thing he said stopped me cold and made me think about my faith. The specific words of our dialogue are unclear now, but I distinctly remember reflecting on his words. After a long pause I said, "I can't just pretend to be a devout Catholic on Sunday and then not live my faith here at work, can I?" He smiled a gentle smile of triumph as if to say, "I knew you'd eventually get it."

I committed a lot of workplace sins and mistakes in the years following that encounter and I continued too often to be arbitrary, quick-tempered and judgmental. However, that meeting was another crucial element of me attempting to shed the chip and develop more tolerance, consideration and affection for the people around me.

That conversation gave me the kick I needed to think more deeply about newspapers and my role.

I never believed I was the best journalist around. In the Star Tribune newsroom there were smarter people, better writers and better managers. I believed my passion for newspapers, people and our readers were the qualities that distinguished me. Even more important, I could live with my decisions, right or wrong. That's the key to leadership.

As the 1990s progressed, the threats to newspapers that have now ballooned into potentially fatal wounds were beginning to show themselves. I developed a reputation for thinking aggressively about those threats, but the truth is I didn't think aggressively enough to turn over the cart rather than just shaking it a bit.

I am proud of my newspaper career because I believe many issues were illuminated better than they might have been and that led to better decisions by the public. My most basic belief is that the light is always better than the dark. I never cared that much about outcomes from our stories but I cared deeply that the issues got explored, debated and resolved the way citizens wanted them resolved.

I will never be an editor again, but if I were, I would focus only on the biggest issues facing the newspaper and the editor. We all spend too much time on things that don't matter much.

POLARIZING FIGURE

The "first half of my life—acquiring security, prestige and identity"—bumped into my mellowing second half in the mid-to-late 1990s.

My resume says I served as of the President of the American Society of Newspaper Editors (2001-2002).

The resume does not tell you how important that position was to me. It does not tell you that being elected to that position legitimized me in my own mind because I had been chosen by my peers to lead a group of editors dedicated to improving the industry. The newspaper industry mattered deeply to me because I believed our work was so vital. The resume does not tell you how difficult the climb to that presidency really was.

Two times the Board of Directors of the organization deadlocked in 10-10 votes for president and I was involved in both. I lost both. The first time the vote changed when I pointed out that one member should not be voting. She was voting for me. That illustrated an important part of my personality: I can't shut my mouth if I think there's a justice issue at stake. I did not assess the political winds before I raised the voting issue. I knew what was happening wasn't right so I blurted it out. The defender of justice role has made me a Don Quixote figure many times in my life.

It doesn't take a high-priced psychoanalyst to figure out why the disabled kid from the small town reacts in a knee-jerk way to anything he considers an injustice. That combative, in-your-face reaction to a perceived wrong against anyone can easily be traced to that grapevine in the neighbor's yard. It has become an essential element of my personality. Depending on your point of view you can label me as a noble fighter for justice or as a big-mouthed obstacle.

The story of the ASNE election also points out another dismaying truth. I can be a polarizing force. Two 10-10 votes involving the same person are, at best, odd. While ties had occurred before they were rare. Twice at least 10 people found other candidates they preferred. Ten others were fiercely loyal and fought until the end. I'll never forget when my colleague, Bill Ketter, approached me after I lost the last time in Detroit. He was so disappointed he was on the verge of tears. I was finally elected in my last year of eligibility.

Throughout my work career some people have been fiercely loyal and others have wanted me to dry up and blow away. That may be because I'm an incredible jerk. It may be that contentious personality. And, it could be that people look at my body and develop certain expectations that I don't meet.

The truth is, first half of life or second half, I was always a bit inscrutable. I don't think I have ever intentionally been contrary or unpredictable, nor is it a contrivance. I just am. Jean said I am still enigmatic to this day. I am moral and boundary-pushing at the same time. I have tithed since the late 1980s but I gamble enthusiastically, I am faith-filled and spiritual, but foul-mouthed. I can be ethical to the point of being a pain in the ass.

I embrace argument and debate. One co-worker said this in an ASNE magazine profile about me. "For McGuire, debate is like air." I love that quote both because of its ambiguity about whether the speaker approves or disapproves, and its accuracy. I always believe debate and argument illuminates, clarifies and sparks creativity and innovation. I dislike acquiescence and passivity. It's why I believe so passionately in transparency. You can't find truth if some parties have a better look at the cards than others.

In the acknowledgement section of his book, What Jesus Said (and why it matters now.) Tim Fallon wrote: *"Special thanks to my lifelong friend Tim McGuire for his editorial expertise, his candid, though sometimes brutal feedback and his loving support."*

Brutal? Brutal? I'll show you brutal if you spend a day in a newsroom. And yet, even my best newspaper friends regard me as astonishingly outspoken. Probably the most important Latino editor of his generation, Rick Rodriguez, who is now a colleague at Arizona State University's Walter Cronkite School of Journalism says I have the biggest "cajones," he has ever encountered. He believes I will say anything to anybody at any time.

That leads us back to an eternal question about people who are different: Is my sense of independence, the need for candor and the lack of fear a product of my disability or something else? Some would argue I am just rude, others that I am a wonderful defender of truth and underdogs. Some would say I revel in being provocative, others that I just don't care what you think because I know who I am.

Discovering who I am has been the great victory of the "second half of my life." I finally arrived at a point where I didn't really much care what people said about me. I came to grips not only with the fact that I am different and my life has been different but I am part of the "other." My solidarity with blacks, Hispanics, gays and other people who are different has grown exponentially since I checked that disability box.

Richard Rohr says we "come home to our true and full self." He says when our "outer performance" days are over we can rest in the simplicity and ground of our own deeper life, we are free to stop our human doing and finally enjoy our human being.

Checking that box was the first time I broke with my life-long belief that I was "just like everybody else." The admission that I was an "other" shaped my politics and beliefs. My increasing acceptance of my "otherness" has radicalized me on issues of injustice toward the poor, gay people and women. My tolerance toward bullies in the Catholic Church and in business has withered. More importantly, I am more confident and comfortable in my own skin. I can just "be" rather than constantly trying to prove that I am good, better or best.

That attitude has allowed me to fully embrace my "second calling." When I retired from the Star Tribune in 2002 I wrote a syndicated column on values, spirituality and ethics in the workplace and did some speaking and facilitating of groups. I also did some teaching through visiting professorships at Davidson College and Washington and Lee University.

In 2005, the founding dean of the Cronkite School of Journalism, Christopher Callahan, approached me about taking an endowed chair at the school. I quickly accepted, was granted tenure and found my second "calling."

The most important thing I do in my teaching life is provoke young people to think. I proudly tell my students: "I am not interested in teaching you stuff, I want to teach you how to think about stuff." That is what I try to do and I think it helps me make a difference in students' lives.

A DISABILITY "RADICAL"

One of the last obstacles to fully accepting my disability came around 2002.

Despite my twisted limbs, my halting limp and my tendency to fall, I never had a handicapped sticker for my car. Acquiring one of those blue placards seemed like throwing in the towel—a form of submission. I hated the idea of admitting my disability was winning. Jean had grown more frustrated with my refusal every year as my deteriorating ankles, my excessive weight and my inherent lack of coordination led to countless falls on the ice and snow.

When I had spinal surgery in 2002 my doctor asked me if I ever fell. I said sure, eight or nine times a winter. He said, "You can't do that!" My response was typically glib: "Sure I can, it's easy." The doctor intensely disliked my humor, and the handicap sticker followed quickly.

Weight is an elephant in the room when it comes to my adult struggles. Since college I have battled to maintain something close to a reasonable weight. Many would argue my disability has been exacerbated by carrying way too many pounds. My excessive girth certainly makes my limp worse, and it has dramatically increased the pounding on my legs and ankles.

My legs are short. That's one of the more subtle effects of all those surgeries when I was a child. Jean and I are about the same height but when I sit next to her I tower over her. That's because my torso is that of a man 5-10 or so. My legs make me 5-3. I offer that as observation, not as an excuse for my obesity. The fact is I overeat and I don't exercise. I could blame it on stress, anger or glands but the simple fact is I don't treat my body well. Only once in my life have I ever really broken the overeating cycle. That was in 2009 when with a combination Jean's healthy cooking and aggressive weight training I lost more than 50 pounds. I later gained much of it back.

Even the loss of that weight did not cure my biggest adult health issue. After my 2002 retirement from the Star Tribune my ankles continued to deteriorate. The doctors said early surgeries had created massive arthritis in my ankles. Being 70 pounds overweight had not been helpful either. As the pain became unbearable in 2010 I decided to have surgery on one ankle at a time. Within months I was a radicalized disability advocate.

The truth is I always felt like a bit of a disability dilettante. When I was a kid, crutches, wheelchairs and braces were either toys, or hurdles to leap to show people I could not be stopped. As an adult I felt that as long as I was mobile I wasn't "really" disabled. People in wheelchairs and other assistive devices were challenged in ways I could not appreciate. I naively believed that the Americans Disability Act (ADA) was a great boon for people using those devices.

The fall of 2010 taught me the ADA does not begin to address the problems of the disabled. To relieve the terrible ankle pain I elected to have the bones in my left ankle fused. The surgery went terribly wrong. The nuts and screws the surgeon had implanted literally fell apart eight weeks after the surgery. Some doctors blamed a kidney infection. My long-time family physician and friend, Dr. Sheldon Burns, believes the rehab routine failed to take my deteriorating Arthrogryposis bones into account. No matter the cause I had to have two more surgeries. Suddenly in my 61st year I was using a wheelchair, a motorized scooter and a modern contraption alternatively called a knee walker, knee scooter, knee stroller or leg caddy. The idea is you put your injured leg on a knee rest and push with your other leg just like my grandson Collin did with his little scooter. In fact, the then four-year-old Collin knowingly patted my scooter the first time he saw it and said with passion, "Nice scooter, Grandpa!"

My leg surgery opened me up to some disturbing new realities. That experience radicalized me about the ADA. It is not the panacea many of us believe. ADA minimum requirements have left a world that is an obstacle course to navigate. The ADA apparently does not require that every door in a new building have an automatic door opener. Many doors in public buildings must be opened manually. I was far more nimble after my surgeries than a quadriplegic or a paraplegic, but I still struggled and twisted myself into a pretzel to open many doors. The only other option was to wait for the kindness of strangers–a risky and demeaning proposition.

ADA minimum standard public buildings and private restaurants are no treat either. There is often no maneuvering room at all. And here's one I would never have thought about: if a stall door opens out, the person in a wheelchair is screwed. You can't close the stall door. Builders should either make sure stall doors open in, or put enough spring on them that they bounce back.

Then there are macadam walkways, stone tile floors and rugs, all of which make navigation damn near impossible on one of these knee scooters. And, don't forget private homes. I was shocked to discover that my own Scottsdale, Arizona, home has a four-inch "lip" at both the front and back doors. I had honestly never noticed nor appreciated that.

The big problem is minimum standards of the ADA are often used as a bludgeon. Architects, contractors and building supervisors know the minimum standards and far too many refuse to take one single step beyond the minimums. I pray there is a special place in hell for anybody involved in construction who ever utters the phrase "well it meets ADA minimum standards." In that room in hell they would all be forced to live for an eternity in a wheelchair in the buildings they designed and built.

A concept such as Universal design may be the answer. Universal design is a concept that would make buildings barrier free and usable for everyone.

I doubt that an experience with wheelchairs earlier in my life would have opened my eyes in the same way my 2010-2011 troubles did. I simply would not have been receptive because it was more important to deny that I was different.

Nothing in this chapter should be read as claiming redemption or perfection. I regained much of that lost weight. I can still be a monumental jerk. I am still too quick to judge and react angrily. I tip generously and Jean and I anonymously buy dinner in restaurants for strangers who we think could use a little boost. Yet, I can be rude and snappish to people on the street.

But there is no question that the second half of my life and my return "home" to appreciating my disability has softened my heart and old resentments have slipped into oblivion. Yesterday needs to be yesterday.

Remember my anger over those false accusations about the high school party? For years I seethed about those sham charges. They made that chip on my shoulder even larger. I am certain the untrue assertions affected my college behavior and it made me a far more skeptical person.

For almost 40 years I actively blamed a particular person for spreading those lies. I am not sure how I decided that person was to blame but I never doubted guilt. When the person's name was mentioned I reddened. Eight or nine years ago Tim Fallon brought the name up in conversation and I spit back some vulgar expletives.

Remarkably, a few weeks after that brief conversation with Fallon, the person wrote me. The timing was spooky. The Spirit might have been at work again. It was the first time I had heard from the person since high school. This was someone whose name could bring me to a boil. My resentments festered for all those years, yet when I received the sincere, self-revealing letter seeking friendship the "second-half" Tim made an easy choice.

I wrote back and it began a correspondence that persists. We met a few years later at a reunion and I found the person delightful and impressive. If that letter had come 10 years earlier I would have probably answered with a delicious, cutting response. Not anymore. Old resentments need to be killed.

I have never asked the person about those false rumors and I never will. I simply don't care anymore. Reveling in the joyful present is so much more fun than wallowing in the hateful past.

During that amazing barbeque in 1992 with Nelson Mandela on an ASNE foreign trip, six months after he had been released from more than 25 years in captivity, a remarkable moment emerged. As my fellow editors asked Mandela all manner of political questions, I observed him carefully. I finally asked the stunningly peaceful man why he displayed no trace of bitterness after his terrible captivity. His reply has lived with me since that day and I hope it has helped shape me.

With no hesitation and with total serenity he replied, "What good would that do me?"

CHAPTER 8

THE ADULT JASON

J ason backed up against the desk in the kitchen like a man facing the firing squad. Fear shone in his eyes. He was facing questions rather than gunfire. Questions make Jason "confused in the head." They are worse than any form of punishment for him.

The 5-4, 200 pound block of man-child was a few months short of 21. He earned this inquiry by acting moody around his always sensitive older sister, Tracy, whenever the subject of Special Olympics weightlifting came up. Jason's tentativeness about going back for a second year convinced Tracy that he "has issues."

I was trying get to the bottom of the problem. That's what dads are supposed to do.

"Weightlifting is strange," Jason said. "Strange" is one of those all-encompassing words that can mean just about anything to Jason. It's usually a strap-on-your-seatbelt kind of word because you know something big and complicated is coming.

"Why is weightlifting strange?"

"I'm grown up, and I'm still going to weightlifting," Jason said, shifting from one foot to another and furtively looking everywhere in the room except into my eyes. He had just started attending a transition school program which emphasized his adulthood.

"Well, Jase, you're one of the youngest guys on the team," I said. "Most of those other guys are older than you are. They're grown-up. They're still there."

"Yeah, but they're handicapped," Jason barked in a half growl, half whine.

I suddenly realized I was in a defining conversation with a mystified Down syndrome man. My deep affection for my sweet-natured son collided with my pragmatism.

"Well, Jason, you're handicapped too."

"But I'm grown-up. I thought I'd STOP being handicapped when I grew up."

Now it was me up against the wall. I could flee or push forward. I pushed forward. Looking down at my own physically deformed body, I said, "Jason, I'm handicapped too, and I'm grown up."

With an anger and frustration I had seldom heard from this gentle teddy bear of a man he snarled, "You're not handicapped, you're married!"

I stumbled and stammered for a response, but Jason was on a roll. "I want to be grown-up so I can get married and drink beer."

At last, something I could handle. "Jason, I'm grown-up, and I don't drink beer."

"I want to start so I can stop!"

Jason's angry entry into adulthood demonstrated to us once again that despite all the stereotypes about sanguine Down syndrome people, Jason is deeply frustrated with his fate. He is not "okay" with his condition and he desperately wants to be like everyone else. His struggle with identity is really not that different than mine. And yet, classic adulthood eludes Jason. He will never be the "grown-up" he so desperately aspires to be.

The older Jason lived in a supervised group home. He had become very different from the adolescent Jason who lived under his parent's roof. He faced choices, conflicts and consequences of a too often unforgiving world in ways his protective parents didn't always allow.

Yet, we are not really talking about an adult Jason. Jason, who is simultaneously 34 and 5, is not an adult like his sister and brother, Tracy and Jeff. He is never going to have children. He will never stress out over a promotion. He will never drink too much beer and make a fool of himself. He will never pursue more education. He will never break up with a woman. He will never marry. He will never exult in loving and cherishing his children.

Jason frequently makes us proud, but always in the context of being a "Down syndrome man." His well-understood limitations are built in. Our dreams for him always have an anchor.

The news is full of Down syndrome homecoming kings, actors, chefs and mountain climbers. I tingle with pride whenever I read of these high achievers. Parents of young DS kids should dream those dreams and grab for the highest rung on the ladder. We applaud and celebrate those triumphant people. We knew from the time Jason was six that he was not one of those blessed children.

Instead, our "adult" Jason is so afraid of lions he made me walk out of the Matt Damon movie "We Bought a Zoo." Our adult Jason travels across country with a carry-on bag packed with a stuffed dog, stuffed Rugrats character dolls and a 15-year-old stuffed coke bottle. Our "adult" Jason can't be unattended for more than two hours because his judgment in a crisis would rattle in a thimble.

I spent my adulthood challenging boundaries and defying stereotypes. No matter how much we might wish, Jason's boundaries are genuine and constricting.

He lives in a group home with three other young men. They have varying degrees of mental disability and there is 24-hour supervision. He participates in meal planning and preparation at least once a week. Group home staff urges Jason to participate in group conversation and activities in the upstairs family room, but he is happiest holed up in his "man-cave" in the basement of the four-bedroom home.

We furnished his room with a single bed, a comfortable rocking chair and a bureau he used when he lived with us. The room's main attraction is high definition television with a DVD player. The chair is seldom used. Jason prefers to sit on the floor directly in front of the chair to watch television. Just as he did when he lived with us, he constantly fiddles with his favorite toy of the moment while he watches DVD's of *That 70's Show, Magnum PI* or any one of 30 or so classic television shows.

Jason still has trouble distinguishing days of the week and often needs to be told when he has to go to work. Since he was a child he has called Saturday "Cartoon Day" and Sunday "Church Day." He proudly keeps track of the days of the month and big events on a calendar. Vacations and holidays confuse him.

Monday through Friday Jason takes what is called a Metro Mobility bus to his work site, Choice. It is one of several job programs for the disabled in the Twin Cities. Choice finds jobs for its moderately mentally disabled clients and offers work projects at its main site. Clients also have access to workout equipment, televisions and conversation areas.

On Mondays and Fridays Jason is bused from Choice to a Lifetime Fitness Center where he cleans exercise machines under the supervision of a job coach. Jason is paid according to his work abilities. Choice and the employer grade each job according to the production of an able-bodied worker. Workers such as Jason are then rated on what they accomplish compared to the norm and are paid accordingly. So if Jason does 60 percent of the work a regular hourly worker does, he will get paid 60 percent of the hourly wage.

The recession was as tough for disabled workers as it was for everybody else. Several employers who used to contract with Choice for workers abandoned that practice when the economy tightened. Jean and I enthusiastically support any business that hires workers with disabilities. Those employers are giving purpose to people who have a hard time finding it.

Before the downturn Jason worked in the community four days a week and he especially enjoyed production oriented jobs. For several recession years Jason got by with the Lifetime Fitness job but in recent months he got hired for two days a week at a restaurant chain called Culver's. He delivers food to tables and cleans tables after customers leave. He loves that job because "I get to talk to people."

On his fifth day Jason also volunteers at an area Nursing Home. He pushes patients to lunch in wheelchairs, serves water and does other tasks as assigned. Jason finds it difficult to stay in good graces at that volunteer job because the television sets which dot the facility are huge temptations. Most of the clients seem to like him and he frequently reports "they tell me I'm such a nice boy."

The group home staff works diligently to fulfill the original promise of "going places and doing stuff." They sign him up for lots of activities geared for mentally disabled people such as dances, bowling and crafts. Every week he goes on what's called a "One on One" with a staff member. He deeply values those solo outings to play laser tag, to see a movie or buy DVDs. They usually include food, but the camaraderie with an adult is even more important to him. Jason is also a loyal friend and often accompanies his closest friend in the group home to his activities, which often include sports. Jason likes to watch sports but he is reluctant to participate.

He seems quite comfortable with his life. It is quite routine, it revolves around his television set and it doesn't offer a lot of what most of us would see as excitement or even purpose. Yet, he changes the world with his smile and positive attitude.

JASON AFFECTS PEOPLE

In 2011, Jason was cleaning exercise machines at a Lifetime Fitness. As usual, his job coach from Choice kept a close eye on him to make sure he stayed focused. TV and daydreaming are Jason's daily enemies when he's working.

On this particular day the male job coach noticed Jason engaged in a conversation with a thirtyish woman. He often chats briefly with customers. The length of this dialogue was out of the ordinary.

Jason and the woman talked for several minutes about our family, the movies he likes and about what he does on weekends. Most strangers only understand about 50 percent of what Jason says so the intensity and the intimacy of this conversation surprised the job coach who later wrote a report.

The woman finished exercising with a smile on her face and left the gym. About twenty minutes later she returned to where Jason was working with a Down syndrome toddler son in tow. She introduced Jason to her son and said, "If he can grow up to be like you, Jason, I will be very happy."

Choice gave Jason an award for positively affecting the community after that encounter. He was genuinely proud of that. His parents were more than a little puffed up, too, but that wasn't the end of the story.

The woman and her young son have become active participants with

Choice. They show up at ice cream socials and other events designed to raise money for the work center. The woman's initial encounter with Jason helped her understand she can find hope for her son through Choice and its clients such as Jason. In an email she told me I have "an amazing son." Jason does that to people.

In March of 2004, my long-time friend, Peter Bhatia, then editor of the Portland Oregonian, visited Scottsdale with his family for some spring training baseball and shopping. Jason was visiting at the same time.

He loves to hang out with normal teenage boys. It obviously makes him feel part of the gang. Jason and Peter's then 16-year-old son Jay hit it off well.

One night Jason started a crazy game with Jay when the entire group was at dinner at Don and Charlie's, a famous sports restaurant in Scottsdale. Sports memorabilia decorates the walls and something triggered Jason to tell Jay he had two strikes and he had better not get three.

For the rest of the trip Jason would warn Jay about the two strikes on him and if he got three, he would be out of there. None of us really ever figured out the joke but Jason found it hilarious. Actually Jay did too. He played along beautifully to Jason's delight. It was another example of Jason bonding with someone over goofiness. Jay figured out early on that if you treat Jason as a friend everything works out well.

Soon after that encounter with Jason, Jay mentored special education kids in his school. That summer he even began working in a developmentally disabled children's camp as part of his school's service program. Maybe Jason made an activist out of a typical teenage boy just by having fun. Jason does that to people.

A postscript to this story illustrates another crucial truth about Jason. In early 2013 I sent these paragraphs to Peter for an accuracy check and he sent back some corrections. One of them contended that Jason said Jay would be *ejected* rather than that he would be out of there. I immediately countered that a) Jason could not pronounce ejected and b) he'd have no idea what ejected means.

Jason is so socially adept that people, who like him, such as Peter, regularly assign accomplishments to him that simply never happened. The better you come to know Jason the more success and accomplishment you unwittingly credit to him. Countless friends and acquaintances believe

Jason is far more capable than he really is simply because of his charm. Recently, a woman who knows Jason was stunned to find he can't read.

His unique impact on friends and strangers is manifested in ongoing games he plays with people.

Tracy was lucky enough to marry a man with a totally accepting family. From the very beginning the Moll family made Jason an integral part of their family gatherings. At one of those early gatherings Ben's father, Duane, slipped Jason an extra piece of cake. Now, every time Duane and Jason see each other at a family party the joking and joshing over a second piece of cake promptly begins. That joke has been an essential part of their relationship for more than 10 years now. And, it always gets Jason an extra piece of cake. Jason does that to people.

Tracy's closest friend in high school was Jill. Jill quickly encountered Jason's irrational fear of thunderstorms. In a vain effort to assuage him she told Jason that her father had always told her that thunder was angels bowling in heaven. Jason never bought that for a minute. Still to this day, every time he sees Jill he asks her if she still believes that bowling angels cause thunder. He always inquires with a tone in his voice that implies "do you still believe that baloney, you poor thing?" That bowling angel's line has served as a tender bond between Jason and Jill for almost 15 years. Jason does that to people.

Years ago, Jean and I were out of town and an emergency made Tracy desperate for someone to watch Jason. Her close friend Theresa agreed to stay with him. Theresa and Jason were doing just fine until they discovered to their mutual distaste that they watched competing soap operas. Theresa wanted to watch *All My Children* on Channel 5. Jason insisted on turning to Channel 11 because he has always been a committed *Days of our Lives* man. He has watched late night *SoapNet* for years so he could feed his addiction. And, when Jason has gotten in trouble at work for sneaking peaks at the television, that soap opera has usually been his irresistible temptation.

Theresa and Jason made that day memorable with their passionate debate and it has continued more than 10 years. Every time Jason sees Theresa, which is quite often, he asks with absolute contempt dripping from his voice, "Sooooo, do you still watch Channel 5?" That silly little joke has sustained their affectionate relationship. Jason does that to people.

He is largely unaware he is an evangelist for special adults. He is far more tuned in to his daily battles for autonomy. His struggles really aren't that different from many adults. They largely revolve around change, control and choices. Sound familiar? Those three issues are scrambles for all of us, but when right and wrong are muddy in your juvenile mind they can be an intractable jumble.

It took a year for Jason to fit into the group home and to become comfortable with his life away from "Mommy and Daddy." In the same summer Jason went into the group home his sister got married, his brother Jeff went to college and his parents prepared to live six months a year in Arizona. The rest of the family found all that change jolting, so you can only imagine what it did to Jason's five-year-old psyche, even though he knew he ought to behave like an adult. That conflict between 35 and 5 is a constant buffeting force against Jason's emotions. He wants to act like an adult but there are some times he would love to climb on his mommy's lap and hold on for dear life. It's easy to see that conflict is tough for Jason to resolve.

In 2005, when Jean and I were moving out of the family house we had owned since 1989, the separation emotions staggered everyone. It was Jason who spoke for the entire family when he plaintively cried out, "I hate change!" Even though he was ensconced in his group home and growing more comfortable by the day, he did not like us leaving the home in which he had found great comfort. As he so often does, Jason was also speaking a larger truth.

His discomfort with change manifests itself when he visits us in Arizona. He looks forward to the trip for months, but after four or five days he wants to return to the comforts of his group home. Routine is crucial for Jason. Anything that interrupts that routine can be tolerated only for a few days.

There has been one change of clients at the group home. Jason truly loved one young client who was so close to normal he needed to move after a year or so. The new client was very different and less mentally developed than Jason. It took years for Jason to get comfortable with him.

He demands that life follow certain rules and he totally lacks flexibility. Despite many years of lectures from his Mother, he is a raging sexist. Doctors are men and nurses are women. Men don't wash clothes or cook. That is women's work. He thinks he knows the rules and it upsets him when they are violated.

When one of Tracy's closest high school friends got pregnant before graduation she felt obligated to tell Jason, but that prospect frightened her as much as telling her father. When she broke the news to him Jason's sense of order and propriety was violated. With judgment and anger Jason barked, "But you're not married!"

Jason is mystified by race and only understands cultural hints he has seen on TV. When he describes an African American to us, he will pat his face and say "different." When he sees a black person on the street, he slaps his chest and calls him or her "homey." I can recall only a handful of people who have taken offense. Most respond with friendly enthusiasm and laughter.

But Jason's greatest trouble with change was more surprising, more upsetting and far more personal.

UNCLE JASON'S CHALLENGE

The concept of being an uncle initially tickled and pleased Jason. The reality has been far more challenging.

He knows in his 35-year-old heart he is supposed to love and treasure his niece and nephew, Kayley and Collin. In his five-year-old mind these little people are serious competition for attention and affection. There was a time everyone in Jason's family laughed at his antics and jokes. Suddenly he found Mom and Dad playing grandpa and grandma and his always-ready-to-help-sister was now a Mommy. The pint-sized rivals were getting the laughs, affection and attention now. Jason despised it.

He has always preferred flight to fight, so his early reaction was to decline invitations to family events when he knew Kayley and Collin would be there. Gradually, he adjusted and accepted their inevitable presence because "fambly" is so important to him.

Another big change occurred when Kayley and Collin started school. With his usual insight he quickly saw that Kayley was smarter than he was. That obviously disturbed him and he withdrew again. Anything that shifts the family dynamic is discombobulating for Jason. Fleeing is the only rational response he understands.

We eventually saw Jason again value time with family more than contention with his niece and nephew. The seven-year-old Collin and Jason often found common play interests. Rather than "pulling rank" as he did with the kids when they were younger, Jason often seems to delight in playing with them. He has even begun to defer to Kayley and Collin by asking them to read things he can't understand.

Jason's difficulty adjusting to a niece and nephew was also an example of his loss of control. Arguably, every sentient being wants control and autonomy. He, like most five-year-olds, has historically had little.

There is no question when Jason was in our home he had a lot of bosses. Everybody told Jason what to do and when because we had high expectations for him. We expected him to eat in restaurants. We expected him to socialize with adults who had money and power. Tracy and Jeffrey did not want him to embarrass them with their friends.

Those high expectations worked. When Jason met President Bill Clinton in 1998, three days after Clinton was confronted by Monica Lewinsky, Jason was friendly, dignified and behaved as if he were 19 and not 5. Clinton seemed entranced and called for a photographer in a place where cameras were banned.

That good behavior resulted from a firm hand from Mom, Dad and Tracy. Jeff was more unpredictable. Sometimes he demanded good behavior and at other times he was more interested in letting Jason be who he is.

There should have been no surprise that when Jason moved into the group home testing boundaries was one of the earliest things on his mind. Remember, in those early days he frequently challenged staff authority by asking if they could make him do something.

The difficult truth is no they really can't or they are terrifically reluctant to "make him" do anything.

The goal of group homes, such as Jason's, is to encourage independent living. To professionals that means the client should make his or her own choices. The client should control how he or she lives.

But here's the rub from a guardian's perspective. If Jason could control his own life and make the correct choices he wouldn't need to live in a group home.

ONE MAN'S SNACK IS ANOTHER MAN'S MEAL

Jason's battle for control erupts over the choices he makes around food, clothes and hygiene.

Most Down syndrome adults struggle with weight issues. Some

experts, such as the Kennedy Krieger Institute, contend "research suggests that children with Down syndrome have a lower basal metabolic rate (BMR) than their same-aged peers. BMR is the rate a person burns calories for fuel when completely at rest—or sleeping. As a result, a child with Down syndrome uses fewer calories while they are asleep and also throughout the day. In addition, adults with Down syndrome (ages 18-20) have finished growing and require fewer calories than they did as a child."

That research represents a serious problem for Jason since he repeatedly argues, "I am a growing boy." He is not growing and his food choices clearly put him at risk. His weight bounces around 205-210, which actually is not bad for someone whose eating and exercise habits are so poor.

Jason eats according to the clock. He has eaten breakfast at 11 a.m. and then demanded lunch at noon. He has more than once conned his way into a second lunch. He loves sandwiches and dislikes vegetables. Early in 2013 he announced to the group home staff "I am not eating vegetables any more. I don't like them." That declaration may well have been more about establishing his control than it was about vegetables.

Yet, it is clear to us that part of Jason's vegetable problem is a "texture" issue. There are certain foods he just cannot handle on his tongue. He dislikes the chewiness of steak but he loves hamburgers. Particular foods are just so difficult for him to chew that he avoids them. No matter how fancy the restaurant, he will usually choose a sandwich because it is easier for him to handle. You can hold a sandwich, and nobody has to cut your meat.

Food definitely gives Jason his best chance to establish control, but his shocking lack of judgment about food is his bigger problem. After his argument that he is a growing boy, he will usually whine, "But I am hungry." Again, his mother contends he has some sort of synapse problem. She says he gets a message that he's hungry when he really shouldn't be. He recently reached into the refrigerator for a healthy snack and at the same time he grabbed a handful of roast beef lunch meat. He infuriates group home staff members when he insists on a sandwich as an after-work snack when he knows dinner is two hours away.

His biggest fights with staff usually revolve around "snacks." If left to his devices Jason would make every snack a meal. He knows the staff is reluctant to order him to put down the roast beef or to choose a banana. The staff is desperately attempting to *teach* Jason about good choices and he has no intention of learning. He is an instant gratification guy. When Jason was at home we kept him on track with raw parental power. The group home is often unwilling to use a big stick so Jason keeps pushing their buttons.

He is just as recalcitrant about exercise. Every year at the required "conference" about his well-being both the group home and the work center set incredibly modest goals for exercise; goals so modest they strike me as a joke. Every year, it seems, he fails to meet them. He established control again.

In fairness we also have to consider the role of modeling. I am seriously overweight and nobody in our home used to exercise at all. (Both his brother Jeff, and his sister Tracy are now actively exercising and watching calories, but Jason does not see that behavior.) And, like any five-year-old, Jason will copy others. The best example of that is the beard he grew after he saw his little brother grew one. When Jeff shaved his beard, so did Jason.

When Jason had the beard he refused to trim it or manage it in any meaningful way. Jean is convinced he thought the beard meant he could drop shaving from his daily routine. He had almost daily battles with staff over keeping it trimmed and looking decent. The beard was a part of a much larger battle landscape over hygiene, shaving and independence, a contest of wills that has seemed endless.

Jean remembers squabbling with Jason over brushing his teeth when he was 12. Rarely a week went by without reminders to brush his teeth, apply deodorant and all the other morning ablutions most teenagers and adults take for granted. To this moment, without supervision Jason will "forget" those morning duties.

He does not really have a "social governor" like most teenagers. He is not trying to impress the ladies and his peers at his job site. Choice and the group home peers are unlikely to complain if his breath or body smells. On the other hand, teachers, job coaches and group home staff are quite often offended by such smells. That's when he gets, in his words, "busted."

Jason's "forgetfulness" over hygiene is a family mystery. It raises two important issues worth discussion: lying and independence.

Lying is my word. It's a word that has always disturbed Jean. To avoid brushing his teeth, showering or shaving, Jason will often just tell people he has already completed the tasks. He will tell staff he has showered when simple observation makes it obvious not a drop of water dampened his shower.

Experts say lying is developmentally normal for a five-year-old. That is a key part of Jean's argument. She contends Jason is just telling people what they want to hear so they're not disappointed. I proffer the theory that the 34-year-old Jason, through his experience and savvy, absolutely knows he is telling lies in order to manipulate the outcome.

There are many great and constant struggles in dealing with Jason, but independence is at the top of the list. Finding the right balance between helping and catering to challenges all of us. When you first start taking parent classes to deal with special children they tell you that you should always be "age appropriate with your child." That rolls off the tongues of the "experts" as easily as "eat healthy and exercise." It's far more difficult to actually achieve "age appropriateness."

SEEKING INDEPENDENCE

Every parent struggles with the question of when to give their children certain responsibilities. Every parent copes with phases their children go through. Imagine a phase that lasts 15 years and you get a sense of how difficult it is to force Jason to be independent. When you've been telling a child to brush his teeth for 15 years, it's not really surprising that you start to hover at tooth-brushing time. Your patience is exhausted and it becomes easier to just make sure certain tasks are done.

Jeff, a highlights producer at ESPN, owns incredible insight about Jason's battle for independence. He says, "Jason has a stubbornness that can be hard to manage." He insightfully points out that "it is not easy negotiating with Jason because he really doesn't understand the concept of negotiation."

Jeff blew me away when he observed, "Jason has always sought independence even though he has never earned it. He does not like being told what to do, which is extremely frustrating, because his judgment, especially about food, is so poor."

That has been the primary difference for Jason between the group home and his time in our house. We watched him like hawks and made sure he was attending to tasks. Sometimes it was just easier to do things ourselves.

In 2004, during a visit to Arizona, Jason made his own sandwiches and cut his own bread, but when he needed help cutting his meat in a restaurant one night he asked our friend Liz Dahl for help without shame. Yet, if we step in too fast, he'll take advantage of us just like anyone would. And sometimes we don't even notice it. One morning Jean started to serve him cereal for breakfast when our friend Bea Favre, a trained psychologist, delicately intervened. She asked, "Jason, do you make your own cereal at home?" He answered "yes." Jean immediately backed off. He made his own breakfast every morning after that.

The staff at the group home often makes the opposite error. They see a 34-year-old man and just can't understand why things are so difficult for Jason and for them. Many of them seem to think he should operate autonomously. We find that frustrating because if he could be autonomous he would not be in that setting.

Jean recalls one evening a few years ago when an emotional staff member called her. The male aide was almost crying as he vented his frustration over Jason's irresponsibility and inability to properly do his laundry. "He really expected Jason to be able to do his laundry as any guy his age would," she related to me after the call. She said, "I wanted to scream at him, Jason is disabled! That's why he needs you!"

Jean did not do that. Instead she told the staffer how to coach Jason and told him to be firm in his expectations. Then she reminded him to keep those expectations reasonable because Jason is different.

I want to be very careful not to cast the group home staff in too negative of a light. Jason would not approve of that. Over the years Jason has been in the Pinnacle home, called Sunset Park, some of his closest friends have been supervisors and staff at the home. There have been some excellent mentors and coaches for Jason and he has valued many of them deeply. Some of the aides see their work as a job, but others seem to genuinely see it as a "calling."

One of the most serious staff problems though, has been turnover. Just when Jason has developed significant bonds with staff members, they leave. Often, we see Jason's behavior get worse after a key departure.

LOOKING SHARP MEANS BEING SHARP

Another significant staff problem for Jean and me is the clothes Jason wears. On his own he makes terrible choices about clothes. He would wear shorts to a Christmas party in Minnesota. He wore a heavy wool sweater to a conference in July. His legs are short, and without his parents around, nobody hems his pants. Jason shows no shame at all when there are holes in his pants or shirts.

If a person with a mental disability looks shabby we believe they will be treated shabbily. Fairly early in my career I often overdressed so I would be taken seriously. Years ago the Star Tribune published a story about an African American middle manager who did not wear casual clothes to the office on Saturday as his peers did, because he was afraid he would be mistaken for the janitor. If Jeffrey goes to work with holes in his shirts or pants his career would be in trouble.

Jason's ability to mingle with presidents and business people has, in part, rested on his good looks and neat appearance. It drives us crazy when he looks like a bum because we want him to be treated with respect. That is one of the expectations we believe have made Jason who he is.

He seldom notices when he looks like a mess and too often staff doesn't either. Our standards for "dressing up" are clearly different from the staff's. I worry there's a bigger, unspoken factor driving the casualness about Jason's appearance. I angrily confronted a staffer about it a few years ago.

That day Jason waltzed out of the house with his typical, almost ceremonial exit, with more confidence than you'll normally see in a Down syndrome man. Jason is a little over 5-4. That makes him a most unusual dude in Down syndrome circles. He is slightly taller than other DS people he encounters, but several doctors have told us Down syndrome people are ALWAYS the shortest person in their family. Not Jason. He is almost 4 inches taller than Tracy, and just a shade taller than his parents.

Jason never really picks his feet up and they slide perilously along the ground just begging to be tripped. He seldom is. The round, Charlie Brown head, the typical Down syndrome eyes, and that ungainly gait shout to the world, that he is not like other young men. Yet there is straightness to the shoulders and the eyes look dead ahead in a way that's not common to a lot of DS folks. His Mother says it's about self-image. Jason's got it and a lot of Down syndrome people don't.

On this day, like most days, he twirled his sunglasses in his hand. He stopped, donned the sunglasses and shot his two pointer fingers directly at the car. Occasionally, he flips two thumbs up. Only then did he march toward the car. That maneuver always makes me laugh but that day I stopped chuckling immediately. He wore a shirt that didn't fit. His pants had numerous holes, the pant hems were horribly frayed. He looked like a beleaguered orphan.

I drove away from the group home that day but I seethed all the way back to our house. Unable to contain my anger I phoned the young man who had sent Jason out of the house. I asked him how he thought Jason looked when he left. He started to stammer. "Would you let your best friend leave the house like that, knowing he looked like hell?" I demanded. The young fellow said, "No, probably not." Building a head of steam I snapped back, "Then why do you let Jason go out like this? Is it because he's Down syndrome and he doesn't need to look any better?'

He said no, that wasn't it, but I am convinced that was exactly the case. Jason never seems to consider his appearance, but when he is dressed up it is obvious his self-esteem ratchets up. If we are caretakers of developmentally challenged people we need to give them the opportunity to look sharp and be sharp.

Perhaps the biggest adult challenge we've faced with Jason has been his sleep apnea. Jean and I learned over 35 years that naked persistence can make most situations at least a little better. Jason's sleep apnea is the clearest example of our total surrender I ever remember.

He has never slept well. We would often find him sleeping, sitting on the floor with his head on the pillow. Often we would hear him rustling when we went to sleep and then hear him watching TV at 5 a.m. Over the years it was clear to us that he could fall asleep anywhere. Invariably, after 10 minutes in a car, slumber beckoned him.

He clearly was not getting enough sleep, but when Jason lived at home that routine was more or less accepted. The workplace was different. Falling asleep at Choice or on a job site simply was not acceptable. Treatment was sought and the diagnosis did not surprise us. Jason had serious sleep apnea. Not only was he missing out on sleep, but he was at serious health risk.

The doctor prescribed a CPAP machine, which is essentially a mask that fits over the nose and mouth. Wikipedia says the biggest problem with the CPAP is "non-compliance." Apparently many adult patients hate the machine and quickly stop wearing it. I knew several friends who had that experience, but I had some friends' wives who swore by the machine because it drastically cut down snoring.

In retrospect, we probably allowed the doctor to rush us into the CPAP prescription. We should have considered more carefully the full impact of the machine on Jason and his psyche.

Hate seems like such a mild word to describe Jason's reaction to the machine. Rather than facing the problem directly Jason took his usual tack: if you want to think I am wearing that contraption every night I will help you believe that. Despite the fact that staff would sometimes find Jason asleep without the mask he assured everyone he had just removed it for a "mimit."

What Jason did not know was that sleep results from his use of the mask were flowing into a computer at the sleep center. When he went for his six month appointment everyone knew with certainty that once again Jason had simply been making everyone happy by telling them what they wanted to hear.

The Sunset Park staff redoubled it's observation to ensure compliance. After several months of almost daily complaints that Jason was using trickery, deception and bald-faced lies Jean and I capitulated. The stress on Jason was obvious. The machine was just too uncomfortable for him. More disturbing, his duplicity was growing worse. We grew tired of staff telling us our son was a "liar." The prospect of him ever being comfortable with the mask was beyond remote.

Despite all that, abdication was profoundly difficult. We knew Jason's health was at stake. Both Jean and I are quality of life folks. The quality of Jason's life and the life of the Sunset Park staffers sucked as long as he was supposed to be on that machine. The white flag was the most loving option.

JASON LOVES TO BOOGIE

As Jason ages two drastically different personas, the hermit and the social animal, grow more prominent and more divergent.

Remember, when Jason was younger he frequently told us, "TV is my life." In his older years DVDs are his life. He has hundreds. Scores of animated "kids" movies are on his shelves but in recent years his favorites are old television shows. He has complete sets of *Seinfeld*, *I Love Lucy*, *Friends*, *Walker Texas Ranger*, *Everybody Loves Raymond*, and *Baywatch*. He assures me he just watches *Baywatch* "for the stories" and not the pretty women in bikinis. Jason is perfectly happy at the group home squirreled away in his basement room with the door closed. He can watch hours of DVDs and only emerge for food. Group home staff wants him to socialize more, but it's a battle. He is happier in his make believe world of television characters, with whom he seems to develop real affection. And, it certainly makes buying gifts for Jason easy.

Even when he leaves the security of his own room he engages in television in an almost exclusionary way. When he visits us in Arizona he enters into a weird ritual that borders on a trance.

He sits on the floor in front of a chair we have positioned about twelve feet from the television. There is no sense in ordering him into the chair. He will comply for all of 37 seconds, until he "forgets."

A barrel table sits to his right where he places his soft drink, sunglasses, his wallet and other essentials. That wallet must always come out of his pocket and it takes on jewel-like status when he carefully places it on the table. His legs are folded in a squat befitting his self-imposed status as a television guru. He is barefoot and his white sweat socks are carefully placed perpendicular to his legs. As he sits transported into the reality of whatever television show he's watching, he carefully rolls each sock into a ball. Only after I got hopelessly frustrated several years ago, did he stop placing said socks in his mouth. He drops them only when his attention, or the quality of the TV show, lapses.

Then he handles the remote as Ted Williams handled a bat. With great skill and total command, he skips through the channels deciding on his interest in a haphazard, slap-dash method that would escape mere mortals. Countless times I have become a bit engaged and bam he's off to another channel. He is almost savant-like in his ability to determine within seconds if the show will appeal to him.

Television can consume Jason to the point of obsession. He is perfectly content to sit in his room and lock out the rest of the world, but the hermit part of his personality is part of a much more complex identity.

Jason loves to boogie. When it comes time to hobnob, he has few peers. At Tracy's wedding reception without any instructions or family discussion Jason took it upon himself that night to visit every single 10-person table. He shook hands with virtually every guest. He made conversation in his limited way and served as a one-man greeting party. No one else, not Tracy, not her husband Ben, not Jean and not me, took the time and expended the

effort to greet everyone. In fact, we didn't even know the master of min-
gling had done the duty until guests started commenting on it on their way
out of the reception. It was clear he charmed the entire reception. Several
guests told us Jason's inspired visit was the highlight of their evening.

One night in March of 2004, Jean and I hosted a party for three visiting
journalist friends. The pool area and the house were full of newspapermen,
a TV personality and several journalism professors. Nobody worked the
room like Jason. Dressed in shorts and a polo shirt he wandered from group
to group in his ungainly way. He easily joined conversations even though
the guests only understood a small part of what he said. Many were stum-
bling through their first Jason experience. As always, his manners were
excellent. He never disrupted conversations, he smoothly joined them.

I squirmed a bit. I wondered what he could possibly be talking about
as I watched from 20 feet away as he laughed and shared with the guests.
The conversations were usually simple, but always charming. Jason has that
special ability to stay north of obnoxious even though his words are not
always well understood, and he does not grasp complex concepts. His ability to communicate interest, affection and engagement can never be dis-
puted. After that party several people commented on what a joy Jason had
been.

It is a sweet paradox that the fellow who can be a hermit at home is
absolutely gifted in social situations. When we introduce him to new people he wins friends for life. More importantly he converts hearts.

Perhaps Jason's biggest stage was my induction as president of the
American Society of Newspaper Editors in 2001, which coincidentally
coincided with his birthday on Friday, April 6, 2001.

As the incoming President I was required to make a five to eight minute
acceptance speech when the organization's gavel was officially passed to
me. I wavered for days about doing something that had never been done
before in ASNE history.

Most of the crowd had read a wonderful profile of me written by my
best friend Gregory Favre so they knew all about Jason. As I stood before
the crowd, I resolved my doubts and made the decision to be bold. I told
the 700-800 members and guests the ASNE gods had arranged for my big
day to coincide with Jason's 22nd birthday. I acknowledged that it was a little strange, but I invited Jason to stand and then I asked the crowd to sing
Happy Birthday.

It was silly of me to worry about whether people would be upset about my request. Happy Birthday has rarely been sung with so much verve and genuineness. Jason was overwhelmed. He quaked, tears ran down his cheeks. He was scared, thrilled and grateful all at the same confused moment. Jason still fondly recalls the birthday when "everybody sang to me." Many years later people in that audience were still approaching me and telling me how important that day was to them. Jason does that to people.

Jason treasures his public interactions and he doesn't want anybody, including me, messing with him. A few years ago we were putting him on a plane back to Minneapolis. He had an aisle seat and I worried that someone might bully him out of it. I told him not to let anybody else have that seat. He took umbrage. With great indignation he said, "I will give my seat to somebody if I want to, I'm nice." I was worried about him being snookered. He was worried about being kind to strangers. Jason can be a great teacher.

JASON'S SPECIAL TAKE ON LIFE

His quirky sense of humor is entertaining but it also distinguishes him. Jason and Jeff can "yank chains" with each other almost as well as Jason and Dad. Several years ago when Jason visited while Jeff lived in Arizona, Jeff needed help carrying his laundry to the car. Without thinking about it very hard, he asked, Jason, "Can you give me a hand?" Jason said "sure" and he clapped.

Then he smiled the sneaky, prideful smile of an imp.

Jason visited us one St. Patrick's Day, just before we sold our Minnesota home. As he walked in the back door, Jean placed a green Irish top hat on his head. Without a pause Jason broke into an Irish jig. He was immensely proud of himself as his mom and dad collapsed in laughter.

Then he proceeded to pull one of his favorite tricks. Without hesitation he strolled to the kitchen table and deliberately sat in the chair I had been sitting in for 15 years. He got the rise out of me he had hoped for, but my stern glare fooled no one. He expertly read the twinkle in my eye. Once his point was made he scrambled to get into his traditional chair, giggling all the way.

About this time I'll bet you're starting to wonder how much Jason is "performing" and how many of his reactions are authentic. I, too, often wonder. Many of his lines do sometimes seem strangely calculated. But, he's supposed to be slow.

Several years ago both boys were in Arizona. As we ate breakfast on a Sunday six days after Jason's arrival in Arizona from Minnesota he loudly announced, "Oh crap, my ears popped." Jean said "Wow that was a delayed reaction." With the typical McGuire lack of reverence, Jeff said, "His entire life is one giant delayed reaction."

Moments later out of nowhere Jason motioned at Jean and me and said, "You and you have a great married life." We think we do, but Jason had never verbalized anything such as that. Because I was taking notes on Jason's visit I immediately wrote that down. Jeff said, "I'm getting the feeling he's talking into the mike."

It was a great line, but like all the humor in our family it had that strange mix of mystery and insight. Jason certainly goes for the laugh, but so does everyone in our family. Jason certainly will suck up to anyone with flattery and affection, but that too tends to be a family trait. Jeff's line was pretty typical too, because Jason is often the cause or the butt of our family humor. He is at or very near the center of all the McGuire action. That could be our nature, but I prefer to think it is Jason's special gift.

Every person in our family knows the greatest Jason adventures are likely to come in a car ride. Conversations of remarkable lunacy, heartbreak and charm are apt to erupt as you drive and Jason figures out life. Since he moved into the group home he has become more tuned into news. He's always been acutely tuned into weathercasts but strangely, the news interest came after he moved away from us.

About a year after he moved he wanted to tell me about one of the staff at his group home, but names can be the most difficult things to understand because mime or word association seldom works. The staff rotates and only a few of them have stayed on the job for a long time so figuring out the name can often threaten to derail an entire conversation. Jason cannot be tricked. He expects you to repeat what you have heard so he is certain you understand. No pretend comprehension will be tolerated.

As Jason tried to tell me about a staffer named Sara getting to work I was stuck on his explanation. It's crucial that I admit difficulty right away when I'm struggling with Jason's language. "Sorry buddy, I do not understand you." There was a time that statement stopped the conversation. Jason would refuse to try to explain. Now he usually looks for an imaginative, alternative way to express himself.

He told me it was on the "news." But that didn't help me. I could see him hesitate for a moment, and then he began acting as if he was driving. I offered that word. He shook his head and pulled on an imaginary air brake. How he knew about air brakes still mystifies me. Suddenly, I realized he was pretending to drive a bus and that he was talking about the bus strike that hobbled the Twin Cities for several weeks in 2004.

The fact that Sara was having trouble getting to work because of the bus strike became obvious to me because Jason showed the determination and resourcefulness to force me to understand.

"That was fantastic Jason. That's the way to explain yourself." I paused and walked into one again. "So, you've been watching the news lately, eh?"

Proudly, he said, "Every night." There was a long thoughtful pause and then he asked me if I had seen another story. Again I was stumped, but I knew he was talking about a girl. Suddenly he waved and said "bye-bye." Jason was asking me if I had seen the story about a *missing* young woman, Dru Sjodin, who was kidnapped and murdered. Bye-bye meant missing to this innocent man who can't imagine the horror of kidnap, rape and murder. With understatement and genuineness he informed me that was very sad. I agreed.

Jason is incredibly loved but, strangely to us, he is often surprised by that.

In 2004, Jason was departing Arizona for Minnesota. We went to our local coffee shop for my coffee and his wild berry smoothie. We talked about how his group home manager, Kristy, was going to discuss a roommate switch. I had earlier told him that Kristy was going to talk to him about the changes. The conversation slowly evolved into Jason telling me how neat it was that Kristy called us. I was amazed at his surprise and told him that Kristy communicated with us often via email or telephone.

"Really?" he asked with dramatic incredulity.

"Of course we do Jason. We care about you deeply and we always want to make sure you are okay."

"Aw dad, that's so sweet," and he patted my hand resting on the gear shift.

A few hours later as he left for the airplane I hugged his neck and said, "You're a great son."

"You are a great daddy," he replied. I was deeply touched.

Jason does that to people.

CHAPTER 9

TIM'S TURN TO CRY

The original final chapter of this book was full of the triumph and bravado of a man who believed to the core of his soul he had overcome two gigantic obstacles in life to find success and emotional acceptance. The chapter included advice on how to deal with life's struggles and it was firm in its outlook that we all face challenges and there are two choices: melt or overcome them.

It began this way:

In the winter of 2013, as I neared the end of writing this book, a friend and colleague, discussed my personal trials in the context of this book. She whispered, "I have never had anything difficult in my life. They say God gives hardships only to those people who can handle them. I feel bad that God must think I'm weak."

Not long after, another woman listened to me describe the book and said, "Well, it's just a good thing those things happened to you because you were able to handle them. God only gives these things to people who can handle them."

Both women undoubtedly meant well but those kinds of sentiments anger me and run counter to everything I believe.

God did not intentionally twist my limbs at birth. God did not make Jason Down syndrome. God didn't cause my 2010 surgery to fall apart. God does not give handicaps and other challenges only to certain select people. Those people certainly aren't chosen because they are stronger than anyone else. God does not "just screw with" some folks because God thinks they are strong enough to handle it.

My experiences over a lifetime and Jason's lifetime have taught me that stuff just happens. It happens to all of us.

A few years ago, a good friend of mine, Dan Untiedt, was distraught over the sudden, almost inexplicable accidental death of his wife. At the wake, the first time he saw me after her death, he embraced me almost violently. With heart-breaking anguish he cried, "Mac, you know this theological shit, why, why did this happen, why did this happen?" He asked me the same question three more times before we buried a woman I liked very much.

I never answered my friend because I feared my answer would torment more than it would comfort. His vain quest for an answer was the same quest my mother embarked on 64 years ago. She simply had to believe there was a reason her first-born was crippled. We all demand to know why karma, fate or God has inflicted these horrible trials on us. I have always told my mother and I desperately wanted to tell my friend, this terrible, horrible thing disrupted his dreams because terrible and horrible things happen to everyone. There are no exceptions. Tortuous hardships are an integral part of human existence.

One of the most influential books of my entire life is a book by Rabbi Harold Kushner, *How Good Do We Have to Be?* Kushner is famous for writing *When Bad Things Happen to Good People.* That is a great book which earned Kushner a lot of attention, but it didn't shape my personal philosophy as much as the "How Good" book written 15 years later.

In How Good Do We Have to Be? Kushner argues that God actually hoped Adam and Eve would eat the fruit in the Garden of Eden. Kushner contends God wanted humans to be different from animals and by eating from "The Tree of Knowledge" humans can experience the very things God experiences.

The passage that resonated most for me from the book is this:

"Animals can experience pain, but human beings, because we have eaten of the Tree of Knowledge, can feel a dimension of pain that animals cannot. We feel loss, dread, frustration, jealousy, betrayal, at levels animals will never know. It is part of the price we pay for our humanity, for our being able to feel love, joy, hope, achievement, faithfulness and creativity."

We have heartbreak and challenge so we can experience joy and triumph. Kushner argues it's an essential part of the plan.

That is the best way I can explain why I find asking "why me" so offensive. I was born with Arthrogryposis Multicongenita and Jason with Down syndrome not because God wanted to punish my parents or me or Jean. Jason and I weren't born the way we were because God thought we were the perfect candidates because of our strength. I believe these are the kinds of challenges we face so as a species we can experience victory and jubilation.

We deal with our obstacles because we damn well have to confront them. There really are only two choices when faced with a terrible diagnosis or a great hurdle. You can go to your corner and curl up in the fetal position or you can put one foot in front of the other, smile and make the best of a bad situation. You always know the bumps, bruises and falls will be there, but you move forward in the hope good things will happen. They often do.

Most disabled people and families of the disabled I know believe their problems pale next to some they encounter in others. That is a human phenomenon. Someone always has it worse, always. I have heard this sentiment before, but I found this on the web in an article called "50 Timeless Life Lessons — If we all threw our problems in a pile and saw everyone else's, we'd grab ours back."

That is the fascinating thing about the two women I described at the beginning of this chapter.

The first woman, my colleague, is a remarkably successful professional who survived a family that put the "dys" in dysfunctional. She told me stunning, heart-breaking tales of the catastrophic role alcohol played in her family. Most of her siblings' lives have been irreparably damaged by that dysfunction, but not my friend. She married a wonderful man and she has fantastic children. She forged a great life and that probably led her to believe nothing terrible has ever befallen her. She focuses on other people's troubles rather than understanding she prevailed over the kind of tragedy that has wrecked millions of other lives.

Similarly another long-time friend marvels at my difficulties at the same time I marvel at her victory over alcohol more than 25 years ago. Her alcoholism could have destroyed her and her family. Instead, she triumphed because of her strong spirit and her ability to put one foot in front of the other, one day at a time.

That's how we all survive obstacles that to others seem insurmountable. We do it because we have to or wither. I got back on that bike 100 times in one day because quitting was not an option. I chased Jason when he ran and Jean spent three years potty-training him because it was the only acceptable path.

Few things surprised me as much in my life as when the special needs consultant, Arnie Grutzmacher, told us that most people seek vengeance because something bad had happened to them. I completely understand feelings of guilt, as fruitless as they are, but vengeance, as Nelson Mandela said to me more than twenty years ago, does nothing good for anybody.

Acceptance isn't easy. I've struggled with it for 64 years but when I achieve it I am more peaceful and it allows me to find true joy in my own life and in Jason's.

A VERY DIFFERENT LENS

I still believe every single thing I wrote in those paragraphs but my lens is very different now. Now I understand hardship, sorrow, grief and destroyed dreams in ways I only thought I did.

On June 21, 2014 at 11:07 in the morning, Jean died.

My partner of 39 years was gone. The woman I had laughed with, been hopelessly irreverent with, the woman I loved deeply for all those years was gone.

Jean's death and the two-year illness that preceded it forced me to reevaluate everything I believed about life's challenges.

Sheer determination and orneriness could not get me through the ordeal of Jean's sickness and death the way it helped me deal with my physical disability. Wit, patience and a take charge attitude helped in Jean's trial but it wasn't the ticket the way it was in surviving Jason's Down syndrome.

People who know me understand I always felt I was in charge of how I dealt with my disability. I always knew I could cry about it or I could embrace it head-on. I could revel in being bobber butt and the rodent or I could shrink away. I could accept every challenge and take on all comers as I tested every boundary or I could choose to be intimidated by my differences. From early age I never allowed myself to ask "why me?" I worked my ass off to avoid playing victim.

In much the same way Jean and I partnered with laughter, irreverence, and tenacity to raise Jason right, to treat our other children with love and respect, and to treasure each other despite all the horrible, depressing statistics about divorce destroying families with a disabled child. Sure, Jean and I had had some moments of hopelessness, but they were few. As I've considered some of the tales I have told, such as chasing Jason through malls and toilet training him for three years, I am amazed at our doggedness and sheer pluck.

From the day in June of 2012 when Jean was told she had non-small cell lung cancer my view on life's challenges was irrevocably transformed. No amount of orneriness or doggedness or pluck could change that diagnosis. And when in January of 2014 we were told that in addition to metastasizing cancer, Jean had myelodysplastic syndrome, a condition that prevented her bone marrow from producing healthy blood cells, it was monstrously difficult for both of us to keep laughing and do that whole "stiff upper lip" thing, but we did.

Jean did not like talking about "feelings." The usual gender roles were always dramatically reversed for us on that score. So, we talked little about where things were heading. For the most part we remained optimistic and full of hope until we were told there was none.

Such an illness, however, takes an incredible toll, even on a rock-solid marriage. Intimacy becomes arduous, long-time roles inexorably change and discussion of dreams and hopes and plans become strained and even inauthentic.

Jean and I always deeply valued control. We knew we were smart, clever and we were seldom stymied. But now the lack of control hung over us like an outhouse stink. That was incredibly difficult for Jean and she sometimes lashed out when her ability to controls things wilted.

Yet, that same hunger for control helped Jean decide the terms of her life and death. She had always done the family accounting. She hung onto that task until about 10 days before her death. She didn't want to give in and not doing the bills signaled surrender to her.

More telling was her reaction to a blood transfusion on May 23. She had had double figure blood transfusions and was in the midst of reaching double figures on platelet transfusions. They were clearly taking a profound toll on her body. She was weak and every move was exhausting. And yet on that day, a Friday, despite feeling as if she had been run over by trains and trucks she announced she wanted to go to the casino.

I was amazed and wary, but her happiness was paramount for me, so off to the casino we went. She played her favorite slots for a couple of hours while I kept a concerned and solicitous eye on her.

The next morning she addressed the elephant in the room and said, "I know you questioned going to the casino last night but I need you to understand. There is absolutely no sense in allowing them to continually give me transfusions if I can't LIVE. If I can't go to the casino or go out with the Brown's tomorrow night, there is no sense going on with these treatments."

The next night, on May 25, we did go to dinner with our good friends Bob and Nancy Brown. Jean was so much her funny, engaging, story-telling self, Nancy expressed total shock two weeks later when I told her the prognosis held no hope for a miracle.

Jean handled her end days the same way I handled my disability, and the way she and I survived the relentless trials of raising Jason, with laughter. There were certainly tears but there were scores of smart-alec comments and even some gallows humor.

We always tried like hell not to judge, but when we saw parents of disabled children with their "mad on," seemingly unable to joke about their lot in life we mourned a little. Laughter does soften the hurt. Self-deprecation, wry observations and appreciating the slapstick nature of raising a disabled child needed to be relished. Humor rescued us from the junk heap of sorrow, regret and despair. Logic, determination and militancy can take you only so far. Then it's time for laughter and joy. Amazingly, Jean retained that attitude as she faced death.

Sure, she cried a little. Jean didn't want to die but she had made it clear that "I have lived a fantastic, blessed life. If it's my time, I will go with no regrets." Her characteristic bluntness and irreverence were present until the final few days.

The day Jean decided she couldn't go any further and it was time to call in hospice care she apologized for giving up. As a couple we never gave up so now I had to tell her it was okay to do just that. My clear message was that nobody expected her to go beyond her limits. I pray to God I never have a sadder conversation in my life.

But then as she listened from the next room to my conversation with the hospice people she re-engaged. The hospice social worker inquired about the home environment in our Minneapolis suburban apartment, "Are there any pets?" I replied with an energetic "hell no." I am not a pet lover and I hate cats.

In the bedroom, Jean turned to our daughter Tracy and said, "There's no way he can divorce me now, let's talk cat."

That night at dinner the family was gathered and the conversation drifted to other topics when Jean, shouted, "Hey, wait a minute, this is supposed to be about me."

That sort of sarcasm and irreverence made it easier for everyone to deal with the saddest moment of our lives.

She worked the same magic with her dearest friend, Janet Sassone. As Janet bawled about Jean's fate, Jean thanked her for the pasta dinner Janet had brought and quipped, "At least I don't have to worry about my cholesterol anymore."

Imminent death was certainly no time to abandon the humor that had sustained us throughout our lives together.

"THE TOUGHEST THING I HAVE EVER DONE"

Yet, I did not do as well with Jean's dying days. I told a few intimates that her illness was without question the toughest thing I ever faced, far tougher than my own disability and Jason's disability.

A marriage of 39 years develops its own rhythms, expectations and responses. A fatal illness changes all that. Jean always said marriage was not a 50-50 deal. She said it was 70-30 and the trick was to keep that 70 going back and forth. In the last few months of Jean's life I gave and didn't get near as much back as I had for years. I am convinced I didn't handle that as well as I should have.

I was angry about it and I fear I worried too much about myself and not enough about Jean. I even uttered to myself those words I've despised more than any other, "why me?"

I have read enough about grief to know that sort of guilt after death is quite common, but it is significant to me that the toughness that got me through my own physical challenges and Jason's mental ones, was almost useless when faced with the fatal illness of my beloved partner.

"Get over it and deal with it in smart competent ways" has been my life's mantra. Yet, toughness and determination to get past your struggles is almost blasphemous in the face of the death of the person you love most of all. I don't want to get over Jean's death. I want to come to grips with it. I want to savor the gift that she was and celebrate the love we shared. I do not want to "get past it" now and probably never will. I will go on with my life, and perhaps even take on a new partner, but Jean is and will always be a part of me.

In fact, that bond between us has been my biggest issue with grief. Some friends who have lost spouses talk about the overwhelming loneliness they face. I have certainly experienced that since Jean's death but there has been another bigger, more pervasive emotion for me. It's "onliness."

I doubt this is an original concept but onliness is bigger than loneliness. When you have been in a loving marriage for 39 years your entire operating context is "what is Jean doing now?" "I wonder if Jean is doing well now." "I like this artist, I wonder if Jean would want to go to that concert?"

Our thoughts on the weekend, our kids, retirement and even trivial things such as dinner, always revolved around Jean and me. Now that Jean is gone there is no one else to consider. It is only me. Only I can decide where I should live. Only I get to decide what I eat tonight. Only I decide when to pay bills and where I should invest.

I recently had a fairly routine medical procedure. The receptionist did her medical privacy spiel and then asked me, as such receptionists had done scores of times before, "Can we tell your medical information to anybody else?" At that moment I was singularly focused on Jean and did not give my kids the credit they deserved. All I could think about was that I didn't want the friend who drove me to have that information. Jean was not there to share things with. Daily, when I look over my shoulder for affirmation or comfort or even disapproval, there is no one there. It is only me, and I hate it. That is onliness and for me it is far worse than loneliness.

Let's look back at those opening paragraphs of this chapter which I wrote several months before Jean died and why, even after the worst loss of my life, I still believe those things.

God certainly didn't decide Jean had to die because I am strong enough to handle it. A lot of people go to pieces when their loved one faces death but they still die.

Jean didn't die because my family was being punished and God certainly wasn't "just screwing with us." I am still convinced, as I should have told my friend Dan, that his wife Ginny and my friends Debbie, Dana, Mary, Barbie, Dick and my Dad died because everyone dies. Everyone gets a turn in the sadness barrel. That is the core of the human experience.

Death is an essential part of the circle of life. Last week a close friend announced the birth of his grandson Bradley. It's an age-old conflict. Jean leaves, Bradley arrives. I am happy Bradley is here to bring joy to so many people but I sure as hell wish I could have kept Jean.

She is gone and no amount of bluster or determination can bring her back.

Since Jean passed I have never asked "why me?" I asked it a few times before her death but I know that loss is crucial to the experience of joy. Jean and I had a fantastic run and it seems apparent from the kind feedback I have received that our love positively affected others.

I miss her like the dickens but celebration of what we had and an ongoing love and respect for her are as far as I am going to get in conquering grief, the biggest challenge of my life.

WISE MAN JASON AND HIS MOM'S DEATH

I found the early weeks of grief mysterious, confounding and disturbing. I described my mind to friends as being "kaleidoscopic." My emotions were totally unpredictable and capricious. Even when I was not thinking about Jean at all, I suddenly found myself sobbing.

If those are the experiences of an educated, successful man, imagine what the death of his Mom is doing to Jason's psyche. And yet, in many ways Jason has been our inscrutable wise man usually saying just the right thing.

From Jean's first diagnosis we were circumspect with Jason. He lives with and works with some obsessive people. Most of them are worldlier than he is, but still lack judgment and social sensibility. We were petrified that if Jason heard the word cancer some of those friends would scare him to death with dastardly predictions.

So we studiously avoided the "C word" but Jason knew Mom was sick because she bowed out of a lot of activities when we were in Minnesota. The fact that we lived most of the time in Arizona and Jason lived in Minnesota made it much easier to minimize Jean's symptoms to Jason.

When we returned to Minnesota in early June of 2014 it was obvious to Jason that his "mommy" was very sick. He saw her twice and she never left the couch in our apartment. His somber expression was clear proof he comprehended the seriousness of the situation but he talked continuously about "mommy getting better."

On Saturday, June 14, a week before Jean died, and the day after she entered hospice care, I knew it was time I leveled with Jason but I had no idea if I was going to be candid with the 35-year-old or with the five-year-old.

His brother Jeff who had been called back to Minnesota to Jean's bedside and I took Jason to lunch. Direct and clear was the approach I decided to use. "Jason, Mom is not going to get better, she is going to die pretty soon," I said.

He did not cry. His eyes cast downward. His expression was solemn, even grave. That look disturbed me to the point of shivers.

Finally, Jason said with poignancy and deep sincerity, "This is going to be hard." The profundity of the observation along with the blessedly sweet understatement of it made Jeff and I laugh out loud. I responded instanta-neously and crudely by muttering, "No shit, Jason, no shit."

Jason then spoiled that particular moment of blinding insight when he lapsed into what may be his most maddening habit. He began asking, as he often does when he hears big news, "Does Grandma know? Does Aunt Mary Beth know" Does (cousin) Sarah know?" Does the postman know? Does the clerk at Walgreens's know? I am exaggerating about the last two but only slightly.

His sister, Tracy, the special education teacher with unending patience, argues the unceasing questions are Jason's way of processing difficult infor-mation. I am more convinced the questions are an indicator of his insecu-rities. I think he fears he's the last to know, and in this case he pretty much was.

I knew I had dropped a huge bombshell on a man relatively unequipped to deal with it, but I had my hands full dealing with Jean's last days. So I left Jason alone while I dealt with hospice and Jean's deteriorating health. Finally on Thursday night, thanks to hired nursing help, I was able to get away to have dinner with Jason. I didn't know Jean would die in two days but I knew the end was near.

I asked Jason if he wanted to see his Mom again. He said no. "Well, Jason, let me ask the really hard question, do you want to be with Mom when she dies?" The answer was crisp, clear and decisive, "No."

There was silence, and maybe one of us uttered something else but then Jason looked me directly in the eye and said, "I just want to have good mem-ories." Since I watched Jean die, and I struggle with that memory, I have wondered several times who made the right choice.

When Jean died Tracy was with me. We grieved for a while, notified rel-atives and close friends and after an hour or so I knew Jason could wait no longer. He was a 20-minute drive away but a telephone call just would not work.

I called from Jason's driveway and asked him to come to the car. I did not have time to take him for one of his favorite smoothies so I told him right there in the car that his Mom had died.

Again, no tears, just that grave, almost haunting straight ahead look.

He was so inscrutable I drove away with the conviction I had made things worse.

On Wednesday night there was a visitation for Jean at a suburban Minneapolis funeral home. Jason was his usual charming self. He worked the room as only he works a room. Several visitors told me he was actively reassuring them in their sorrow, consoling them with assurances that we would be all right.

That night Tracy saw the first of two signs of palpable grief. A video specialist had taken our family pictures and put together a powerful DVD portraying Jean's life. I sobbed non-stop as I watched it. Tracy said Jason got quite teary-eyed and then walked away. She pursued him and asked him if he wanted a copy. He adamantly refused and did so several times since. He did not seem to want any tangible memories and that concerned me.

I never saw him cry at the funeral. Numerous people who were watching me very closely throughout the funeral told me later that the way Jason comforted me by stroking my back and shoulders is their most poignant memory of the ceremony.

But Tracy did see Jason's tears flow. Jeff gave a powerful eulogy for his mom and held up beautifully throughout, until he returned to his seat where he broke into uncontrollable sobs. That set Jason off, according to Tracy, and he cried considerably. We haven't seen tears since.

Jason has apparently decided I am his biggest responsibility. He has told staff at his group home that he "has to be strong for Daddy." When he says that, he flexes his muscles like a strong man. I have tried to disabuse him of that notion but that seems to be his chosen role.

As we said goodbye the day of the funeral Jason grabbed me by the shoulders and said, "You'll be fine daddy."

For many weeks after Jean's death he did not bring her up in conversation. I know he saw me silently sobbing a few times but Jason's focus seemed to be on the good memories.

Four weeks after Jean's death I gently approached Jason by saying, "Are you okay buddy? You don't seem to mention Mom at all. He looked at me and shrugged, "It's over. It's time for me to move on and it's time you did too, Daddy."

I was surprised and amused but a little pissed all at the same time. Jason's pace of acceptance was much too fast for me.

It now appears Jason just needed time. About eight weeks after Jean passed Tracy was driving Jason home and she noticed he was quietly brooding. "What's the trouble Jason?" He responded with his always frightening, "I've been thinking."

"What have you been thinking?"

"About Mom stuff."

"What kind of Mom stuff?"

"I miss her."

I cry every time I think about that story, but it was a huge relief that Jason had started to face his sadness.

WRITING THE ENDING AND SEEING THE BEGINNING

Throughout this book I stressed that I don't offer Jason or me as models of anything. A woman named Liane Kupferberg Carter writing on the Huff Post Parents website beautifully articulated my thought on that contention on February 22, 2013: "Once you've met one person with autism, you've met one person with autism." The same thing applies to Jason and Down syndrome and my Arthrogryposis. And now it applies to me and my grief. There is nobody like us. Our experiences and our challenges and our responses are unique. My grief journey is different from every one before me.

Jean's death represents an ending but it also must mean a beginning. I sobbed so much writing these words I could not see the computer screen. As hard as it is to accept, the sun has been coming up every day since Jean died. Jason and I do have to move forward—at our own chosen pace.

Despair is a pretty comfortable crutch but it is certain to collapse of its own weight. Jim and Anita were filled with despair when I was born. I think that is clearly the wrong path. Self-delusion and phony optimism are just as dangerous. Life without Jean is not going to be popcorn and lollipops but I will find a way just as Jean and I did raising Jason.

We understood parenting a disabled child is different. For years a framed copy of Emily Pearl Kingsley's poem "Welcome to Holland" hung in our guest bathroom. We thought it declared to visitors our philosophy on raising a special child. Kingsley says having a baby is like planning a dream trip to Italy. She compares finding out your child has a disability to waking up to find you've landed in Holland. Holland is not horrible, but it is not Italy. It's critically important parents of a special needs child understand their trips are going to be different. Not necessarily tragic, but different.

Jean and I got angry on at least a weekly basis but we found we had big, overwhelming fits of anger every seven years or so. Especially when we thought we had settled into a routine, new behaviors and innovative frustrating acts would simply piss us off. Let's face it, three years of toilet training could tick off Gandhi. I've known anger over my condition throughout my life. Being mocked or being unable to do things everybody else does is maddening. However, that anger usually leads to peace and comfort. To paraphrase Kushner, if I don't know anger I can't know contentment and triumph.

The hole that Jean has left is devastating and life changing, but it can't be life stopping, and it can't be laugh-stopping. She would have hated that.

The first reading at Jean's funeral mass was from Ecclesiastes 3:1-8. That's the basis of the song *Turn, Turn, Turn*. The message of "to everything is a season" meant a lot to both Jean and me.

I was not ready to write this book until early 2013. My views about my own disability and on Jason's, needed time to percolate. If I had written about Jason when he was 7, 14, or 21 the book would have bristled with anger. At other times it would have oversold the parenting experience. There is tremendous benefit at looking at the entire journey from a 50,000 foot perspective. It takes perspective to appreciate it.

The wild card in that readiness to write this book was Jean's death. Certainly I thought about delaying it for a while to gain a better understanding of where our family will be without our sweet, guiding light.

I go forward knowing that we will find the strength we need. We always have because we all do what we have to do to survive and move on. It's a mystery where the strength comes from, but it usually comes.

I will go forward knowing that nobody can map our journey like we can, despite all the wise, well-intentioned counsel I get. My mother, Anita, admits that her biggest mistake after I was born was listening to all the advice everyone was so willing to give. Nobody knows your struggle. Everyone will be convinced they could do it better. It doesn't matter if they could. The gift and challenge is all yours.

Having a disabled child seems like a tragedy when it occurs. You have after all landed in Holland when you had your heart set on Italy. My mom and dad were smart enough to recognize and celebrate all the gifts that accompanied my handicap. Their son was pretty smart, he was a good speaker and he was tougher than nails. Jean and I realized Jason was socially savvy, funny as hell and that he changed every room he entered for the better. There are some really good things about Holland and neat things can happen there.

I have tried to use karma, fate and God interchangeably in this book. The fact is blessings and good karma can be absolute gifts for the parents of a disabled child if you focus and appreciate them. If the bad thing that happened becomes cancerous, your whole life can be terminally ridden with depression and defeat.

Jean and I never gave in to despair. I am deeply proud of that. I am just as proud that we faced our challenges holding hands just as my parents did. This book is the story about Jean and me holding hands to deal with the challenges Jason presented. That chapter has ended.

Jason, Tracy, Jeff and I will move on, one step at a time just as we always have. We will do it with laughter, irreverence and even joy.

The joy will come from the memories of Jean and all the years we spent together. They will sustain us and drive us. We know that because Jason saved his greatest wisdom until the moment Jean was interred in a Columbarium, a Catholic device to store ashes of the deceased. After the priest concluded his prayers, the parish administrator moved to close the vault.

I stopped him because I wanted to say one final goodbye. I moved to Jean's wooden urn and placed my hand on perhaps the most sacred box I have ever touched, sobbing uncontrollably at that final encounter.

Jason, the man with an IQ of 52, the man who can't read or write, the man fueled by thousands of TV shows and movies, stepped forward to comfort me. With his hand gently resting on my shoulder, Jason pointed at his head and then his heart and said, "Daddy, she's here and she's here."

And, that's how we will move forward.

AUTHOR'S NOTE AND ACKNOWLEDGMENTS

The book was always intended to chronicle a family's struggle to cope with a child's mental disability and to show a family's triumph over that circumstance. And it was always meant to also be funny and irreverent because that's how we've lived.

The "Jason book" took a dramatic turn in December, 2001. False starts had piled up like the firewood in my garage that we didn't touch for seven years. Six months before my retirement from the high-pressure job as editor of the Minneapolis Star Tribune to write columns, speak, and work on "the book," I presented a seminar at the Poynter Institute in St. Petersburg, Florida. I did a storytelling exercise focused on my personal life stories. Those stories included one about Jason, but most of them were stories about my own disabled childhood. I laid bare the struggles, the discoveries, the acceptance, the anger and my relentless push to be accepted as normal, whatever normal is, or was, at that time.

Only when a couple of kind participants pointed out the power and significance of my own stories did I think of telling Jason's story intertwined with mine. Because, of course, it is. I owe a deep thank you to Karen Dunlap, Chip Scanlan, Al Tompkins, Roy Peter Clark and the Poynter Institute crew from 2002 for convincing me my own stories had worth.

When I got home from that trip I started to tell my wife Jean about my new realization and she said, "You know I've been thinking, you ought to make the book the story of both you and Jason." Jean was a few beats ahead of me and she usually was. Her sharp intellect her persistent humor and her total dedication to our family are the soul of this book and our family's story. The inscription on the niche that holds her ashes says "Jean Fannin McGuire...The heart of our story." She was the heart of this story too and her role as partner, editor, collaborator, cheerleader and taskmaster also made her the book's prime mover.

I have no intention of entering the hot button arena of abortion, but I can say unequivocally that I believe our world would be an inferior place if there were no Down syndrome children. The pursuit of the perfect baby would deprive our world of real joys and triumphs. I hope the optimism that is inherent in this book may provide intellectual and emotional fuel for making those life-changing decisions.

The language I used reflects difficult choices which disability advocates may find objectionable. I deeply believe in sensitivity and I never use any language with the intention of offending. I do use words that some may dislike but only in quotes or in the context of history. Many families deal with reality more than propriety, and in 1949, and even in 1979, language was not the issue it is now.

I hope the humor, drama and triumphant human spirit portrayed in the stories of a man and his son engaged, entertained and provoked. Telling our stories has been challenging because memories are elusive. The memories recalled are mine. They are my best effort to be honest and accurate. I have found that even Jean and I remembered things differently. Things that were a big deal for me never hit her radar.

People involved in some of my stories may remember them differently and in some cases I comment on those colliding memories. The memories reflect my perspective and my perspective alone, unless I refer to contemporaneous notes or specifically assign the memory to someone else. The story of my birth is obviously based on recollections from my mother and father.

My mother has been an absolute champion throughout this process. She was invaluable as a source. Her inner strength and the power of her partnership with my dad have inspired me all my life. I am convinced I would be a different person without their determination, guidance and prayers.

Thelma Fannin, Jean's mother, has always been one of Jason's strongest advocates.

Our other two children, Tracy and Jeffrey, guided and shaped Jason, and their strong assistance on this book has been deeply appreciated. I always feel their love and support. My siblings, Marty McGuire and his wife Jan, Mary Beth Thompson and husband Ron, and David McGuire and his wife Laura have assisted me through their entire lives and their stamp on this book is unmistakable. Tracy's husband Ben Moll, and the entire Moll family, deserve a special nod of appreciation for the affection they have shown Jason.

Friends have been crucial on this journey and mine are remarkable. However, Gregory Favre is special beyond belief. In my early 40's I was finally able to find wingtip shoes that would fit me. Gregory actually sent me flowers to celebrate that fact. That is just one example of the loyalty and affection my long-time horse racing partner has shown me. Gregory has been catalyst, mentor and close friend for more than 35 years. He has been a true partner along with his wife Bea in our Jason journey. Gregory brought the same tireless commitment, thoughtfulness and affectionate attention to detail that have marked our long friendship to the editing of this manuscript.

I also benefited from the candor and insight of Leonard Downie. Every suggestion he offered made me realize again why the Washington Post did such amazing, prize-winning work during his tenure as Managing Editor and Executive Editor. The most difficult aspect of this book was writing about me. Len saved me from myself with his sharp pen. Favre and Downie made this book immensely better. If it doesn't measure up after their wise advice, that's on me.

Farley Chase, a New York book agent, also added valuable editing advice. We weren't able to sell the book to traditional publishers, but that, too, is on me. Farley is a grade A agent.

Christopher Callahan, the founding Dean of Arizona State University's Walter Cronkite School of Journalism, has been muse, counselor and valuable friend. He made the connection to his close friend Mitchell Zuckoff, the outstanding author of 13 Hours, Lost in Shangri-La and Frozen in Time. Mitch made invaluable editorial contributions for which I am grateful.

Thank you to Ian Punnett, Kristin Gilger, Jaqueline Petchel, Elizabeth Mays and John Dille who offered excellent philosophical guidance along the way.

I am grateful for Meg Herbert's cover and for Brandon Quester's technical expertise. Their assistance down the home stretch has brought the book to reality.

Special thanks for the lessons taught by every staffer and editor who crossed my path at the newspapers for which I worked. Joel Kramer, Pam Fine, Will Corbin and Keith Moyer deserve special mention. The students and faculty at the Cronkite School have been stalwarts. Professor Rick Rodriguez and his wife Emelyn have always been there when I needed them. Senior Associate Dean Marianne Barrett also deserves my thanks.

I owe incredible gratitude to my dear friends who have had strong roles in this book and may not realize it, Ed Bailey and the late Dana Bailey, Peter Bhatia and wife Liz Dahl, Bill and Chris Cheevers, Pat and Cindy Dawson, Mike and Donna Hackett, Tom and Kathy Hayden, Frank and Ann Hughes, Tim and Carla Fallon, Brian Murphy and Pam Mower and the late Deb Murphy, Fran and Brooke Reidelberger, Arnie and Terrie Robbins, Jim and Laurel Ward, and Dan and the late Ginny Untiedt all have affected me in deep, untold ways. Special thanks to Janet Sassone for the support she offered Jean for so many years.

Both Jason and I owe a huge debt to countless teachers, special education advocates and specialists who have guided and shaped us both. We thank all of them. My special gratitude also goes out to all the people in our lives, from waitpersons, to clerks, to good friends, who instantly accepted Jason. They made our journey easier.

Finally, I thank Jason, the profound teacher, the jovial sidekick, and the personification of unconditional love.

And through our tears we all thank our beloved Jean.

Made in the USA
Lexington, KY
06 April 2018